Alice Brown

Stratford-By-The-Sea

A Novel

Alice Brown

Stratford-By-The-Sea
A Novel

ISBN/EAN: 9783337029210

Printed in Europe, USA, Canada, Australia, Japan

Cover: Foto ©Thomas Meinert / pixelio.de

More available books at **www.hansebooks.com**

AMERICAN NOVEL SERIES.—No. 4.

STRATFORD-BY-THE-SEA

A NOVEL

NEW YORK
HENRY HOLT AND COMPANY
1884

STRATFORD-BY-THE-SEA.

CHAPTER I.

A LONG stretch of level country, bordered on one side by the sea, sweeps away until the imagination begins its guess-work where the eye is forced to stop, at a thick fringe of pines in the far background. Here and there, perhaps two miles from the sea, are farm-houses in picturesque groups of threes and fours, forming the little town of Stratford-by-the-Sea.

This quaint corner of the old township dates back to colonial days, and almost to colonial primitiveness of life, though, like many another place and people, it has retained certain forms and customs of its ancestors without their accompaning rigidity of virtue. But, alas! true as this is in the main, many a good custom is unhappily obsolete ; there are scolds in Stratford who have made no acquaintance with the ducking-stool, and an occasional worthy member of society dares absent himself from church without fear of a penalty. I have been told, too, that various young people there strangely bewitch one another's hearts and affairs without going to the stake for it.

The little place is given its locative termination to distinguish it from the great township of Stratford, of

which it was once a part. Stratford-by-the-Sea is
merely a remnant, a fragment broken from that large
tract of New England which at present has no existence
except in the country records. The township had, in
its first youthful pride, kept what are now independent
neighboring villages, quite concealed under its own
name, but, as its age and feebleness increased, they
had broken away, one by one, until the only relic of its
former greatness is the poor little town bearing its name.
The resemblance between the parent and its dismem-
bered parts, as they became individuals with titles of
their own, grew more and more faint. The one poor heir
of its name was the only faithful follower in its footsteps. Stratford-by-the-Sea never advanced very far
in any line of enterprise, for the best of reasons,—it
steadily abjured the new. Year after year it remained
placidly stationary ; the farmers on the uplands con-
tenting themselves with patient mowing and reaping by
hand, where for miles around any thing but machine
labor, where machinery could be used, had become a
thing of the past.

The people had a marked trace of that curious dia-
lect which seems often an effect of sea-air, a broadening of the vowels and a rough burr of consonants.
Certain characteristic oaths were in vogue, from which
the exquisite simplicity of their use removed every
trace of profanity. The picturesque compound of
farmer and fisherman was wont to push his tarpaulin
away from his grizzled locks and ejaculate roundly, "By
Righteous ! By Mars !" and " O King !"

Old-fashioned and time-worn touch as every part of
the town bore, there was a perpetual beauty in its elm-

shaded roads and houses garlanded with woodbine. This was in summer ; but its winter winds held a bleak, invigorating severity, and from January to January there was, nearest the sea, the grandeur inseparable from a rocky coast with ambitious waves. A winding little river cut off the " Stra'forders," as they were called, from their neighbor Scone, of whom they were madly but good-naturedly jealous. Scone possessed a good harbor and had once sent out whalers, which the men of Stratford could never do from their bit of rocky coast. Scone even entertained yachts, and when the yachtsmen staid over night at the smart hotel, there was excitement enough to have lasted a Stratforder all his life.

Stratford seldom had a glimpse of strangers. Summer boarders came over from Stowe, the town on their left, for a day's picnicking and curious exploration, with probably the same feeling of remoteness with which children, taken to the sea-shore for a day, enter the wigwams of an Indian encampment. It was the one dream of Stratforders, the favorite method of working off their ambition, that of moving across the river to Scone and engaging in the whirl of life there ; catching fish for the hotel in the time of summer boarders, peddling it in the adjoining towns, and drying it for market. Not one of them had ever done it, and, with equal probability, not one had reached manhood without having at some time dipped into this Utopian plan, perhaps with an inward shame at having been led away by too wild a scheme. On winter nights, when some half-dozen men were congregated about the stove in the little office and parlor of the Sea View, their piercing

eyes and weather-beaten faces duskily seen through the smoke, one would take his pipe from his mouth to say :
" Wal, neighbor, if ever we should move away from here—" and so on, though a line of brilliant prophecy, which one and another took up in an ecstatic fugue. But no one had ventured to become pioneer, and Stratford was still in her unbroken sleep, dreaming restlessly of an awakening, but too deep in slumber to rouse herself and work out her own deliverance.

One November day, the broad road leading to the sea was swept by a gale of wind, and the few remaining leaves rustled along with the nervous eagerness left old age in its last revels.   Two pedestrians, a boy of fifteen and a girl at least five years older, were stoutly breasting the wind, talking in the high-pitched voice necessitated by the boisterous weather. The boy was slight in figure, with a pale face whose habitual expression was nervous and eager.   The forehead was almost too highly developed, denoting an intellectual strength quite out of proportion to the delicate mouth and chin.   In the hint of lines about the last two features there was, indeed, super-sensitiveness, which might, under harsh criticism or defeat, harden into angry pride or despair. He was talking eagerly and volubly.

" Betty, you don't seem to have a bit of ambition. To be sure, you're only a girl, but that isn't the worst thing in the world."

His sister smiled ; she was too often in a state of quiet amusement at his extravagances to exclaim at them.

" Much obliged for your encouragement, Philip. But I own it ; I haven't any more ambition than—that squirrel. See what a tail ! Bless you, Mr. Gray Fuzz ! But tell me, Philip, what you'd like to have me do."

"I don't know ; something splendid. But you haven't any talents, have you now ?" he added, thought-fully. Elizabeth laughed outright at the hopeless candor of his tone, not in the least offended by it.

"Not one," she owned frankly. "It would puzzle even you, Phil, to make a girl.famous who doesn't want to be, and couldn't be if she did. What will you do about it ?"

"I don't know yet. Hold on ! Yes, I do ! When my book is published and I am famous, you shall keep my house and look after the company. Poets and painters, Betty ! And when some great actress has taken my play, the very first night, when all the house applauds and roars, you shall sit with me in my box and look pretty in a white dress. O, Elizabeth, won't it be grand ?" His assurance was manly ; his enthusiasm boyish in the extreme.

"Very fine indeed," said Elizabeth, rather sadly, clasping his small hand closer ; " but you seem to have forgotten Grandmother."

"I didn't ; I never forget her," he said, frowning, a note of obstinacy in his voice.

"You know she would never let her money go towards carrying out such plans. You'll have to be a minister or not have an education."

"I sha'n't do it ! " he cried, in boyish petulance. "I'll write my play and succeed before she knows it ; and then let's see any one interfere with me. Betty, how I should like to go to her and say, Grandmother,

I've earned a thousand dollars, and I can earn just as many more."

"Yes, dear, but you know that would be too much for any body but a wonderful, wonderful geuius to do, almost greater than any one that ever lived. No, you must go away to school."

His heroic mood had passed with the moment. "I suppose it's so; of course it is. We've talked about it a thousand times, and always come back to the same place."

"Yes, I am really sure of it," said his sister, in a tone of patient kindness. "I didn't think so once, but being in Weston has made me change my mind about a good many things. Now, there was Professor Gorham—he used to visit Mr. Lunt—and Philip, he had spent years studying little passages in Shakespeare, and trying to find out what some of the words in old English books meant. I believe hearing him talk made me see what a hard thing it is, and how much study it takes to write any thing that is not silly nor weak."

They had reached home, a large house, which, being originally unpainted, had grown black through lapse of years, and was destitute even of blinds, or a spray of woodbine to relieve the monotony of its walls. Most of the Stratford houses had the bare branches of wood-bine, a prophecy of summer greenness, but this one only indicated comfort and cleanliness, with no pretense at adornment.

The two went up the narrow path in silence, but just as they reached the heavy front door, Elizabeth paused, and looking into the boy's face, said, rather wistfully, but with great tenderness:

" I haven't hurt you, Philip ? You know I didn't say you would fail."

" Not a bit of it," he answered, cheerily, though his first self-sufficiency was wholly gone. " You're a pretty good sort of a girl, Betty."

The door which Elizabeth opened led into a wide hall, with a sitting-room on its right, made neat by thrifty braided rugs. On the left was the typical country parlor, which was always closed except on the rare occasions of funerals, and Thanksgiving celebrations, at which latter time neither the roaring blaze in the fireplace nor its flicker on the brass andirons was sufficient wholly to relieve the pervading gloom. There was in one corner a coffin-plate, framed under glass, and beneath it an ambrotype of a youth with large serious face and staring eyes. The picture was made rather ludicrous than otherwise by the old-fashioned coat, small even for that spare figure, by the high collar and large ciavat ; but there was a pathos about it, too. Life must have been so over-full of seriousness and responsibility for the boy that you could only be grateful to the coffin-plate for saying that " Jeremiah Nye died ———, aged nineteen years." Entering the sitting-room, where Philip was alternately burning and blowing his fingers at the air-tight stove, one would draw a fuller breath in the more home-like atmosphere, and remember to be thankful that the furniture had daily use.

An old lady, upright and muscular, though near her eightieth year, sat knitting near the fire. She was the grandmother, or, as the neighbors said, "th' old Ma'am," the backbone of the family, as she believed, and cer-

tainly its controlling head. Her features were cut
with a generous squareness ; there was something
strong and massive in her entire build, while an un-
shaken spirit looked out from her spectacled gray eyes.
Her hands were whiter than those of housewives usually
are, and as they clicked the needles regularly, there was
a steadiness in their movement quite as characteristic
as the nervous indecision sometimes to be marked in
hands. After her grandchildren had come in, she
looked at Elizabeth disapprovingly from time to time,
and finally said, in a voice not at all harsh, but rather
chilly : " Elizabeth, why don't you take some work,
and not sit down in that way ? Any body would think
you hadn't a thing in the world to do."

" So I haven't, Grandmother," the girl answered,
quietly. " My blue dress was finished this morning.
The loops are on and the pocket in, and you know I
always leave the pocket for a week or two ! "

" There's the mending," said Madam Nye. " I put
two shirts and a pair of stockings in your mother's
basket. I wish I could understand how any boy of
Philip's age manages to wear out so many stockings.
If I didn't keep knitting all the time I wonder where
he'd be ? "

No one answered the latter suggestive remark ; perhaps it left too broad a field to the imagination. Philip
had taken up a book, and Elizabeth, going to the large
cupboard for the basket, sat down to her mending.
There was no trace left of her activity and vigor in
breasting the wind. It is the time to watch her now,
when her face has settled into its ordinary expression,
lighted by no response to excitement from without.

She is a slender girl, with heavy brown hair drawn straight back and twisted low in her neck. Her mouth is sweet and childlike, with lips neither red nor full. One misfortune compensates for its presence by lending a peculiar grace of its own ; she is slightly near-sighted, and that gives her an intent look, her body the least possible forward bend which is only graceful, and her whole appearance something eager and impressive.

"Your mother is coming," said Grandmother, as she rose to get her measuring-stocking. "She's been gone all the afternoon, at one house or another."

The two looked up with their first show of interest in what she said. Almost immediately Mrs. Nye came in ; a woman with delicate features and fine, light-brown hair. Hers was a worried face ; you would say it belonged to a woman who had learned to distrust the future, and was so used to unpleasant surprises that there could be few shocks for her now. Her eyes sought the children first, with a smile that was as brightly answered. Elizabeth rose and hung up the faded plaid shawl, as if she must do something in dumb affection.

"Any news ?" asked Grandmother, without looking up.

"No ; except—" with a quick glance to note the effect, "except that John Craig's son has come down and opened the house."

Madam Nye laid down her work, an angry sparkle showing itself behind her glasses. "He here ? What for ?"

"I don't know," answered Mrs. Nye, uneasily; she had the air of considering herself personally responsi-

ble. " He came to Stowe last night with two young
men, and they've been out gunning to-day."

" Does he own the house now ? " asked Philip.

" Yes, he does," said Grandmother, bitterly ; " and
no danger of his being any different from his father.
John Craig was the ruin of your father, dragging him
into speculation and coaxing his money away ; and
now I suppose his son's come down to enjoy it."

Elizabeth and her mother sighed rather wearily, the
one over her work, the other looking into vacancy. It
was an old subject ; they had all had the chance of
becoming tired of it.

Philip ventured, " He can't find much fun in that
old barn of a place, and it's almost unfurnished, too.
Besides, Grandmother, I don't see as he's to blame :
he couldn't help his father's leaving him the property."

" You don't know any thing about it," said the old
lady. " Don't try to find excuses for gambling ! "
And having regained her composure, she knit on stern-
ly. A cloud seemed to have risen over the house.
The news had evidently a deeper significance than the
mere fact of one man more or less in town would
seem to warrant.

Elizabeth and her mother set the table for tea, and
the meal was eaten in silence.

CHAPTER II.

PHILIP had gone out to split kindlings for the morning fire and his mother followed him ; she was used to little devices for seizing uninterrupted half and quarter hours with her children. Grandmother, her knitting laid aside for the few minutes it left her hands daily, sat by the fire in the sitting-room. She was usually in her chair at this time between daylight and dark, always upright, and always wearing a certain severe and retrospective look. Those who had seen her so for years, day after day, had a portrait of the stern woman not to be dimmed by time. Once seen, indeed, she impressed herself on your memory. You could never say, " Yes, I saw Madam Nye once, but I quite forget how she looks."

Elizabeth, just completing her dish-washing in the large kitchen, heard a quick and decided knock at the door. She took the lamp, and holding it above her head to illuminate the outside darkness, opened the door, standing for a second with her head bent forward, and the rays brightening her hair.

" I beg your pardon," said a voice from the darkness, one peculiarly courteous and appealing. " I'm afraid I can only introduce myself as a beggar. Could you give me some bread and butter ? "

Then, as if overcome by a humorous sense of the nature of his request, the unknown supplicant burst into a laugh full of enjoyment. Elizabeth smiled too. She could by this time distinguish, at one side of her shaft of light, a man dressed in shooting-cap and jacket.

"Come in ; we have just been to supper, but we shall be glad to get you some,—that is, unless it's a joke," she hesitated, for he had stepped inside, within the range of the lamp, and she discovered that he was not after the manner of Stratford men : still less did he belong to the nondescript species known as tramps.

"I assure you I am in deadly earnest," he said, taking off his cap and going at once to the stove, while Elizabeth closed the door.

He had taken in at once the beauty of her white arms below the rolled-up sleeves. Beauty could never escape his notice : hungry, tired, and bound on the least ideal of errands, instinct kept alert the keenness of glance many an artist acquires only by practice. Nor was a picturesque detail in the homely furnishing of the room overlooked.

"Let me introduce myself. I am Oswald Craig, and I own the large house on the other side of the street. You know the name ? Ah, I see you do," for Elizabeth had given a nervous little start and glance in the direction of the sitting-room. It had never chanced that any of the Craig family had come in contact with her own since the death of her father, and with a knowledge, all too great, of her grandmother's spirit, she half expected an immediate outbreak.

"I came down from Boston this morning with some fellows, to shoot sea-fowl, and found the place exactly what I wanted ; so I made up my mind to stay and camp, and my friends went home. You know the tra-

ditional idea of camping?—to shoot your own birds,
catch your fish, and do your own cooking. But,"—
with a shrug of his shoulders, "I'm not prepared to
play primitive man, with no fowl, no fish, and not even
a frying-pan. So," with such a rapid transition to his
former pleading tone that Elizabeth laughed again,
"will you please give me a piece of bread and butter?"

She had laid the cloth on the kitchen table while he
talked, and placed on it a second supper. She felt
quite at ease with him. With most people she had a
reputation for reserve and perhaps dullness, but Oswald Craig always adapted himself too thoroughly to
the situation to allow discomfort near him.

"You are very kind," he said, drawing his chair
quickly to the table, as soon as her preparations were
finished.

Elizabeth, after pouring his tea, began to put her
dishes away, and Oswald talked and ate with equal
interest. Just as he finished Philip came in with his
basket of wood, his mother following with a few sticks
in her apron, seeming to find in them witnesses to jus-
tify her for having been out of the kitchen. Both
started and looked curiously at Elizabeth for an explanation of the phenomenon of a stranger at home at
their table.

"Mother," said Elizabeth, "it is Mr. Craig, who
has come down for gunning and decided to stay longer. My brother Philip," she added, as he turned
from shaking hands with her mother.

"You see I've had the usual luck of sportsmen," he
said gayly; "I've nothing to show for my day's work

but a fair amount of stiffness and a tremendous appetite. And, worst of all, having no means of staying the latter, I have boldly begged your hospitality."

"You're welcome, I'm sure," said Mrs. Nye ; they were all standing somewhat awkwardly. "Won't you take a chair, or—come into the other room ; we always sit there evenings."

Elizabeth and Philip exchanged a quick glance ; hers contained a little shrinking from a probable encounter with Grandmother ; the boy's held only amusement. Philip's way through the home annoyances was daily smoothed by a keen sense of humor, of which Elizabeth was quite destitute. Events always presented their most literal and serious aspect to her. The mother, too, looked about with a slight sense of alarm after having committed herself by the invitation ; but if there was any hope in her mind that it would be refused, it was to be disappointed.

"I shall be glad to spend an hour with you, if you will allow me," Oswald answered, promptly. "Company and firelight seem very attractive, when one thinks of the empty walls and close rooms across the way."

Elizabeth, light in hand, led the way to the sitting-room. She thought, with a slight relief, that Grand-mother could not have failed to hear every word of the previous conversation. "At least she knows who he is," thought she. Can any one, except those who have endured the daily trial of being watched and judged by some one who has the power of pricking the sensitive flesh with innumerable pins of criticism, know how an outbreak is sometimes dreaded in families ?

Elizabeth, for it was always she on whom the burden
of disagreeable explanations fell, introduced Craig to
her grandmother. The young man bowed in his easy
manner, with perhaps an added deference. Madam
Nye said, without glancing at him,

"How do you do? Elizabeth, hand me my knitting
and put the candle on the light-stand." The request
was portentous; in seasons of great domestic calamity,
Grandmother, tacitly refusing communion with the rest
of the family, had a candle on a small stand by her
side, knitting there in silence while the others occupied the table.

Oswald appeared to be quite unconscious of the chill
in the social atmosphere, and while Elizabeth quietly
carried out Grandmother's commands, made himself
comfortable in the easiest corner of the not very luxurious sofa. "Such a delightful day, Mrs. Nye," he
said, easily, with a familiarity which a Stratford man
would not have attained after six months' acquaintance.
"There is such a strong taste of salt water in the whole
town that I shall stay for more of it. May I hold your
yarn, Madam?" turning suddenly to Grandmother,
who had finished her ball and was untwisting another
skein.

"No, I am much obliged to you; I can do it myself," said the old lady, with a severity which was not
the less marked for including every one. "Elizabeth,
turn the back of that chair round here."

But Oswald was before her : he placed the chair,
and seating himself opposite her, took the skein gently
from her and put it over his own hands.

"Now which way shall I turn it? You want to get

at the end, do you not?" He held it deferentially, turning to go on with his day's experience to Mrs. Nye.

Perhaps even in so small an encounter as this, it was the first time Grandmother had been worsted. His good-natured, imperturbable way of taking things for granted was something to which she was not accustomed, and having hesitated at the decisive first minute, she could not retrieve her failure. Scorning to glance at the others to see how they took it, she began winding steadily.

Craig had by this time taken to discussing the town.

"A strange, bare waste of a place, isn't it? And yet, it's a rare field for an artist; though I should feel sorry to have a view of the coast hung in my room. It would keep me frozen." The remark held a great deal for Elizabeth; the sea made her uneasy, and the low level of the entire view had always oppressed her. Sometimes a hint from a book gave her a quick inspiration of a different life, one in which there should be deeper color and warmer air, but the picture soon faded; she had not enough imagination to utilize it into permanent comfort.

"We don't have any time to think about artists," said Grandmother, her monotonous tones startlingly severe after the modulations of Oswald's. "The Creator didn't make the world for men to paint!"

"Ah, there you are right, of course. I do not pretend to account for His designs, and therefore I couldn't contradict you, if you were not." All this with a humility which removed from it the sting of sarcasm.

"Are you an artist?" asked Philip, boldly.

"I? Oh no. I suppose my father thought I had no talent in particular, and so I was educated for nothing in particular."

Immediately the three impartial ones among his hearers felt that to be able to look neutrally on all professions while abjuring them was a very superior ground of action to take.

"But perhaps at the same time I ought to confess," he went on, gracefully indicating Grandmother as if a more elaborate explanation were due to her, "that I really haven't any talent which would have paid for cultivation, or it would have developed itself."

The old lady had finished her skein, and the visitor moved so that he could rest his head easily against the woodwork of the old fashioned fireplace. It is an undeniable fact that good breeding gives a certain tone to form and expression, which no mere beauty can ever grant. Elizabeth gave a quick look at his fine head, the grace of his attitude, and thought, with a momentary depression, that he was not of the Stratford stamp. He had come to them for an evening's entertainment; they could give him nothing else. His world, being an unknown one to her, was all the more marvelous and unreal.

"Do you think I can get a boat to-morrow?" Oswald asked, turning to Philip. "We had some trouble in finding one, to-day. The worst feature I know about your Stratford fisherman is that he's so grandly dignified. I talked half an hour with an old fellow, this morning. Would he let me have one of his boats? Wal, he couldn't say; Jim was out in it now. Jim's own was hauled up—keel smashed in; if Jim got in

in time, why, yes, we might have it ; we might as well
have it as to let it lay idle ; shouldn't go out himself ;
had a lame hand. But when would Jim come in ?
Wal, that he couldn't say. He'd been out a matter o'
two hours or more—might be in before dinner—might
not. Couldn't we signal him ? No, too far ; Jim
wouldn't see it; besides, he was a neighbor and ought
to have the boat if any body did. And so on, with his
hands in his baggy pockets, looking out over the sea
all the time in that speculative way, as if he expected
an argosy which would add to his lordly sense of possession."

"It must have been Si Davids," said Philip, delighted at the touches from life. " Si's the most independent fellow on the coast."

"And did you get the boat ? "

" Yes, Jim fortunately came in and the old sea-king
cheerfully said we might as well have the boat, if Jim
didn't want it ; Jim agreeing, we went. I have felt
all day as if my fate hung on the decisions of Jim."

"Are you going out to-morrow ? "

" Well, I don't know. I tried to make a bargain for
to-morrow morning, but the man said he guessed not ;
we might happen round and if Jim didn't feel a mind
to go out, all well and good, we might have it ! But you
see I don't want to wander about on any such uncertainty. I want to be out by daylight, when the birds
are flying."

" I'll tell you what," said Philip, his face quite bright
with interest,. " I know of a boat I can get you. It's
a little way up the shore and you wouldn't know where
to find it, but if you'll tell me what time you want it,

I'll row round to the Point and have it ready for you
there."

Grandmother's face, albeit not lifted from her knitting, wore the stern look that the others knew so well,
and Mrs. Nye felt bound to remonstrate.

"Philip, you may get cold being out so early : you
know how damp it will be, and your throat—"

"Yes, I know it, mother," broke in the boy, excitedly ; he could not bear to be denied. "But I'll wear
my thick comforter and—yes, I'll tie it over my mouth!
Won't that do ?"

"I should be sorry to take your offer, if you really
ought not to go," said Oswald, politely, adding, however, "How would it do to say we would start from
the Point half an hour before sunrise ?"

"That will be all right," said the boy, delighted and
fearful ; the latter because a word from Grandmother
or Mrs. Nye would shatter his fine plans.

"If your mother is quite willing,—" said Oswald, appealing to her ; and she could say no more.

"I only want to be sure he won't catch cold : his
lungs and throat have always been very delicate."

"He shall not ; I give you my word." He probably
did not think it necessary to state his method of preventing this result ; and so deep was the impression made
by his manner that it did not occur to Mrs. Nye to doubt.

"Now, if we are to be off so early in the morning, I
must say good-night." Oswald went on the sensible
and wholesome principle that too much of any one experience is likely to prove tiresome. He had enjoyed
his half-hour with these people, but an hour might
transform them into bores.

"But where do you sleep?" asked Mrs. Nye, hesitating between housewifely instinct of hospitality, and natural lack of confidence in her own suggestion.

"I have sent for blankets from the little hotel—shall I call it hotel? The place where they have very thin steak fried in very fat lard—and I shall go there to breakfast. When I am in the woods I like to deny myself comfort; it gives me a genuine feeling of camping. I shall see you in the morning, Philip? Good-night. I thank you for a pleasant evening, Mrs. Nye, and you for charity!" he added, with a laughing glance at Elizabeth, as he passed her.

He had bowed and found his way to the outside door before they could do more than make up their minds to rise in returning his good-night. Stratford farewells were longer; a Stratforder was wont to stand at the threshold making a few last remarks on the weather, or on current topics; he did not feel it well to be precipitate.

When the door had closed behind the visitor Elizabeth took the lamp from the table and placed it in the window, so that its rays would stream out on the path : as she did so she saw Oswald turn, in the track of light, and take off his cap to her. There was a silence after he had gone, one somewhat heavy with unexpressed opinions. Philip and Elizabeth were much excited over the stranger, and their eyes spoke eloquent volumes to each other, saying, "If Grandmother would only go to bed!" but Grandmother, according to an exception she sometimes made, knit monotonously on past her bedtime, without a word or look for any one. Her face was impassive; it would have told no story to an observer unused to reading it, but to the members of the family it spoke her severest displeasure.

" Philip, hadn't you better go to bed ? " said his mother, mildly, at ten ; and the boy, knowing there would be no chance of seeing his mother or sister alone, took his candle reluctantly. Mrs. Nye wound the clock, and Grandmother fastened the doors, a duty she would trust to no one else, and in silence betook herself to her own bed-room.

CHAPTER III.

THE next morning Philip was awake before dawn without any help from any one, though it was usually a concession to duty to leave the warmth of his bed; he dressed hurriedly, with a pleasant excitement. He did not remember the woolen comforter, but having buttoned his jacket closely about him and put on his cap, stole down the stairs carefully, that no creaking board might carry the tale of his progress to Grandmother's bed-room. As he was going through the dark kitchen, a figure came softly and quickly out of the pantry. Philip's heart gave a bound; though it was almost time for daylight, he could not but feel that he was on a secret and mysterious mission.

"I've been waiting ten minutes," said Elizabeth, coming toward him. "I wanted to see you last night and ask what you were going to do, but there was no time. Whose boat shall you get?"

"Oh, don't you bother," said Philip, his courage rising as some one else took an interest in the situation. "I'll find one. But I must be off, because there's just time to get round to the Point, and he'll want to be out by light. How I wish I had a gun! What do you suppose he thinks of a fellow who lives right here and never has chance to shoot a loon, from one year's end to another?"

" Never mind that," said Elizabeth, prudence getting
the better of her interest ; " this is quite enough to do
without thinking of guns. I wonder how you dared
promise, and right before Grandmother, too ! But
we can't whisper here. I came down to put you up
some bread and butter, because you won't be back till
long after breakfast."

"I don't care about breakfast," answered Philip,
the anticipation of a morning with a sportsman, and
present consciousness of doing something daring, bringing out all the boyishness in his nature : " I sha'n't
have time to eat. But I'll take it ; put it here in my
jacket pocket. Good-by ! " And stealthily opening
the kitchen door he went quickly down the path, and
then began to run.

Elizabeth, standing to watch him, could hear the
quick, sharp footsteps on the frozen road long after
she could see him ; then, remembering that the draught
of keen morning air was blowing across the kitchen,
she closed the door and sat down by the window to
wait the time for making the fire.

Philip kept up his first speed till he was out of breath,
and then dropped into that staggering step in which
one loses the time gained by too long a run. It was a
mile by the road to the sea, but he was not bound for
the beach most frequented. Si's small house, which
was over-run by children but seemed to expand miraculously during the summer months when the children
spent their time outside, tumbling in the sand, was so
near the sea that the five minutes walk down the little
foot-path in front of it, brought him to his boats, drawn
up on shore. One, alas ! was old and battered, a bare

brown wreck of what it had been, with the bottom broken in and huge cracks gaping in the sides : Si had a tenderness for it he never confessed, but tacitly owned by the care with which it was drawn up out of the reach of the highest waves. ,Another boat was not fit for use, having had the rowlocks broken. Si was not famed for the dispatch with which he did the repairing necessary to life. But the third was in good condition : it was the one which had been used by Jim for the past week ; the one which had been promised Jim to-day, but which, when that worthy sportsman came to find it, would not be there.

Philip had made his plan in a moment, the night before ; he knew there was no other boat available within a short distance, that the fish houses made the nearest point at which one could be found, and had boldly resolved to take this away before any one else had it. Si might be angry, but he couldn't stop to think of that till it was all over. Philip's temperament was all impulse, disguised somewhat by his studious habits and capacity for dreaming, but it occasionally broke out in little acts of daring audacity. By the time he reached the shore he was out of breath, but did not pause until, with an effort almost beyond his slender strength, he had dragged the boat out into the water and was pulling away from land with all his might. There was no danger of rocks just there, but he needed to pull out a short distance before taking a straight line to the Point.

Every boy in Stratford knew how to row : it was as natural as for a sea-bird to fly, but Philip had done less of it than most boys of his age. Hard and severe as

Grandmother's nature was, and fully as she believed in a rigid moral discipline, she did not push him out of doors to fight with and manage the elements. Perhaps the thought of " Jeremiah, aged nineteen," present to her mind oftener than any one knew, even those who said she " took his death hard," warned her to be careful of the boy. So Philip had never been encouraged in the sports which develop manly force, had indeed been forbidden many of them which seemed to involve danger, and the boys of his own age were not sufficiently attractive to tempt him into stealing away to join them.

By the time he began to pull toward the smooth inlet at the side of the Point, his slender hands ached with their grasp of the oars. When within short enough distance, he could see Oswald finding his way over the pebbles to the foot-path, having struck which he came down over the Point at a swinging pace, with his gun over his shoulder.

" On time, aren't you? " he said, as soon as he was sure Philip could hear him. " Here, bring your boat round so I can get in from this rock. So ; now we're all right. You breathe as if you'd had a pull ; let me take the oars."

Philip was glad to relinquish them, though too proud to do it otherwise than slowly ; seated in the stern, and already carried far out from shore by the steady strokes, he had time to look at the oarsman, whom he had a curiosity to see by daylight. The face was a pleasing one, with no ill features ; the eyes brown and the hair, closely cut, of the same color. If Philip had been more experienced in the world of human nature, even if he had been a believer in physiognomy, he would have read at once certain other signs of character which were then invisible to him. He could not help seeing that the firm hands and blue-veined wrists showed a careful keeping quite foreign to what he ordinarily saw.

"We went out here to the left, yesterday," said the young man, " because we saw the gunners there ; of course it must be the best place or they wouldn't choose it, but I mean to strike out to the right this morning. If it's a mistake, there'll be plenty of mornings when I can profit by it."

" Shall you stay here long ? "

" Oh, I don't know," answered he, carelessly, keeping his eyes, now very keen, on a sweeping survey of the sky, "until I get tired of it, probably ; there's nothing in Boston to go back for in the next week or two."

" I wonder people should ever come here, except in summer," said Philip, growing talkative after the pleasure of having his plan succeed. He was a garrulous child, ready to talk with any one who showed the least interest or possibility of sympathy. " I don't like Stratford in this weather ; it makes me shiver."

" No, I fancy I shouldn't, for more than a few days," said the young man ; " but it's invigorating for a while, like a cold bath.—By the way, do you have good surf-bathing here ? "

" Oh yes," said Philip, quite eagerly, " people, that is every body but me, go all along the south beach, over there ; but I know such a nice place further on, where the water comes into a deep inlet in the rocks and stands there and gets warm. There's a big place almost like a cave, behind it, where I leave my clothes ; it is so much nicer than taking them off at the little house up there ! "

" I wonder there are not summer boarders ; your friend Si told me they were very few."

" Well, you see there's no hotel here but the Sea View, and Mr. Sims says it's no better than an old-fashioned tavern ; and there's nobody with money, nor any enterprise, so nothing is done. Mr. Sims says all the houses are so poor that nobody would have any courage to come and build, because it looks like such a God-forsaken place that they would be afraid it wouldn't pay. Do you think it looks like a God-forsaken place ?" he asked, suddenly.

Oswald laughed, resting on his oars a minute and looking at the sky. " What a queer little chap you are ! Well, yes, if you want the truth, it is, rather ; but then I have noticed that almost all towns at this distance in the country have a sort of dead-and-buried look. Now I should think we were out far enough ; we'll drift for a while."

He drew in the oars and sat waiting, scanning the sky. Philip would not shiver, but he wished he had worn the comforter.

· · · · · ·

" Well ! " said Craig, at last, " this proves it. To-morrow morning we'll go out where the natives do, and take care to be there early. Did you have any breakfast ? I meant to go round to the hotel for some, but it would have been too early to get any thing."

" No, and I'm hungry," said Philip. " Oh ! " with a

sudden thought, "Elizabeth gave me some lunch ; let me see if I have lost it out of my pocket."

No, there it was ; a square little package that proved to consist of slices of bread and butter, gingerbread, and cheese. Philip spread it on the seat before him.

"This is a find," said Oswald, helping himself to bread. "How did she happen to think of it ?"

"Oh, I don't know ; she thinks of every thing for me," remarked the boy, with a well satisfied sense of possessing a sister who had done the proper thing, under the circumstances. "She understands things you tell her, too ; most girls don't, you know."

Oswald was looking at him for almost the first time that morning ; his attention before had been given undividedly to the birds.

"What kind of things ? " he asked.

"Oh, every thing ! Never laughs when you tell her what you mean to do, or—Will you tell me something about theaters ? " he asked, suddenly, looking very soberly over his bread and butter.

"Why do you care for them ?"

" I never saw one, but I want to know all about them. I got a paper at the Sea View the other day, and saw they were playing Hamlet; is it very beautifully done ? "

"The critics say no," said Oswald ; he was ready to indulge the boy, perhaps in payment for the amusement Philip was innocently affording. Beyond that, the slightness of a new experience did not detract from the warmth with which he met it.

"Bellingham takes the part, and Bellingham is made up of a stage stride and pompous mannerisms. Besides, he's too fat; you can't imagine Hamlet's porcelain soul in that kind of envelope."

"And how does the theater look?" asked Philip, having met, for the first time in his life, some one who could answer his questions without being shocked at them. "Is it a great building with the stage at one end?"

"Have you never been inside one?" said Oswald. "You must go, if you care for the stage so much. Yes, it is a very large building with two balconies, in a semi-circle, so, like my hands. The stage is here, where I put this piece of wood."

"And it has a curtain?" said the boy, eager to urge him on.

"Yes, the one I am thinking of has a great crimson curtain that goes down quite near the foot-lights, and behind it is the drop-curtain that falls between the acts."

"And Hamlet, tell me about him; what does he wear? And how does the ghost look? Can they make him very terrible?"

"The poor ghost! no," laughed Oswald; "he is made up of a big voice, some armor, and is illuminated by a spectral sort of light; nobody looks at him, except perhaps the servant-girls and coachmen in the gallery. Every eye is on Hamlet."

"And is he pale and frightened? Please go on."

"That depends on your actor," said Oswald, entering into the boy's interest and seeing that he need not bring the subject down to a tale for his amusement; "he may be all bravado; a solid, beef-eating Hamlet, who would track a ghost to earth as quickly and with

as much relish as he would a fox. He may be only
an actor who has learned to mouth the part, but is
not student enough to spend years in dissecting it,
and he will fall into an abject terror. But once in
two or three life-times, you may find a man who has
such power of sympathy as to put himself into Hamlet's
frame of mind ; and if his own mind is fine enough,
his emotions sensitive in response, his conscience
abnormally developed, and his will unequal to any
steady strain upon it, that man may come near to an
understanding of Hamlet. Then, if he have a respectable figure, and a nose that is not a snub, a severe
theatrical training, and a vivid talent, perhaps he may
venture to play the part."

Half of this was over the head of Philip, but he did
not like it the less for that ; more than most of us object to scientific nomenclature which possibly leaves
no very clear impression on the mind.

"Is it very hard to get a play accepted ? " asked
Philip in a voice that sounded unnatural to himself ;
it seemed to him it must publish to the world the fact
of his dear ambition.

"Oh yes," said Oswald, so carelessly that the lad
felt a real surprise that he evidently had not seen the
personal drift of the question ; "unless one has influence at court, or enough talent to write a sensational
play that would take with the multitude and run for
the season. He might understand stage management
well enough to get up scenic effects and produce one
of those brilliant plays that have enough noise and
thunder for the ear, and blue and green lights for the
eye, to be popular. But who wants popularity ? All

this is clap-trap, you know ; if you come to real play-
writing, that is another thing."

"Another thing because it would be so hard to do ?"
asked Philip, with almost hurt emphasis. " But if one
wanted it more than any thing else ; so much that he
would be willing to wait a long while to be known ?"

" Well, he might have all that without any brains,"
said Oswald carelessly, taking up the oars ; "brains
do count, after all, you know. I believe I'll row in
shore. How good that gingerbread was ! Your mother
—or was it the sister ?—was very thoughtful."

Philip sat silent all the way in ; like many conscious,
sensitive people, he was easily wounded on the score
of his personal wishes and plans. Elizabeth was the
only one to whom he had ever spoken of them, and
she always believed in him. This was the first doubt
that had ever entered his world of visions. Oswald
noticed the change in him.

" If you are willing, I'll leave you at the Point and
take the boat round," said Philip ; he had his own
reasons for wishing it.

"Just as you like. Shall I give you the money to
pay the man, or will he let us take it again and pay for
it all together ? "

" That would be the best way," said Philip ; he had
no intention of braving the probably irate Si, so far as
to offer him money to pay for the trick. Oswald
could do that for himself, if he chose.

" I shall see you again," said the young man. "Come
in and sit by my fire with me. I've had roaring ones
made in two or three rooms of that old house. Come
in and keep me company."

"I should like to," Philip said, forgetting his depression of the past minutes in the prospect of longer talks with the stranger. "I will if I can."

Oswald left him at the Point, and he, looking back as he rowed away, saw the well-knit figure fast disappearing over the rocks, the gun over the shoulder picturesquely outlined against the sky.

Fortunately, no one was down by the shore when Philip drew up the boat. He was rather glad, not because he shrank from confession, but he was cold and tired, and the joke did not seem quite as funny as it had done. By the time he reached home he was quite chilled, and thought of the kitchen fire with more interest than of any thing else.

No one was there when he went in, but as things were all in order in the room and the clock ticking soberly, sole watch over the scene, he knew that, the work being done till dinner-time, the three women were busy in the next room.

It makes one tired, both mentally and physically, to think of the hours they spent sewing or knitting, day after day and month after month, in an unbroken silence. It is to be questioned whether the mind does not lull itself to sleep in such monotonous pricking of the needle, as the bodily eyes close in weariness after fastening themselves on one uninteresting object after another.

CHAPTER IV.

O SWALD spent his day at the Sea View where, after eating a dinner especially adapted to the place, consisting chiefly of fish-chowder, he took his seat by the fire and talked with one after another of the men who dropped in to smoke. They interested him warmly, and he was so talkative and conciliatory in hope of drawing out their own originality, that after he was gone there were strong beliefs expressed that he was a politician, who had an ax to grind.

"Why," said a bent and grizzled figure in a blue jacket, Charlie Reeves, an old man who seemed to have retained the boyish diminutive of his name chiefly on account of its inappropriateness, "you remember when Josh Rowe was murdered in his cider-house? Twenty year ago it was, but there ain't a man in Stra'ford that hain't had the particulars of the story told him. There warn't a clue to the murderer, you know, and jest at that time there come down to this very tavern, boys," bringing his brawny hand down on a chair to emphasize the reality of its being the identical furniture that was there twenty years ago, "to this very tavern, a slim, slick young chap ; butter wouldn't melt in his mouth. The fust Sunday he was here, he went to meetin' and set in Elder Fry's Bible-class. Talked with every body, he did ; talked with me !

Said he was interested in murders ; wanted to know
all about it; and if you'd believe it, when I told him all
I knew, he'd set and shiver !   Wal, he staid round
here ten days, talkin' to one and another, and most of
all with Bill Holmes ; and then, one day, we was settin' here, right here in this keepin'-room, boys, and
Bill Holmes come in and sez, kinder reckless, as if he
thought best for folks to hear him, ' Give me a glass
o' whisky, old man, I'm goin' up to Boston on the ten
o'clock train,' and before any one could ask a question,
' So you are ! ' sez a voice like the snap of a whip. We
all jumped an' turned round, an' there, where we
thought he was settin', stewin' over the fire an' askin'
questions in that low voice of his, was the stranger ;
he was standin' straight as a gun-barrel, and you'd a
thought he'd grown six inches.   ' Yes, you shall,' sez
he, ez cool ez you be now, ' and I'll go with you.'   An'
with that he walked up an' slipped a pair o' hand-cuffs
on Bill's wrists.   Bill cow'd down an' never said a
word ; an' in the spring he was convicted of murder
in the fust degree.   You see, boys, the feller was a
detective, and he had come down here o' purpose to
ketch him.   Now this one goes on talkin' jest ez he
did, and don't seem to have no more business on his
hands."

Here Charlie paused and looked with cool triumph
into the fire, as if he had proved his case conclusively
but was too modest to look up for applause. The
circle of men had gone on smoking gravely, giving
confirmatory nods at certain points of the story. They
had heard it more times than it would be well to estimate, though not as illustrative of this particular per-

son, but no one gave a sign of impatience at the last
recital.

Next spoke Jim Bolton, a good-natured young fellow, who managed to be very happy with his wife and
six children in a house of two rooms, and bore with
the most beaming good-humor the epithet " shiftless,"
applied in no very severe reproach, but as the result
of criticism by the town in general.

" Must ha' been a politician after office," he said,
knocking the ashes of his pipe into the saw-dust bed
in which the stove was set ; " never had a stranger
make me talk about myself as he did, except Emmitt,
when he wanted to be senator. Kept holt o' my hand
ten minutes, Emmitt did, askin' how my family was,
before I got a chance to answer him."

" What did you tell him, Jim ? " asked a youth of
nineteen, who felt highly honored at being admitted to
this conclave, and who knew, as did all the rest, the
coming answer.

" Told him I was much obliged for his int'rest, and
that my wife and child'en was all down with the small-
pox. Lord ! how quick he dropped my hand and
skulked off," and Jim's voice broke into a ripple of
laughter.

A smile passed round the circle ; an old story was
as good as a new one—in fact, rather better ; it was
more in harmony with the current of Stratford life ; a
new and startling recital would have been like a
heavy stone thrown into the calm waters, making waves
instead of ripples.

But one man had an interest in making Oswald's
acquaintance. Si had intended to use his boat him-

self, that morning, and had gone to the shore only to
look for it in vain.   Great was his astonishment when
Jim, who he supposed had borrowed it, came down for
that very purpose, and it was not until some gunner
solved the mystery by saying he had seen the stranger
out in it, that the wonder ceased.   Si waited to see it
brought in and give the stranger a decided expression
of his opinion.   He was of that easy nature which
could forgive almost any dereliction for weeks, and
then when it happened to impress itself on his mind,
would suddenly pounce upon the offender.

He watched for the boat's coming in, but a
friend with a bunch of brant and teal over his
shoulder, big enough to make any sportsman's eyes
water, passed through his back yard and stopped
to talk ; and Si, forgetting his resolve in the excitement of telling his grievance, was deeply absorbed
at the very moment when Philip was drawing up the
boat and running home across the rocks.   When Si,
taking his foot down from the saw-horse and his hand
from his knee, had finished his narrative, he found, to
his surprise, the boat in its place.   But the sturdy sea-
man had a strict sense of justice and was not to be balked of his purpose ; so, learning that Oswald was at the
farm, he took his way there, saying nothing to the men
who inquired about the loss of his boat.   The house
was quite dark, as he approached, save for a glow of
ruddy fire-light playing across the small window-panes.
Si knocked, and after waiting a suitable time for an
answer, walked into one of the large, square rooms
opening from the hall.

"Come in," said the voice of the young stranger,

lazily. " I don't know who you are, but you're welcome."

After the moment necessary to accustom his eyes to
the gloom, Si could see the young man's figure, stretch-
ed on a buffalo-robe before the roaring fire. The old
house, left untenanted for so many years, had not
known a fire for so long that it must have been quite
shaken on its foundations with enthusiasm, at the roar up
the wide chimney and the tongues of ambitious flame.
Si seated himself gravely on a straight-backed chair
near the door. " I come to ask you about usin' my
boat this mornin'," he said, every word pointed and
emphasized to the young man's ears by the broadness
of the vowels and the rolling of the " r " s. Oswald
was instantly conscious of a pleasant interest and a
wish to detain him, there was such a delicious newness
in his speech.

"About paying for it? I knew I should want it
again and so I thought perhaps we had better settle
for it all together ; was that all right ? "

" Not the pay for it," said Si, still keeping up his un-
discouraged pursuit of justice. " The amount of the
matter is, my boat's my own ; I don't allow no man to
take it away 'thout my leave. It don't make no difference 'bout this mornin', but if you are goin' to stay
in these parts you might as well know it."

Oswald began to wonder what canon of social usage
his innocent and unsuccessful excursion of the morning had violated.

" Was it because I sent the boy—what's his name ?—
Philip, to ask for it ? But you see it was a good deal
more convenient than to go myself, and to tell you

the truth, I didn't know whose boat he got. I told
him you wanted to use yours to-day and he asked me
to let him find one. I didn't even notice it was the
one we had yesterday."

Light dawned on Si and he began to smile broadly.
You must remember that in the exceedingly primitive
and remote town of Stratford, slight events were often
obliged to magnify themselves in order to create a
proper interest in life.

"Wal, that's the master!" said Si, with a deep drawn
breath; "the master! If it had been one o' the other
boys I shouldn't ha' been surprised; but Phil, he passes
for a young deacon."

"Do you mean that he took it without permission?"
asked Oswald, laughing. This little affair interested
him, too; the very atmosphere of the place seemed to
inoculate him with its floating germs, breeding interest.
Any corner of life made him a home.

"He didn't look like a scamp, but I suppose all boys
are, more or less; I know I was."

Si was still smiling, "I don't know ez I care, now he
done it; an' Jim didn't want much to go out, this mornin', either. Any body likes to accommodate a neighbor fust, you know."

"Yes, I suppose so. What is Jim; a fisherman?"

"Wal, no;" said Si, argumentatively, thoughtfully
inclining his head on one side and stroking his leg where
the fire scorched it. "Jim ketches a few fish in the
summer, for the Sea View, and shoots a few birds and
pots lobsters. He's one of them fellers that jest keeps
body and soul together, and wouldn't work more'n that
to save you. But Jim's a good neighbor, and a fust-

rate hand if any body's sick ; he lays out every body in town."

" Married ? "

" Yes, and six child'en, too. It's well for him that his wife is jest like him, for a capable woman'd make it hot fur Jim. Lord ! I've been there in the mornin' when there warn't nothin' in the house to eat but a couple o' lobsters, and they was all as chipper as you please ; one child arter another tumblin' out o' bed ; and Tishy settin' on the door-step with the baby, as cheerful as if there warn't nothin' in the world to do ! "

"Well, it's a comfortable way to take life," said Oswald, putting his hands under his head and settling into an easier attitude. " A good many of you people here in Stratford seem to get along without much worry, as far as I've seen you."

" I've thought o' that, myself," Si said, with an air of having heard for the first time from another, a thorough-ly original proposition which had long been revolving in his own mind. " I've wondered sometimes,- if 'twas as easy to get a livin' in other places,—not to be rich, you know, but to get a livin',—as it is here. What would be the use of a pile o' money here ? there ain't no stores but Jerry's, and a man can't spend much on dried apples and molasses. I s'pose it's different in thicker settled places."

" Yes," said Oswald, gravely, with a keen relish of such homely reflections, "most of us are not satisfied unless we either have a fortune or have spent two or three. But tell me more about the people here ; this Philip's family, for instance, what are they ? "

"Wal, there's Mis' Nye an' 'Lizabeth an' the son,
—the boy that lets boats ! " with renewed appreciation of the morning's occurrence, " an'.th' old Ma'am.
She's the devil an' all ! "

" The grandmother ! yes, I've seen her. Does she
rule the family ?"

" You'd think so if you'd lived in the town ez long
ez I have, and knew all the inns an' outs of the
neighbors' business. You see it happened in this way.
Old Mis' Nye was always used to havin' her own way ;
she was the youngest to home, an' they always hu-
mored her more than the others. The old minister
was one of the real old brimstun sort and didn't give
his family no rest from week's end to week's end ;
they had to set up straight and never speak o' nothin' more like folks than praisin' the Lord. But Jane,
this last darter, was a good deal like him an' had the
same iron temper, and so he begun to let her have her
own way over the other child'en, an' when she was
growed up she kep' it ! Her husband was a sort o'
quiet man, an' she had the money, too, so things
come into her hands agin ; an' then her child'en
walked in the path the old lady marked out for 'em.
Jeremiah didn't live long to do it ; he died when he
was studyin' for the ministry. Abner stood it ez long
ez he could an' then he died, too."

" I should think the grandchildren might prove to
have minds of their own," said Oswald.

"But ye see, she allers had the whip-hand," said
Si, proving his case by means of finger and thumb,
dimly seen in the fire-light. " She allers had the
money. Abner went into speculations an' lost all but

the house-lot an' the timber land that belonged to old
Mis' Nye ; lost all he had, ye see. So th' old Ma'am
has had to take her money to support 'em all ; they've
had to feel it, too ! "

" Is the old lady very rich ? "

" Yes, I suppose she's a rich woman. The Nyes
have always been well on't,—money an' bank-stock
an' railroad shares. Lawyer Sims, over to Stowe, gets
her dividends out ; he's close-mouthed ; never can get
him to tell how much the old woman owns, but I guess
it's a good deal. She's done a good many things for
'em all ; sent 'Lizabeth to school over to Weston, and
I s'pose she'll do the same for the boy. He'll have to
be a minister to keep up the family, or th' old Ma'am'll
worry him into consumption ; all the Nyes are given
that way."

It had been some time since Si had found an interested listener who was not perfectly familiar with
the facts he was relating ; it inspired him to loquacity.
He would have been greatly surprised, at the end of
the evening, to know how much time his speech occupied ; but like most people who are garrulous, the
only impression left on his mind was that Oswald was
" a sociable fellow."

The two smoked a pipe together ; the young man
only half hearing some of the old sea-dog's reminiscen-
ces, but wrapped in an agreeable atmosphere of smoke,
warmth, and indolence. Si took his leave at ten, prof-
fering the use of his boat, with great cordiality, for the
next morning, because Jim was going to Stowe to see
about getting some shoes to make.

" Lord ! he'd never finish a set, if he got 'em," parenthetically, "but it does him good to try to do suthin', once in a while ; makes him feel like other folks."

Oswald accepted the offer of the boat ; but the next morning found him also on his way to Stowe, in the only wagon belonging to the Sea View.

His mood had changed ; and, no longer caring for sea-dreams or fowl, he was on his way to Boston by the early train.

CHAPTER V.

THE most apparent effect of Philip's day with Oswald was a bad cold ; a less visible result, a pleasant excitement in remembering that he had gained a fragment of real information about the theater. This was the first person he had ever met who bore the air of having an intimate knowledge of the life of which the boy dreamed. The last few years had been filled with dreams, assuming the more gigantic proportions as they depended so entirely on imagination for their growth. At first he had brought them within the scope of known facts ; dramatic life existed and men had written plays, but as a younger child he went no further than imagining himself listening to Shakespeare (which he knew better than any school-book), on a real stage. But once give the rein to imagination, especially if the mind has been starved of experience of life, and where will one stop ? Philip had, at least, that tiny germ of genius which will grow fit to cope with deeds if circumstances favor it—a passionate desire to create. The capacity for work might not be there, nor the power of mastering technicalities, but the longing was strong.

He had been hemmed in from all intercourse with life outside Stratford by circumstances which he was too young, if not too irresolute, to overcome. There were few books at home, and all but his dear Shakespeare were calculated to fit a religious bent of mind. What could have been expected ? Healthy mental growth was impossible for want of good food ; was it any wonder that the rootlets of fancy should suck the juices of the unknown and find their way luxuriantly into untrodden soil ? Since he must color his thought independently of outward suggestions, there was every reason that his intense nature should make the hues as rich and varied as possible.

Elizabeth was never shut out from his gorgeous and cloud-topping palaces. Because she listened not only with patience to his visions, but with interest only second to his own, he invited her in and made her, with himself, actor in his brilliant pageants. He was to do, while she was to share the fruits of his work. Sometime, as he told her, there would be a play full of power and pathos, to take great cities by storm, and Elizabeth would sit beside him while he should receive the praises of crowded theaters. He was glad he was still young. It could not be many years before the play would be written ; and there was a childish triumph in the thought that people would speak of his youth while they wondered the more at his genius.

Oswald's coming was something tangible as floating sea-weed from that unknown land. That some one spoke of theaters as places, actors as living existences, was almost like having a dream begin to come true. To Elizabeth, the advent of the young man was something beyond the ordinary, though no romantic fancies were connected with it. But the days

were unusually lacking of interest, that fall ; she had
seen no faces but those with which she had been
familiar all her life. And this was a handsome face
that broke the monotony, at last ; one with warm brown
hair and eyes, and a soft, youthful outline of feature.
Whatever disagreeable characteristics he might possess,
which no one could be expected to guess from an
evening's acquaintance, Oswald had the exterior and
carried the air of a fine creature ; and as such he might
easily inspire with active pleasure a nature open to
beautiful influences. Elizabeth, therefore, felt a
momentary pang of disappointment when Philip
brought the news that he was gone ; a feeling quite
overbalanced by the boy's passionate regret.

"I wanted to see him again,—I thought he would
stay !" he cried.

"I suppose he only came down for a few days' gunning," said Elizabeth. "It wouldn't be very comfortable to stay long in that bare house, you know !"

"But he had just begun to talk to me about the
things I wanted to know," mourned Philip, the pathos
of his tone in no wise lessened by the hoarseness which
was a reminder of his morning on the water. "I
couldn't ask him all the questions I wanted to, then,
but I meant to go on ; he liked to talk, I know he
did."

Grandmother had not deigned to notice that Philip
had a cold ; whenever he took one in a legitimate way,
by carrying water or wood, or sitting in the chill and
draughty church, she harassed him with remedies ;
but the present case was quite outside her sympathies.
On the subject of his absence that morning she main-

tained a silence which betrayed the state of her mind only too plainly.

Philip was nursing a secret project more daring than he had ever seriously entertained. Oswald's few words had clung to him and fixed their impression; he was convinced that there ought to be a foundation of reality for his dreams, and he set about the only practicable, as well as the hardest, method of obtaining it.

Grandmother could make his vision real. It had grown to be a habit of thought in the house that if she chose to do a certain thing she would not need to be reminded of it, and, if she had no intention of doing it, a reminder would only involve unpleasant consequences. But now Philip would take his fate in his hand, and ask her to help him.

Sunday afternoon, when the greatness of the under-taking had so grown upon him that his heart beat to suffocation whenever he thought of it, he resolved to speak. His mother and sister were at church, and, having excused himself from going out on account of his cold, he was, as usual, by the fire. Madam Nye finished her chapter and sat with her hands, those strong, square hands, folded in her lap as they never were except at the command of her creed. Her face was a little harder than usual, this morning. Philip imagined it always was, on Sunday, and wondered if it were because she chose to read the sternest parts of the Bible then, or because observance of the day was more effective and strictly religious if the face were a fit index of the heart. Perhaps if one could have traced her reverie, he would have found a page of

history in which there was one chief actor, the pale
" Jeremiah, aged nineteen." Philip thought nothing
of this ; he did remember Jeremiah, but only in connection with his own cause. Here was a son who had
been educated ; why should the grandson expect less ?

His heart beat fast, and he saw only an indistinct
blurr of print upon the paper he held. The stillness in
the room was alarming, and, when he spoke, his own
voice startled him with its strained, husky effect.

" Grandmother, my uncle Jeremiah died when he was
away at school, didn't he ? " Madam Nye started.

" The date is in the Bible, after his name," she said ;
" it's on the coffin-plate, too."

" Was he a very good scholar ? Mother says he was
called one of the brightest boys that ever went to the
Academy."

" Your mother knows no more than she's been told ;
she never saw him. But folks told the truth when
they said that."

" He went to college, didn't he ? "

" Why do you ask me such questions ? " said the old
lady, bending her keenest glance on him.

" Because I want to go away, too, and Elizabeth says
you could send me."

" So Elizabeth talks about my money, does she ?
Does she want some of it herself ? "

" No, oh no. That is, not as I do. But I must
have a chance."

" Have you made up your mind to be a minister ? "

" No, Grandmother, no : I never can. But I shall
do something you will be proud of—— "

" Yes, nobody knows what. Well, you can remember this, that when you're ready to consecrate yourself to the Lord, I'll put you through college. Till then, not a cent of my money do you lay hands on."

She turned to her Bible again, while Philip sat sick and choking, counting the ticking of the clock and wishing Elizabeth would come. He told her the conversation, carelessly, that night, covering his hurt, this time, under defiance. The wound had healed a little, with a new and rebellious resolve.

"But I've got a plan," he said, while Elizabeth looked at him in silence, too sorry for words. "I've made up my mind. I shall tell Grandmother I'll do what she says, and then when I've got my education— why, by that time my play 'll be written and I can have my own way!"

"Lie to her? Lie to any body? You shall not, if I have to tell Grandmother about it myself!" said Elizabeth, rapidly. Philip looked at her in angry astonishment.

"I thought that you cared what became of me. It seems you don't," was his parting shot, as he turned away and walked into the house.

CHAPTER VI.

THE following days were hard for Elizabeth to bear. Philip had no patience with her scruples. If they had touched a less sensitive spot in his own life, and his imagination had not strained toward one point until almost any means of reaching that seemed justifiable, he, too, would have shrunk from deceit. As it was, he could not forgive any one for not seeing how vital it was to him to have just this one thing. To do that, was to help him attain it ; therefore it must be that Elizabeth had not really understood when he believed she did. Still, he could not carry out his plan without her consent ; not quite because he feared her threat of telling Grandmother, but because a need of her approval had become second nature to him. He could no more run counter to it than to his own convictions. Consequently, while tacitly yielding to her, he vindicated his independence by making her thoroughly uncomfortable. She could only try moving him to the old kindness by little appealing ways, which apparently had no effect.

Grandmother was the same, only a little more severe to both the children. She had not forgotten that they made plans in which her money figured, and what she would or would not do was taken for granted. Mrs. Nye did not trouble herself about the new chilliness

in the atmosphere. She was so used to taking a dep-
recating attitude towards things in general, that there
had ceased to be in her mind any curiosity as to the
reason for sudden changes. You do not stop to consider the immediate cause of two or even three degrees' fall of the mercury. If people were disagreeably
silent it was sufficient for her to try, by various con-
cessions, to prevent an outbreak.

Philip came in one day, saying that the winter term
of the Academy would begin next week. Was he to
go?

"Why yes, you went last winter ; all the boys are
going, I suppose," said his mother, hesitating, and
glancing at Grandmother for confirmation, which was
not given. "Don't you want to ?"

"I don't know as I care," said Philip. "It won't
make much difference, I guess."

Grandmother laid down her knitting, a portentous
sign. She usually felt silence to be her most effective
weapon, but there were times when speech was also
required. This was one.

"There seems to be a good deal of change in you
lately, Philip," she said. "Nothing is made to suit
you, as far as I can see. Perhaps if you could find
things ready to your hand, instead of having to stoop
to pick them up, you might be better pleased. I thought
you wanted to go to school."

"I do," said the boy, respectfully enough. "But
I've been to the Academy three years, and every time
I'm put back to the same place and made to go over
the same lessons, till I can say them by heart."

"So you ought to know them by heart," said the

Grandmother, going on with her knitting. "We could say the whole catechism from beginning to end, when I went to Master Winthrop's, and you hardly know your Ten Commandments. Elizabeth remembered them better than you did. A boy that is going to make his mark in the world wouldn't be likely to let a girl get ahead of him."

"That isn't fair. The Ten Commandments are not every thing," burst out Philip, and stopped as quickly, checked by his mother's glance. "It isn't the Ten Commandments I want to study."

"The amount of it is you don't know what it is you do want," said Madam Nye, with severe composure. "You want to get hold of something that won't take time and trouble. Money that don't come by work is a curse, and it's likely to be so with learning."

"But don't you think he'd better go to the Academy, Grandmother?" said Mrs. Nye.

"If he belonged to me I shouldn't have him lounging round home while other boys are at school," said Grandmother; a general remark which, from her lips, was equivalent to a command, and Philip was not sorry. It was something to be out of the house.

He was in a frame of mind which would allow him to think of nothing but his own disappointment; perhaps he might even have been excused for making poor Elizabeth feel the weight of his ill humor.

Just then came a letter from Stowe, saying that Aunt Mercy Hardy was ill. She was Madam Nye's sister, a woman who had been only a breathing mechanism for the last ten years. Shut in from the outside world by deafness and blindness, she had, by dint of

perfect quiet, preserved the shattered old body till its
ninetieth year. The old servant wrote a characteristic
and laconic letter, saying that the old lady "couldn't
live much longer. She had spells. And could some of
the family come and stay? She herself would take
care of Mrs. Hardy. It wasn't the work, but she
couldn't bear to be there alone. And then it didn't
seem proper!" There was, evidently, to her mind,
something contrary to all precedent in spells not presided over by blood relations. Grandmother read the
letter aloud.

"Yes, Hannah'll know better than any body what
to do for her," she said slowly. "But it's true enough,
somebody ought to be there. None of us ever died
with only hired help in the house. Elizabeth, if you've
got feeling for what's right, you'll want to go."

"I?" said Elizabeth in surprise, lifting her head
quickly from her sewing. "But, Grandmother, I
shouldn't know how to take care of her."

"Don't you see that Hannah says she will do all that
herself? What would there be left for you but staying there to be company for them?" said Madam Nye,
rather sharply.

"It would be pretty dull," said Mrs. Nye. "Wouldn't
it be easier for Elizabeth to stay and keep house, and
let me go?"

"Yes, if she wants what's easy. Young folks seem
to, now. But there needn't be any talk about it. I'd
go myself—perhaps a journey in the winter wouldn't
kill me—but if it did, it would be a pity for you to have
two old women on your hands, instead of one."

"O Grandmother, let me go if I can be of any use,"

said Elizabeth, not in the least in the spirit of submission, but impatiently willing to accept a doleful winter for the sake of present peace.

But Grandmother said no more that night, and Elizabeth went to bed, hoping her own rash offer would not be remembered. She had a tender heart, but old Aunt Mercy seemed very far away, while Philip and her mother were here and needed her. Home was not very pleasant, but she had not had experience enough outside its walls to hope that other places might be kinder, or much idea that any life was very highly colored. To be sure, there were Philip's visions and her own fancies, but it was impossible for her literal mind to forget how unreal they were. Philip believed and rejoiced in them. He could have eaten a crust and persuaded himself that a bowl of nectar would make up for it to-morrow. But if Elizabeth had sought to draw comfort from the same idea, she would have tried conscientiously to believe it and then have laid it aside as a very pretty conceit, but one not at all affecting the probabilities of things.

Her last three years had been spent, with occasional vacations, in the family of a Baptist minister at Weston, who eked out his salary by taking boarding pupils. Of the three girls who were with her there, Elizabeth would have been able to say that they were very good. If you had urged the question, she might also have owned that they were very dull. And the same verdict could be given of the entire place. Of such dead respectability had it been, that no association which she cared to renew had clung to her when she came away. Directly after breakfast the next morning, Madam Nye called her as she was carrying the dishes from the table.

"Elizabeth, come here. Did you say you would go to Stowe?"

"Yes, Grandmother," said Elizabeth, with a sinking heart.

"Then get your stockings down and I'll see if they want mending. You ought to be ready to start by day after to-morrow." And so she was.

Philip was not told until night, for he had been working at a neighbor's all day. He had occasional fits of earning his own living otherwise than by castle-building. Elizabeth wondered if he would forget his resentment now. His mother told him the news while he was piling a basket of wood for the great kitchen box, and Philip stopped midway in reaching after a stick to ask with sudden interest, "Betty going away? For how long?"

"I don't know. Perhaps she will stay while Aunt Mercy lives, and that may be all winter. Don't say you care any thing about it before Grandmother, for it's all her doings."

"But it's a shame!" cried Philip, excitedly. "Aunt Mercy's older than Grandmother, and perhaps she is twice as cross. How could you let her go?"

"You know I couldn't help it," said his mother, a shade more depressed under criticism, from which she never appealed.

"Well, I'm tired of this place," said the boy, sitting down on the wood. "Every thing goes wrong. I wonder if it will as long as we live!"

Mrs. Nye went quietly into the kitchen, and told

Elizabeth to go out and speak to him. Philip was
looking at the chips he was absently handling, quiet
tears rolling down his cheeks. He did not look
up.

"Somebody ought to stop Grandmother from always
having her way!" he broke out passionately. "Perhaps you are willing Betty should go, mother. You
must be, or you'd say she shouldn't, but I won't stand
it! I want her here!"

"Why, Phil!" said Elizabeth, her voice full of tenderness and delight that he really cared. "Why, Phil!"
There was nothing more to say. Sobs came fast, and
Elizabeth was on her knees beside him, with one arm
round his neck.

"But I couldn't help it, you see," she was saying,
only selfishly glad that he was sorry. "Grandmother
asked me, and you know every thing would have been
worse if I had said no."

"But you sha'n't do it!" cried the boy, still sobbing.
"After you are gone who will there be to talk with me,
and care about what I'm going to do? Though you
don't care as I used to think you did."

"Now, Philip, you are unjust!" suddenly indignant.
"You knew why I made you so angry, when I would
have given any thing to have you pleased. It was only
because I couldn't bear to have you do a mean thing,
and I knew you would see it as I did, when you could
think about it."

"Well, it's very likely you're right," said the boy,
doggedly, beginning to gather up his wood again.
"But it seems queer that every thing any body wants is
always wrong! I want to read Shakespeare Sunday,

and it's wrong ; I want—but never mind, it's of no
use talking over things if you're going away."

"But you must know I do care, Philip," said Elizabeth, quite in despair. "There isn't a question of that.
And if I could do any thing, even speaking to Grandmother, you know I would. Shall I?"

"No, she told me enough. I know just what to
expect from her."

"Then," said Elizabeth, "do try to take courage
from something, from waiting a little longer, or from
just hoping something must come because you want it
so. And it isn't as if you were going to stay here in
the house with nothing to do ; you'll be with the boys
and have something to study."

"Yes, Latin sentences and spelling from Worcester!
And somebody from Stowe will come to keep the
school, of course, a fellow all blue neck-tie ! No, it's
all well enough for you, Elizabeth. You don't want
to do any thing, and it doesn't hurt you to sit in the
house and sew. But it's enough to kill me to see my
chances go by."

Elizabeth was hurt, but too sorry for him to waste
much pity over her own sensibilities. It was true she
had no definite ambition, and a warmer home atmosphere, with a chance of knowing some of the best
things of life, was all she asked ; yet, because her own
demands were less, was she incapable of understanding this other longing, which she had read day after
day, till it seemed a part of her heart, too ? But she
could not protest without making him still more impatient, and soothing him was worth far more than
justifying herself.

"I shall write often," she said, after a pause. "And perhaps you'll get time in school to answer, if you don't want to do it too often at home. I suppose Grandmother would call it silly."

"Plenty of time," said Philip. "That's the trouble. Yes, I'll write, and if you hear of any thing to do to earn money, you'll send me word? Nobody could hinder my running away."

Elizabeth promised, and they immediately grew happier. A vague allusion to a possible resource was like a new hope, and made the sky grow bright. Though the evening was exactly the same as usual, with constant knitting and few words, it seemed more cheerful than any had been for a long time. Elizabeth went to bed with a light heart, knowing, too, that the next night would find her at Stowe.

. . . . .

After he had watched her drive away in the old Sea View buggy, Philip dreaded to go into the house again, and wandered down to the shore. There, just hauling up his boat, was Si. He waited for Philip to come up, a tall, gaunt figure, in a rough jacket, with his oars over his shoulders.

"Young sir, I want to settle with you," he began, with no sign of amusement about the mouth left visible by the grizzled beard. "Who took my boat last week, 'thout sayin' 'by your leave'?" The joke was very stale for Philip by this time, and certainly his present mood was not the most favorable one for appreciating it.

"I did. I wanted to go out in it."

"I s'pose you're master sorry now?" with a keen

look to note the amount of hypocrisy in the lad.
He had had dealings with Stratford boys before this,
finding them profuse enough in penitence when justice
overtook them.

"No, we had a good time. Yes, though, I am sorry
if you wanted it very much. Did you, Si?"

"No-o, it ain't no matter now, young man," his
features relaxing from their enforced magisterial
frown. "But don't you never try that game again.
Mebbe it wouldn't work so well a second time. What
d'you think o' thet young feller?"

"He was splendid! He knew all sorts of things."

"Thet may be," said Si, taking his way along the
shore, Philip following. "But don't you make up your
mind in a hurry. It don't pay. When a man knows
too much, you can't help stoppin' to wonder where he
got his learnin'. I shouldn't be surprised if thet feller'd had thousands o' dollars in his life, an' spent
'em all on folderols."

"But he doesn't look as if he'd spent any being
bad," said Philip, whose ideas of dissipation were best
illustrated by Job Haddons' bloated face. "Any way,
he's a right to his own money."

"Yes, if he's come honestly by it; but I don't
believe he's used up much strength earnin' it. He
looked 's if he knew the ropes pretty well. When
you're as old as I be, you'll look twice afore you make
up your mind 'bout folks."

Si turned up the path to his own house, leaving
Philip to keep his way on the beach. The mention of
Oswald was sufficient to send his thoughts dreamily
along the current that had so often borne them since

that morning with the stranger. A sudden inspiration
came to him ; might not Oswald come again, and
would he not help him ? Philip was young enough to
trust any one who carried the recommendations of a
fine manner and beautiful brown eyes. And he was
led on further than his individual confidence would
have taken him, by the impetuous faith which belongs
to youth in general. Your young enthusiast finds it
hard to believe that the world at large does not take
his own estimate of his plans.

He caught eagerly at hope, and was again happier.
Grandmother was not the one all-powerful person in
the world, though her dollars, undiminished by distance, bore a more distinct money value than any
which might flow from a possible, unknown kindness.
Still, hope of the unseen is vastly more comforting
than hope connected with some result we partly guess.
You may plan your tower as high as you please, if you
are not obliged to stop now and then, and wonder if
there will be bricks enough to finish it.

Speak scornfully as Philip might, there was
some comfort in being at school, even studying the
too familiar arithmetic and spelling. Stratford
Academy was, like many others in similar New
England towns, dignified by a title of very delusive
importance. The school met in a bare room over
the Town Hall,—a room heated by a stove of
most impulsive temperament. In the morning, it
never deigned to make an effort towards preventing
the girls from muffling themselves in shawls, while
they held their pencils in stiff fingers, or the boys, sto-
ical as they might be, from turning up their jacket

collars ; but in the middle of the forenoon, it grew so
hot with zeal and hemlock wood that the very walls
and ceiling steamed.   There was but one term for the
year, and that in the winter, when the boys could de-
vote themselves exclusively to ciphering.   For some
years, the teaching had been done by young men who
had begun an education at some well-known institu-
tion, but whose thirst for study had not urged them to
advance beyond the first conjugation.   Having "been
away to school," it became the duty and pleasure of
the youth to prove his gratitude for such advantages
by putting their fruit to use in ways cut off from the
masses.   Consequently, he never allowed himself, at
least until this temporary pride of life had worn off,
to think of manual labor ; but in summer, took the
prettiest girl in town driving in a very smart buggy,
and in winter, heard the lessons recited in some rural
Academy.   This poverty of instruction was not peculiar to Stratford, but a misfortune it shared in common with dozens of country towns which were more
open to intercourse with the world ; the wave of edu-
cational reform and experiment had not, a few years
ago, touched any of them.   It was according to long
established precedent that boys and girls should, winter after winter, drone through the explanations of
tediously complicated "sums," acquiring a certain
dexterity in the use of figures and phraseology, which
was not without its value.   In fact, any innovation on
that time-worn habit would have been regarded as a
waste of the town's money.   I am not sure that these
sturdy committee men were wholly wrong.   Their
course of training doubtless gave a less graceful finish

than would three months a year of the oral instruction
with which certain schools are rife. But there were
developed the bone and sinew that yeomen need.
Book and pencil given, with the command to learn this
paragraph or " do" that problem, there was no idea of
help in the mind of teacher or scholar until victory
had been proved improbable by the erasure and patient re-making of several thousand figures.

Let no indignant protest rise to your lips, O educa-
tional pioneers, who would simplify and sugar-coat
Sanskrit if you could ! These are heterodox opinions,
but they are humbly submitted as exponents of the
truth that a mistaken training may have its advantages. These children might not have much versatility
of mind, but they gained a toughness of mental fiber,
a habit of self-dependence, which the disciples of your
school gymnastics will probably lack.

It was as Philip had said, the classes (and there
were at least thirty, not more than two or three pupils
having the same text-books), began with every term
at the same place and went over familiar ground.
The older scholars (youths with ambitious collars to
which their necks were all unaccustomed, the acquaintance being kept up through these winter months, and
renewed from Sunday to Sunday during the rest of
the year, and girls with crimped hair and much be-
ribboned throats), had a general idea that Latin was
the necessary accompaniment to an academic course.
Exactly what place it held in the practical work before grown men and women, they could not have told.
It is not even safe to state that many of them knew
quite what part the language had played in the world's

history. It was, indeed, popularly supposed to be a recent invention or compilation for the use of schools. Consequently, if the instructor's knowledge went far enough the pupils were able, at the end of their course, to translate the sentences at the beginning of the grammar.

This term, Felix Kewe, a stranger to every body in town, had taken the school. Lawyer Sims had seen and strongly recommended him. The district fathers had a respect for the lawyer's opinion which led them out of their usual distrust of strangers, though they did not scruple to say that the young man had "come from nobody knows where." But it was generally understood that he had finished his college course, and would teach some months before choosing a profession.

CHAPTER VII.

THOUGH Felix Kewe had no idea that he was charged with a divine revelation, he had implicit faith that he was a man with a mission. And the belief was relieved from any possible savor of spiritual pride, by the equally strong one that all men had missions. His own he recognized with ardor. He was a man who had had experiences enough to give him something more than a one-sided view of life, and consequently was not likely to be led away into fanatical courses. Felix had been very poor; indeed he was still; but there had been times in his life when he knew the vacuity consequent on one meal a day, and the depression that haunts life in a fireless attic. For several years, in his boyhood, the world had left him to his own devices. He had a dim recollection of his mother as a fragile woman with a sweet voice, and the most distinct memories of his father. He had died when Felix was a boy of ten, and the child thought of him with a kind of passionate worship. All his happiness had been connected with his father; the two lived together in a rare and beautiful intimacy.

Raymond Kewe was a man to inspire devotion in any one who was allowed to approach his life closely. He had fine tastes, and being peculiarly reserved in temperament, would have chosen to live the student's life, apart from men. That was not possible; he was

only a book-keeper at Burbank's, and saw no possibility of becoming any thing else. He was deeply in love
with his wife, and, after her death, life became too hard
a problem to struggle over longer.

He had, fortunately, owned a little house at Cambridge which was sold, and the money, with his small
life insurance, was invested for Felix. The father's
provision was that the boy should be sent to school
as long as the money lasted, and, as the interest might
not be sufficient for all unforeseen expenses, the principal was to be used as it was needed. It was, as Raymond Kewe said to old Mr. Burbank, only of importance
that the boy should be fairly started in life. By the
time the money was gone, he would have found out
whether he deserved the start. So Mr. Burbank, as
his guardian, sent him to a boarding school where the
tuition was what he might have paid for his own son ;
but it was not adapted to the size of Felix's small fortune, which diminished too fast. Mr. Burbank meant to
discharge his trust faithfully, but he had only seen the
boy once, and consequently had no very definite idea
of him as an individual. He was a busy man, and Felix's existence seldom occurred to him except on paying the quarterly bills, when he said, perhaps, " That
boy must be growing fast. I wonder what Kewe
meant to make of him ! "

Professor Mellen, the principal of the school, knew
the state of the case, and when Felix was fifteen, wrote
that the boy would only be satisfied with a college
course. Was that possible with the amount of money
still left ? The answer never came ; for, in less than a
week, the elder Burbank died. His affairs proved to

be in confusion. Professor Mellen was not a rich man. The best he could do for Felix was to give him advice, and find him a situation as office boy in Boston. He hoped it would not be permanent ; that he might be able to recommend him to some one in authority, who could help him on. But Felix, though he wrote from time to time and always mentioned the same desires, did not complain, and the Professor had not time to remember him very actively.

Nobody has known the story of those years in the office, because nobody could be told the fervor of desire, and the discouragement that walked hand in hand with every day's duties and through the dreams of each night. All that could be known was that Felix worked from seven till six and, after that, spent two or three hours over his books—the time varying as did his weariness, sometimes studying with a glow which seemed the prelude of success, and often, with bitter tears, trying to understand what only a word of explanation could have made clear. Money became the slave, the possession of which would entail that of all good things. He hoarded it jealously ; the smallest sums were magnified, until he was exultant in finding that, without too great discomfort, he could omit his dinner from the programme of the day. He did very little wailing over his fate, even as a boy ; indeed there was no time. He felt, rather than saw, as an older person might, the necessity for conserving force toward better ends than complaint.

In two years, the Burbank estate was settled, and Felix was notified that the rest of his money would be paid him when he chose. With a delight more boyish than any emotion he had dared indulge for years, he gave up his situation, talked with Professor Ryder, and so reached that gentleman's favor by showing clear common-sense, that he took pains to give him definite advice. In pursuance of that, Felix began study at Cambridge. The next year he entered college and managed to stay there. He heard of Stratford Academy through Lawyer Sims, who had chanced to visit Harvard in the way of sight-seeing.

Felix had carried through his years of hard work a growing wish to be of use in the world. He was born with that sympathy for suffering and desire to help which is inherent in some souls, and it had been fostered to a passion by his own contact with working people. That had trained this natural instinct, which was like a delicate sense responsive to suffering, by giving him a practical knowledge of what life forces people to bear. He nourished and tended theories of living ; with his pity, there was an enthusiastic faith that life need not be so bitter, if religion could be made an intentness on doing, which should leave no time nor heart for moaning over what fate had done. So the resolve to become a minister had been in his mind for years ; he had no theological creed or bias, but made his choice simply because a minister was recognized as having something to say for the good of the soul, and people expected to listen to it. Having a lesson to teach the world, or good thing to share with it, and being neither poet nor philosopher, he had no way but to stand honestly before it and speak. And he meant to do this without prefix of title, without sanction of synod or laying on of hands.

When he opened school on Monday morning, Philip did not look at him with a great deal of interest, beyond noticing that he had a muscular, rather gaunt figure, and a pair of powerful gray eyes. The face was made up of prominent, bony features ; and though there were hollows under the eyes, they were signs of hard work and study rather than ill health.

School had not been in session more than three days, when such a moving of the dry bones of learning took place as sent every young academician home with strange and exciting tales of the master's notions. It seems that Henry Barrell, who was approaching his twenty-first year, and had only come to school because he could get no shoes to make, appeared, one morning, with a battered copy of a Latin grammar, saying he meant to study it. Felix did not object, but the incident led to a familiar talk before they went home that night. It was clear enough for every pupil to think it addressed to him individually. The substance of it was, that one who is in school only three or four months in the year can not afford to waste his time over ornamental flourishes. What Stratford scholars needed, was a knowledge of the practical branches necessary for the making of good citizens, who would sometime vote on town improvements and school laws. Extra time might well be spent on history, but never on the elements of Latin. He owned that if any body insisted on an unnecessary study, he should be obliged to teach it, but he could not help hoping that every pupil would show a solid common-sense, in willingness to be guided. This fragment of a speech gave the impression that at least he knew what he was talking about.   There were various interpretations of it at the different homes.

"Sounds well!" was the sententious verdict of the Sea View, and that was as cordial an agreement as could have been expected in Stratford. The consequence was that a new plan of study was organized, from which the superfluous adornments of the Stratford mind were thrown out altogether. Something of a struggle ensued in ridding the programme of a few books to which the school was greatly attached, but even that was accomplished, and only three boys clung to their Latin. One was Henry Barrell, who would not be turned out of his course from pure obstinacy, the second, a boy who had bought a new grammar and wanted his money's worth. Philip was the third. Felix put them in a class together, and took the first opportunity of seeing them alone to ask their reasons. Philip's turn came last. He went to the battered desk, just as the last stragglers filed out, tying their comforters as they went. Felix looked searchingly at the pale, sensitive face, as he asked his question.

"I wanted to keep on with it because I mean to go to college," answered Philip, steadily.

"Then you are not included in what I said to the other boys. Have you always had it in mind to fit yourself for college, or have your friends made the plan for you?"

Philip grew a shade paler ; he half expected to be discouraged or smiled at, when his baseless plan should come out.

"They can't help me at home, and I haven't any money. Nobody has made any plans for me, except myself, but I shall do it!"

In spite of himself, his eyes filled with tears. Felix saw them and understood. His sympathetic nature gave him the key to many others ; indeed, he leaned so far on the side of understanding sorrow, that it was only common-sense which kept him from exaggerating the need of pity.

"I see," he said, kindly, as he rose to go home. "Well, if you need to depend on yourself, the best and only thing to do is to fill up this winter with hard work." Philip's heart was won. Here was something definite to do, and he began earnestly.

At the end of a week, as they were leaving the school-room, Felix called him back and said, " Wouldn't you like to come in and see me this evening? You know I board at Mrs. Potter's."

" Yes, sir, I should. When shall I come?"

" After tea, if you will, and come up to my room."

Philip ran home and carried in wood and water with an enthusiasm hitherto unknown. Having told his mother previously, he took care to mention the master's invitation at the table. Grandmother frequently felt injured at having things happen of which she had not been warned. She became more silent every day. Elizabeth was her favorite, and, strange paradox as it may seem, when Elizabeth was at home Madam Nye was so much more comfortable that she could afford strength for being more actively disagreeable.

Mrs. Potter's was a small house, about half a mile from the Nye farm, and when Philip reached it, there was a bright light in the dormer-window above the sitting-room. Mrs. Potter was a fresh-cheeked, plump little housekeeper, with smooth flaxen hair ; a woman

whose feelings lay so near the surface that the slightest
appeal to them was sufficient to excite a flow of tears.
She opened the door for Philip, the lamp in her hand
illuminating the round face, and making it more like a
winter apple than ever,—moreover, a kindly apple that
would rejoice at being eaten on Thanksgiving evening.

"Yes, he's just gone up-stairs," she said. "He told
me he was expecting you. I'll hold the light. There !
he's opened his door ; now you can see."

"Mrs. Potter," came Felix's voice, "Mrs. Potter,
please don't have any thing to do with the well. I'm
coming down again."

"You stay up there with your company," said the
little woman, beaming at his thought for her. " 'Twont
hurt me a mite to bring in a little water. I've done it
before now." And the sitting-room door closed behind her.

"Come in," said Felix, waiting for him in the door-
way. "Sit down a few minutes and make yourself
comfortable, while I go down-stairs to help Mrs. Potter a bit. She thinks she might as well keep on doing
what she always has done, and I'm trying to entice her
out of bad habits." While he was talking, he drew
the only easy-chair near the fire for Philip, who had
taken rather an uncomfortable straight-backed one.

"Perhaps you think it would have been more polite
to do my chores before you came," Felix went on.
"And so it would, but we staid a little longer at table
than usual, and then I ran up here to be sure it was
warm. Here are one or two of the latest papers, and
some books ; not the latest books, though, which is all
the better for them. Now excuse me."

He ran down-stairs, and in a few minutes Philip heard the bucket of the old well go down with a whirl and rush. He looked about the room before taking up a book. It was rather a small chamber with a sloping roof, under one side of which it would have been possible to assume only a devotional attitude. The floor was carpeted in a red and white pattern, and the large chair covered with gay chintz, while the bed boasted a log-cabin quilt. This was unmistakably the "best chamber," though the warmth from the little air-tight stove, and the table covered with scattered books, gave it a homelike, cosy air, which perhaps no other best room in Stratford could boast. Philip took up a bulky brown volume from the table, and found it to be Mill's Political Economy. The sight of a new book gives the young student a certain excitement and thrill of curiosity, for may it not contain some truth he has been seeking? Philip was disappointed to find only words which bore no more meaning to him than a mathematical formula. Before he had time to look further, Felix came back.

"Now I'm ready to be comfortable," he said, putting on the well-worn slippers again, and seating himself. "No, please, keep that chair. I don't like any thing on rockers. They make me slipshod and sea-sick. I'm no more used to lounging than a soldier. I remember seeing a play some years ago, where a sergeant has to march across the stage, turn, salute, and give an order, and he was so like a ramrod that we laughed more at him than at the play. Sometimes I am afraid of being unpleasantly like him."

Philip's interest rose at once.

"Did you live where you could go to the theater? Did you go often ?"

"I lived in Cambridge. No, I didn't go often because I hadn't much money to spend in that way."

"Was it because you didn't think it would be right to spend it so ? Grandmother wouldn't !"

"Oh, I should have been glad enough to do it if I had had more," Felix laughed. "But there's always a choice for people who are not princes in the Arabian Nights. The question was, should I spend the little I had on the theater or save it toward my college course."

"But it was a great thing for you to give up so much !"

"Not at all. Why, how you bubble over with praise and blame !" said Felix, looking at him with some amusement. "There's nothing heroic in a man's deciding what is worth most to him in life, and then giving up less important things for that."

"Why," said Philip, it striking with the force of a new revelation that circumstances could be hard for other people as they were for him, and in precisely the same way. "So you had a hard time to do it, too ! Do you suppose I ever can ?"

"I wish you could tell me about it some time," said Felix. "Now, if you are willing. Perhaps I have been in the very place where you are." Philip was ready to pour forth the whole story. He gave neither confidence nor interest piecemeal. The account was very full of Elizabeth and how she helped or hindered him.

"Elizabeth is your sister ? Yes, I knew it, though

I had forgotten for the moment. Mrs. Potter has spoken of her. And so you came to think it would be necessary for you to know more. Why do you want to write plays?"

"Why, that is the only thing I care about, and I mean to be famous."

"I believe you must have a higher object than that in your mind," said Felix, gently. "Though perhaps you are too young to recognize it if it is there, or feel the need of it."

"What, please? Isn't it high enough object to want to do any thing for the pleasure of it?"

"Not the very highest, I think, though even that people can't feel all the time. They must be thankful if they keep it somewhere in their minds and can pull it out and look at it occasionally, as a pilgrim does his relic. What I meant was that the desire to do good work ought to be a sort of religion, doing it because it is the best way one has of enriching the world. Now shall I give you advice?"

"Oh, if you would! I don't even dare talk with any body but Elizabeth, and she can't help really, but only be sorry."

"That's a good deal, too. Now you are fifteen, you know very little, but have a great deal of ambition."

Sure as Philip was of his desire to be told the truth, and familiar as he thought himself with his own deficiencies, he was conscious of a momentary resentment at this plain statement of his ignorance.

"It is to be proved whether you have the genius for work which is the only possible thing to develop ability. If you like, I will give you a start in Greek, besides keeping on with the Latin, and I can tell you, of course, what other directions to take. Now this isn't helping you to money, but the best thing you could do now, if you had a gold-mine, is to begin the course of study."

Philip's eyes were dancing.

"Do you think I can succeed ?   Yes, I know you do, or you wouldn't offer to help me ! "

" It is best to work for every thing worth having as if it were possible," said Felix, equally afraid of giving baseless encouragement and failing in practical help. " But I am sure it will do you good to work."

Philip heard only the words which answered his own desires, and went home happy.

CHAPTER VIII.

THERE were two religious societies in Stratford, which were not exactly rivals, neither claiming an exclusive knowledge of the path to heaven. There was, on the contrary, a most amicable feeling between them, though the Methodists were sure the Baptists failed in sundry minor points of doctrine, while the Baptists were equally confident that their Methodistical neighbors were lax in having but one prayer meeting a week. But great events like revivals or praise-meetings were sure to unite them, as was the case this winter, when a traveling band of Evangelists came from Scone where they had made a stay of ten days, with, one of them nasally said, "a profit of forty-three souls." They began a systematic course of exhortation urging to repentance, and graphic depicting of the consequences of hardness of heart.

There were meetings held every evening in the week, at which Baptists and Methodists mingled their tears, prayers, and confessions without a thought of sectarian boundaries.

Philip would not have thought twice of the meetings had he not been compelled to take them into consideration in a manner which roused his ire. Coming home, one afternoon, from school, the early twilight making the time seem far later than it was, he sat down at once to his Latin translation, which he had ambitiously lengthened, day by day. The other boys had long before dropped out of the class, quite satisfied with their brief sip of learning. Grandmother was standing by the stove, cleaning an old-fashioned brass candle-stick, melting the tallow and carefully wiping it away.

"You'll have to get your chores done early to-night, Philip," she said, slowly fitting in a long candle. "Your mother'll want to be at the meeting early to get a front seat. It's dark enough to carry a lantern, too ; I guess I'll clean it for you now."

"O mother," said Philip, putting down his book, "you don't want me to go with you, do you ? I can't spare the time."

"Can't spare time for the Lord ? " said Grandmother, in her most weighty and lifeless voice. "The day may come when you are obliged to. Beware, lest you provoke Him to anger."

Philip was too much absorbed in his own affairs not to be irritated by interruption, which seemed particularly ill-timed. Indeed, it probably seems so at any present moment when it occurs.

"I don't believe the Lord would rather I should go to prayer meeting than get my lessons," he said, with his head so far over his lexicon that he was ignorant of the effect of his words. "If He doesn't want me to go right on doing what I ought to do, and not stop to hear somebody preach, I haven't—"

"Stop ! " rang through the kitchen. He looked up, startled, to see that the old lady had put down her work and was standing with her gingham apron grasped in one large hand, while the other rested heavily on the kitchen table. Her square, bony frame was trembling with indignation.

"You shall never say another word like that, while you are in this house! The next time I hear a blasphemy against the Lord, you go. My father would turn in his grave, if he knew any of his family could fall into such wickedness."

The habit of obedience is strong, and though Philip had, more prominently than any other emotion at the moment, the sense that he was unjustly treated, he said nothing ; a glance at his mother, too, who was making biscuits at the table, her hands trembling too much to cut them, was a powerful restraint. Grandmother walked into the sitting-room and did not come out until she was called to tea. There was silence throughout the meal,—one of those silences which, in families, are so much harder to bear than storms of words. One coming in would have felt that the storm had been there. After tea, Mrs. Nye followed Philip into the shed, and said, in a trembling undertone, "You will go, Philip? She'll be real put out if you don't."

"I can't help it, mother ; I must get my lessons. More depends on that than any body knows,—any body except Mr. Kewe."

"But I have to be here alone with her all day," said the mother, a tremulous note in her voice, the precursor of tears. "You are at school, and Elizabeth,— I do wish Elizabeth would come home ! "

The boy was touched, as much by the homesickness in his own heart for Elizabeth, as by hers.

"Don't cry, mother. I'll go, yes, to a dozen

prayer-meetings, and if Elder Jones isn't there, I'll go
round and borrow his wig and preside."

Mrs. Nye's coming tears resolved themselves into
the accompaniment of a laugh.   She was timidly conservative in matters of religion, but she could not
believe that the powers of heaven would militate
against her boy's nonsense, much as they might
concern themselves with other matters quite as
trivial.

"That's a good boy, and we'll go early so as to see
our way."

In consequence of their zeal they found themselves,
half an hour afterwards, in the pew directly behind the
one left vacant for those who would go forward for
prayers.   Every body came.   Jim Bolton was there,
with his wife and four of the six children, the two
youngest having been left in charge of Granny Eld-
ridge, who had asthma and dared not venture out. Si
was there, looming up tall and broad-shouldered in the
corner ; the Academy boys and girls were out in full
force ; and it was evident, from the number of men
rendered miserable by coat and neckerchief, that the
Sea View sitting-room must have been left unadorned
by a single lounger.

There were three Evangelists,—one thick-set and
heavy, who sang hymns with a scowl ; one who wore
spectacles, and acquired by means of them and the upright fringe of yellow hair surmounting his forehead,
a peculiarly owl-like expression ; and a wiry, nervous
man, with a tongue moving so fast that it might rea-
sonably be supposed to flicker.   The meeting was
like a thousand others held before and since. After

the vigorous singing of a hymn, Christians were invited to rise. It seemed to Philip that the whole body
of the church was coming to its feet. Being so near
the front, he could not see that any one was seated
except himself, and when his mother slowly rose also,
his heart began to beat so that it sounded loudly in
his ears. There was an unpleasant excitement in being
the only sinner in a church full of Christians, the only
one in danger among the saved.

"Every one ! every one !" said the exhorter, in a
monotonous chant, fixing his eyes on the boy, who was
unfortunately in the range of the vacant pew ; the
singer began sonorously. The time seemed hours before the Christians were allowed to reseat themselves ;
it was probably several seconds. Those who desired
prayers were then asked to stand, and Philip continued
sitting. One after another of the young people he knew
passed, sobbing, into the anxious-seat, while his heart
beat louder and louder, and his lips grew painfully dry
and parched. In the eyes of the people his silence
betokened hardness of heart. In reality, it resulted
from pure nervousness and lack of any guiding impulse,
except the one to sit still because that involved least
trouble.

He had never thought of religion except incidentally, as necessitating a great many disagreeable sacri-
fices and deprivations ; it consisting in taking a
mournful view of life, and spending perfectly quiet
Sundays, broken only by reading of the Scriptures.
He knew, too, that if one were not a member of the
church, he was inevitably doomed to eternal punish-
ment. His Grandmother and the other people who

held the strictest views on the subject must be right ;
probably he was very wicked to sit there, not even saying he was willing to be prayed for, but he felt that the
very effort of standing, and consequently bringing all
those eyes to a focus on himself, would be unbearable.
He drew a long breath of relief when the meeting was
over, and they reached the fresh air.

Just before going to bed, while the three sat round
the stove, Grandmother looked searchingly at Philip,
who, with chin on hand, was thinking of the evening
with exceeding repugnance, and said, with startling
distinctness,

"Philip, are you under conviction of sin."

"No, Grandmother," said the boy, starting with a
hunted look, as if he had just caught sight of a new
pursuer. "I think it is all dreadful ! I wish people
would let my sins alone ! "

"So a good many people wish," said the Grandmother, wrapping her large freestone in careful folds
of flannel, and holding the compact bundle in her lap
while she looked at Philip with the eyes of a physician
accustomed to the symptoms of the soul.

Philip's sleep was not a peaceful one ; it was not
broken by dreams, but before he lost consciousness,
sins, fears and punishments assumed monstrous shapes
before which he trembled. He was not conscious of
great personal depravity, but only of a helpless feeling
that he had been born into a world full of very dark
places, into which one might fall if he did not walk in
certain paths, and that the paths themselves were so
narrow and unpleasant as to make life a hand in hand
journey with fear, and in such straight and cramped

armor that one's breath must always be drawn with difficulty through closed visor.

There were other pale faces at school the next day besides his,—some of them tear-stained and all very solemn. There were, to be sure, a few irreverent souls among the boys, who dared speak lightly of the Evangelists, but they became such a despised minority that their worldly spirit died weakly out, and they contented themselves with snowballing more vigorously than usual, while the opposite party sat about the stove at noon. Felix felt the brooding excitement in the air, but did not trace it to its source. He had been unusually busy with his reading for some evenings, and, so absorbed, had no further knowledge of the town affairs than that there were to be several prayer-meetings in succession at the Baptist church. He was therefore quite in the dark, and only said, as he passed Philip's desk, "Does your head ache?"

" Yes, sir."

" Then I wouldn't try to do any extra translation to-day. It will come all the more easily to-morrow."

Felix had yet much to learn of Stratford ways. At recess, Dora Chester, who was of a sentimental cast and would probably, with a more facile use of rhymes, have written poetry to be estimated only by long measure, but who now relieved her over-charged sensibilities by prose composition on Hope or the Seasons, came to the desk to ask, " Mr. Kewe, do you love the Saviour ? Are you a Christian?"

Felix's eyes were opened in an instant to the meaning of the general air of other-worldliness.

" Not a church-member, if that's what you mean,

Miss Dora," he said cheerfully, going on with the evolution of a long "sum." "Did you mean that?"

"Yes, sir. I thought of course you'd have found the Saviour before this."

As the week went on, the gloom deepened. There were scoffers in town who still pursued their accustomed walks of life, yet the majority subordinated secular affairs to this annual balancing of their spiritual accounts. In school, Testaments were secretly substituted for text-books. Much as Felix might disapprove of a fever of emotion, it was still a religious one, and he had too much reverence to attempt killing it violently. Philip was besieged on all sides by admonitions and urgent requests to go forward for prayers. That attack on the subject of his sins made him uncomfortable, roused in him an unpleasant fear that such discomfort proved his guiltiness. Perhaps that enigmatic phrase "under conviction," already applied to him. And while repugnance to the whole subject and fear of being drawn into the ranks occupied his mind, Grandmother watched him keenly, and read, for the morning chapter, fiery Jeremiads and gloomy denunciations, until Philip's flesh crept with a horror of the supernatural.

The week passed and the revivalists were gone. Every one breathed a little more freely; even the most zealous were glad to feel themselves justified in indulging in less intense emotion. The new converts, including three-fourths of the Academy pupils, held prayer-meetings on every available occasion, and preserved an habitual expression of solemnity. Had Felix been content to wait, things would have righted themselves, as

they always do after a strain ; but in his zeal, quite as
hot, in its way, as that of the Evangelists, he believed
it his duty to add his influence to that of time. He announced to the school that he would hold a meeting
in the room that evening. The scholars looked at each
other in astonishment. It had been a growing prej-
udice among them that the master was not " a professor." Felix caught the glance, and, with ready tact,
went on, " I see no reason why I should not talk to
you as well as any preacher who has as much in his
mind that he wants to say. Perhaps you do not all
know that I intend being a minister myself, within a few
years."

In an hour, a wave of strong approval swept over
the community, and the best coats and gowns were
donned without delay. As Felix went up to the school-
house at seven, he overtook Si, who, with stertorous
breathing, and huge, seven-league strides, was steadily
pursuing his way.

" Goin' to convert 'em all over agin ? Wal, I guess
they need it."

" Perhaps not," said Felix, " I merely had something
to say and took this opportunity of saying it."

" I've nothin' to say agin religion," said Si, as they
plodded on. " Nothin' ; 'twouldn't become me either,
thet ain't never been a professor and only knows one
side on't,—but I can't abide the airs o' the new converts. What did they do but come and hang over me
at the meetin' till I felt like a great shaggy dog jest
out o' the water, being pestered by a couple o' little
black-an'-tans. Says I, No, I've got sins enough, Lord
knows, but the Lord's goin' to settle his own 'count, I

guess, 'thout my standin' up to be prayed for. You
know Jim Bolton ?—Know he got converted ?"

"I know who he is," said Felix, "but I haven't been
to the meetings, and guess more than I hear about
them."

"Wal, Jim, he does it reg'lar every time there's a
revival. Sort of an obligin' fellar, you know, and can't
bear to hurt any body's feelin's by sayin' no, an' jest
as reg'lar he backslides after the revival's over. Makes
me think of what my mother said about a man that
done the same thing, and when he'd been converted
seven times, old Mis' Parsons come in and says, 'Sam
Gridley's found the Saviour agin, and he's so happy !'
Marm was tryin' out lard, and she went on skimmin'
away and says, 'Better cut his head right off, then.
Don't let him have a chance to backslide !' "

They were going up the hall stairs at the conclusion
of the anecdote and Felix was conscious that his face
wore a broad smile, which ill accorded with the general
hush and solemnity of the assembly. Old and young
were there. The stove was almost red-hot, attesting
the zeal of the scholars who had the room in charge ;
kerosene lamps were lighted, and well-worn hymn-
books lying on the desk. Felix perhaps made a mistake in not opening the meeting formally with singing,
but he was only conscious of the message he had come
to deliver ; moreover, he was quite unused to the
orthodox mode of proceeding.

"You have been excited about your sins, this past
week," he began, taking his place near the platform ;
"the excitement was followed by an exhaustion which
you mistook for peace. One step beyond that lies

your ordinary and comfortable state of mind. Unless you are careful, there is coming a greater danger than that of going on sinning—the danger of believing you are safe forever, and so can drink sacramental wine and eat the bread of the communion while you slowly drift back into slothful living. Believe me, there is no need of spending your strength and your tears in be-wailing past sins. The only true conversion takes place when a man realizes he has not always been faith-ful to the right, and swears that, henceforth, he will choose his duty before every earthly good, putting aside pleasure and personal comforts for its sake, without hope of reward. What hell is there for him if he refuse ? The fact that he has made it harder for some other soul to live happily and grow strong ; the remorse that lies in knowing he is out of harmony with the beautiful universe. While rain, and snow, and fire, and vapor obey the laws which render their operations beneficent, he is every day transgressing the Divine mandates.

" Do you not see, the hell of feeling a personal re-morse at having committed sin, is a slight pain com-pared with the knowledge that this sin has created some misery in the world which was not there before ? The first touches you alone ; the second reproaches you with having injured all men.

" You have been sorrowful and cast down. I have seen it in school ; even the young people are impressed so deeply by this haunting dread of a wrathful God, that they cannot give their minds to their every day work. I have heard it repeated dolefully, that " this is a dying world." It is not, unless you mean that physical

death is here. Our bodies change into other elements,
as one tree dies and grows up again into new forms of
life. Whether we live again as the same individuals,
I do not know, but of this I am sure ; that the world is
all life, instead of a deceitful appearance of life
wrapped about a ghastly skeleton of death.

" You have all had trouble, except, perhaps, those
who are too young to have felt it, but to whom it will yet
come ; sickness, discouragement and death have crept
into your houses, and lingered like unwelcome guests.
But believe and ye shall be made whole. Believe in
one another, that life is full of hope, and that these
sad and cloudy days bring nearer a great and general
good, that they are all needful for working out that
good. Rejoice every day, be kind to one another, and
put aside this horrible phantom of an angry God and
a waiting hell. As well as if I had been shown the
truth in a vision, I know these fears are needless."

A man fired with an idea can hold and sway his
audience, though the influence may be but temporary.
Felix believed with all his heart in what he was saying.
His eyes glowed and grew black with the intensity of
the emotion behind them ; his voice was full of the
pathos which, sent warm from the heart, melts the lips
which are its messengers to softness and eloquence.
He had the personal magnetism which moves men ; a
growing consciousness that it was so sustained him
through the words he had to say, and gave him a triumphant belief in their worth.

People went out slowly, after he had finished, no one
venturing to deliver an opinion. After the first criticism had been made, others would follow in flocks.

Philip had been deeply moved. The master was his oracle of wisdom ; now he had spoken with authority and had become a spiritual leader. The boy went home with his volatile spirits at the top of the wave. Life was simplified ; he had been told for the first time, that it might be right to be happy.

CHAPTER IX:

W ERE there many testimonies ? " asked Madam Nye, the next morning. "Who led in prayer ? " "There wasn't any prayer," said Mrs. Nye, as unconcernedly as she could.

"No prayer ! " repeated Grandmother, putting down her knitting, which she had taken for a few rounds before breakfast. "What do you mean ? I thought it was a meeting. Philip said so."

"Yes, he did, but it wasn't a common meeting. It was like a lecture, you know. He preached a little sermon about what people ought to do after revivals. Pretty good, too, I thought."

"A lecture on sacred subjects, and not begun by asking the blessing of the Lord ? That's something I never heard of ! "

"He said we needn't be afraid of any hell, either," said Philip, mischievously.

"If that's what he thinks, the town had better get rid of him," said Grandmother, slowly. "And the children ought to be kept out of school."

As may well be imagined, Philip realized that further pursuit of the subject might not be quite wise.

Comments on the previous evening were various, but nowhere was such a faithful exposition of the real popular sentiment as at the Sea View.

"Seems to know his own mind, any way," said Jim
Bolton, who took a lenient view of opinions diametri-
cally opposite. "I like thet in him, though he don't
seem to take much stock in savin' grace."

"I'll tell you what I've been thinkin'," said Sam
Peters, taking the cautious side of the road. It was
a constitutional habit; he was never known to row
on any but the smoothest sea. "Air we jestified in
keepin' a fellar in town thet'll put such ideas into the
young folks' heads? Now, I've allers been used to
hearin' thet there's a hell, an' somehow I shouldn't
feel easy to give it up. But I take it from what I've
heerd that he don't deny there is one," waiting for
confirmation, which was given by two or three nods
around the circle. "No, I took it not. He only says
't aint jest the hell we've been used to. Now, on t'other
hand, I don't see," taking out his pipe which was to
serve as an emphatic aid to gesticulation. "I don't
see why thet shouldn't be so. There's hunderds of
things changed sence I was a boy. Why, when we
kep' bees, Sir never was easy 'thout there was a sprig
o' tansy near the hive, and now nobody thinks o' usin'
it. We allers used to kill our pigs on the full o' the
moon, but Seth got into the way o' doin' his butcherin'
any time the weather was fit. So now why shouldn't
there be some change in religion?"

"Thet's a kind o' dangerous thing to say, an' you a
professor," said another. "Why don't the Scrip-
ters change ef it's sootable to say one thing to-day an'
another to-morrer?"

"Now, I ain't a saying there *is* such a thing as veer-
in' an' tackin' in religion," said Sam, deprecatingly,

but still anxious to present the subject with as much
liberality as possible. "I was only a sayin' it might
be so, as it is in other things. But on the ground thet
a man hain't got no right to take up new doctrine, I
say air we doin' our duty by the town in lettin' our
child'en hear such new fashioned notions?"

"The young fellar's likely to be in the right on't,"
broke in Si's deep voice. "He's got a good deal o'
common-sense on his side, an' learnin' too. I never
went to college myself, but I'd bet on any body thet
knew enough to prove what he said by the book."

Si's word was of great weight, and concluded the
speculations for that day, at least. For a man to be of
exceptional stature, capable of holding his tongue at the
right time, or knocking down an offender if necessary,
sure to bring a boat-load of fish or a brace of birds,
does him as good service in a community like Stratford
as exceptional intellectual gifts may elsewhere.

Felix saw a change at school, in the fact that some
few of the scholars shunned him with an air of distrust, which he read perfectly. They were unable to
make up their minds whether he was the inculcator of
dangerous unbelief, or a harmless individual who
took a different view of life from that of their
fathers and mothers. But the majority showed an enthusiastic regard for him. Philip wrote Elizabeth
glowing accounts of the master, which led her to ask
for more definite reports of what he really said. Her
letters to her mother, which must be read to Grandmother, were tame items of information in regard to
Aunt Mercy, and what she herself was doing. Hannah
was very good to her—too good, in fact, because she

would not let her do any housework. Aunt Mercy required very few services. It pleased the old lady to
have Elizabeth sit with her, she herself by the fire, in
the helpless apathy which accompanies extreme age,
occasionally asking a question in a cracked, high-
keyed voice. The questions were usually concerning
some long past event, which Elizabeth might have
heard mentioned, but which had no real existence for
her. She was conscious of an eerie feeling that she
was living in a world of shadows which had been substance once, but had died out and left her only their
thin, querulous voices echoing from the past. Sometimes she sat sewing for hours, every nerve alive with
anticipation of that questioning voice again, in reply to which she must probably shout, "I don't
know, Aunt Mercy." She was compelled to live
within herself; a life of reflection which no young
person would choose, being forced on her by soli-
tude and the absence of interest in her surround-
ings. Philip's letters were welcomed like no other
interruption of her day. They were hopeful; he
spoke of talking over his plans with Felix, and the
fact of present help in study; then of the hopeful
things Felix said of the possibility of making life
worth living happily as well as dutifully. This last
was like a breath of out-door air, a ray of sunshine
striking athwart a darkened room. It held no definite
solution of what were growing to be serious problems
of life for her. Philip's accounts were rambling, glowing with a new ardor rather than defining any logical
creed, but they sweetened her moods. Finally she grew
to piecing out the fragments of thoughts he sent, from

her own mind. When Philip wrote that Mr. Kewe was giving a course of lectures, and that they were exciting all sorts of comments in town, she began to look eagerly for further particulars.

The truth was that Felix had conceived the daring idea of giving a set of lectures on morality. While he held that the only permanent good can be done by building up physical and moral cleanliness in men by slow degrees, he was yet strongly impressed by the power of the word alone. Perhaps it was not possible for him to greatly benefit the people of Stratford in his short stay there. Real teaching demanded time, a life full of effort, and he was convinced that his own star called him elsewhere. These people were stolid and bigoted, not stifled with misery nor sunk in crime, and he longed for a work among those who sorely needed comfort. Would not the best thing here be to rouse an enthusiasm for good deeds, by personal appeal, leaving it to take what form it might?

People came to the lectures unsuspiciously, and Felix, realizing the importance of not creating a panic (which would only serve to drive away the conservative, leaving, perhaps, a few dare-devils who would listen to him as long as what he said disagreed with popular opinions), meant to be sufficiently careful of his phrases. Beginning with the physical basis of good and évil deeds, he electrified the staid members of Stratford society by a new version of the time-worn doctrine of the influence of Adam's fall. He uttered some truths startling to ears accustomed only to Scriptural axioms served up year after year in the same dress,—sometimes a sad masquerade, it must be owned.

A few of the more pronounced among his unfavorable
critics staid away from the second lecture ; others
halted in opinion, and went with the majority of the moment, while a third class, composed chiefly of young people, were ready to become his loyal disciples. At length,
in consequence of some statement a trifle more heterodox than usual, a wave of excited feeling rose against
him, and it became a question of public interest whether
it was not the duty of the town to refuse him shelter.
A self-appointed committee of two resolved to visit
him and settle the matter. A judicious questioning
must force him to show decided colors, for, however
ready Felix had been in avowing principles, he let
points of doctrine altogether alone, neither denying
nor affirming. Deacon James and Cyrus Pearson had
talked much together on this question of the day.
Perhaps the suggestion came from them, or possibly
originated with some citizen less willing to undertake
responsibility ; in any case, one crisp, clear night
found the two, in the full dress of gingham neckerchiefs and Sunday suits, at Mrs. Potter's door.

"Yes, he's here," said the widow, a little fluttered.
"Walk right in and I'll call him. Cold, Deacon, ain't
it ? I'll try to get this stick in. It's a knot that
wouldn't split, an' bein' hard wood, it keeps the fire.
Is your folks well, Mr. Pearson ?"

"Tolable well. Abbie's had a cold, but she allers
expects it this time o' year. Oh, here's the master,"
as Felix came in from the kitchen with another hard
knot, a stubborn, gnarly mass that defied splitting from
every one of its knobs.

"Good evening, gentlemen," he said, heartily, put-

ting down the stick to shake hands. "Glad to see you.
Mrs. Potter, will you have this in now?"

"No, I just put one in. I'll go out an' do my clear-
in' away; the folks have come to see you."

Felix devoted himself accordingly to the entertainment of his visitors, neither of whom seemed quite at
ease, though he supposed their silence to be only the
result of unaccustomed clothes, and the responsibility
of making a call. The conversation drifted from the
clear sky to the sea, and the need of a new town-hall.
Then there came a pause. Cyrus, feeling that the
moment for making a plunge had arrived, began with
his fluently nervous speech.

"We called to talk over a little matter o' doctrine,
Mr. Kewe. I don't suppose you'd feel behindhand
in statin' your convictions, should you?"

Cyrus was a thin man of a uniform color, having
sandy hair and a face ash-like rather than pale. He
was wiry animation beside the Deacon, who simply
represented so many pounds avoirdupois. His large
frame, heavy face surmounted by black hair, large
hands, and slow utterance, made up a vast whole.

"Convictions?" said Felix. "Certainly, if I have
formed any. On what subject?"

There had been no doubt in the mind of Cyrus that
his meaning would be caught at once. To be asked
for more explicit explanation was embarrassing. He
fidgeted in his chair for a moment, and then turned
to the Deacon, saying feebly, "I b'lieve it's your turn
to speak now."

The Deacon had been slowly drawing up the heavy
artillery, which was as slowly bent upon the opposing

ranks. "We've heerd it said you was goin' to be a minister o' the Gospel, an' nobody's ever mentioned your denomination."

"Oh, I see," said Felix, settling himself gravely to the subject. "No, I don't at all mind telling you that I'm of no denomination. I do not belong to any one church, though my belief inclines towards Unitarianism."

"A Unitarian, an' not quite that, nuther!" broke out Cyrus, treading on the heels of Felix's speech with startling promptitude. "Then what do you believe?"

"It will not take very long to tell you. I believe in doing right for the sake of one another and the conscience that is within us. If you ask me if I believe in God, I cannot answer yes, because I know you think of Him as a person. I have not yet been able to decide whether I consider this wonderful something to be personal Deity, principle, or a mystery animating the universe. After all, the name makes little difference. You call him God, and a great philosopher calls him the Unknowable. You mean the same thing."

"Do you believe in the savin' blood o' Christ?" asked the Deacon, ponderously.

"No ; I believe that his example did the world incalculable good, and that, as example, he has benefited me ; but I cannot think that his death has any thing to do with the forgiveness of my sins."

"About the need o' conversion," said Cyrus, growing momentarily sharper and more ferret-like. Now that the first embarrassment was over he felt as eager for investigation as the Grand Inquisitor himself. "Do you b'lieve it's necessary to jine a church?"

" No."

There were a few more questions with prompt, grave answers, and the two men took their leave. The next day they had a long talk with the members of the school-committee, one of whom called on Felix immediately after and announced, in a somewhat shamefaced manner, that "the money hadn't hel' put as long as they'd expected, an' school 'd better close next Friday."

CHAPTER X.

SO the school closed, in the midst of indignation
and approval. This was Philip's first great loss.
He had grown in a few weeks to feel that, as the beginning of the solution of his haunting question came
from Felix, the same judgment was to be his pioneer
through deeper thickets of the same forest. With a
child's wholesale despair, he was sure that there was
nothing left him but renouncing ambition and walking in the path towards which he was led by circumstances.

"Nonsense!" said Felix. "I'm not a demigod.
See, Philip, you are in as deep a difficulty as Æneas
and Ulysses ever were. Suppose you give your mind
to the problem of getting out. It will be a fine thing
to do."

"But what can I do—study alone?"

"Yes, and when you strike a snag write me, and
we'll see what can be done in the way of pen and ink
teaching. I shall be in Cambridge, but not long, I
hope, for I want above all things to establish my little
church."

"I thought churches were all ready, and ministers
had calls to them."

"Usually, yes; but no church would call me and
let me honestly say that I am neither priest nor

Levite. I only want to help a band of people who
shall come together for the purpose of doing good
works. If I were a member of any religious denomination I should feel obliged to uphold articles of faith
which I cannot affirm."

"Do you mean that you wouldn't preach from the
Bible?"

"Not altogether; that is why the most liberal of ex-
isting creeds would still be too binding. I should take
truth found any where—truth irrespective of authority
—for my foundation-stone; it might sometimes be a
text from science, sometimes from a religion popularly considered pagan, and often a thought dropped
by a child or a working-man."

"But I don't see——" began Philip, perplexed.
"Isn't any of it true? What I've always heard, I
mean."

"Much, ever so much; but the religion of the
future is a higher and better thing. See, Philip, the
last ages were those of belief without question. When
priests described Heaven and hell, the pictures were as
real to them as this beach and the sea-waves are to you
and me. Then, when there were greater and more and
more numerous discoveries in science, people (and the
wisest people too, mind you,) grew to believe only
what they saw with their bodily eyes, or could touch
and experiment on. Now, one age leans as far one
way as the past one did in the opposite direction,
because people can't believe in any thing with all
their hearts without making some mistakes. And in
counteracting past mistakes, we are likely to make
just as many different ones."

"So," said Philip, delighted to deduce a conclusion, "if people don't believe enough now, they will believe too much by and by."

"Exactly. We are an age of doubters, and the next will be one of superstition. I am inclined to think its credulity will be in reference to spiritualism. I believe that holds truth which will be one step in the elevation of the race, but before the real heart of it speaks to the heart of the people, there will be vulgar expounders of its apparent miracles ; there will be as much superstition as the old age of witchcraft ever held. So thoughtful men have a duty, to see that the common dependence on material truths shall not degenerate into skepticism and hardness, and, on the other hand, that no superstitious falsehood gain foothold. We have our responsibility in forming this coming religion ; we have no right to sit down and fold our hands, waiting for the next prophet."

.   .   .   .

The winter went on slowly, with more variations in the physical atmosphere than in its social one. There were at least alternations of gray and sunny days, with the occasional purification of a storm, but no change enlivened the Nye household. Philip was too absorbed in study and letters from Elizabeth and Felix, to have much time for complaint, or, more fortunate deprivation still, for adding airy towers to his unsubstantial castles. At length, when the first change from settled dreariness and cold to the sweet-tempered spring might be looked for any day, word came that Aunt Mercy was dead.

"I shall go to-morrow, Eliza," said Madam Nye.

" I've expected it this four weeks, and my clothes are
all ready to pack. I'll have my hair-trunk brought
down and set by the fire. I shall want four or five
changes. It's always best to have enough."

Mrs. Nye, inwardly wondering why the short journey
would necessitate so many suits of raiment, brought in
the precisely folded packages of linen, venturing to ask
no questions, but suggesting that she and Philip could
take a valise together.

" You and Philip ! Where are you going ? " asked
Grandmother, pausing in the inventory of a box of
night-caps, to look up sharply. " Eliza, you are old
enough to show more calculation. Since I came to
this house, it never has been left alone for a single day
or night. Are you willing things should go to ruin,
while you are at the funeral of somebody not your own
blood-relation ? "

How could Mrs. Nye believe in the conclusion suggested, unless it should be confirmed by the plainest
English ? In the past ten years, Grandmother had not
been away at all, and this poor, depressed little woman,
who for a quarter of a century had been trying to fit
her thoughts and feelings on the model prescribed by
this martinet, felt like a child grown drowsy and stolid
over his book, who is suddenly promised weeks of sunshine and acres upon acres of green fields.

" Go to my blue chest, Eliza. Here's the key," taking an imposing bunch tied with a twisted blue cord
from her large pocket. " And in the right hand side,
down by the till, find the bundle done up in a Watch-
man. They are the clothes I want put on me when
I'm laid out. I'd better take them with me, for if I

should be called away while I'm gone, ten chances to one you'd bury me in my every-day clothes and never find these till you began to rummage my things."

Mrs. Nye held the bundle rather gingerly, when she came back with it.

" Do you think there is any need of taking them for so few days, Grandmother ?" she said, timidly. The journey had a funereal aspect that her kind heart longed to relieve.

" I shall stay longer than two or three days. You don't seem to consider that the property will go to me and I shall have to settle it up. I may be gone a month."

A month of freedom ! Mrs. Nye had always done Grandmother's bidding patiently, but she now set about speeding her departure with a helpful alacrity which approached officiousness. If Madam Nye had not been engrossed by other and weightier subjects, suspicion would have risen in her mind as to the cause of such extreme cheerfulness. When she was ready for the journey and awaiting the Sea View buggy, her appearance might have provoked a smile from the lips of irreverent and light-minded youth. A black dress of fine material, rusty with age, a shawl of voluminous folds and a large bonnet within whose projecting brim lay thick ruffles of lace, completed her costume. She sat by the window when the buggy arrived, grasping the basket in her lap with both hands, an attitude which will be found, on observation, to accompany the fact of being unused to journeyings.

" Don't throw matches around, Eliza," she said, as severely as if that dangerous occupation formed Mrs.

Nye's favorite pastime. "And you'd better try out
the lard next week. Philip, tell the man not to scrape
the end of my trunk on the wheel. Run, before the
hair's all rubbed off ! "

And so she slowly accomplished the ascent into the
buggy and drove off, her last audible words being a
request to Sam, the driver, that he should leave his
whip at home. Sam's most potent argument against
such a course lay in calling attention to the visible ribs
and evident lameness of his horse, but he was only able
to effect a compromise by which the whip was to be put
under the seat and taken out when imperatively needed. Mrs. Nye and Philip went slowly into the house
with a great outward show of propriety, but the door
had no sooner closed on them, than the boy gave vent
to an exuberant "Whoop !" It seemed a startling in-
discretion, and made him wonder at his own daring, in
the very face of the knowledge that there was no one
to object.

"Why Philip," said Mrs. Nye, unable, from long
habit, to help reproaching herself for laughing. "Be
careful ! They're not out of hearing yet, and I shouldn't
wonder if she forgot something and came back."

For answer, Philip only took her about the waist and
skimmed across the kitchen floor with her. During
the next few days, Mrs. Nye developed traits which
filled her boy with surprise. She came out with queer
little jokes, and mild attempts at playfulness, as timidly as if she were furtively glancing over her shoulder.

"It is time for a letter from Elizabeth," she said
one afternoon, as Philip came home from the store.
"She ought to write and tell how Grandmother got

there ; but then, if it hadn't been all right we should have heard before this."

An hour later, Philip rushed in, falling over the staid and respectable Maltese cat.

" She's come, mother ! The wagon has just stopped ! " he gasped, not stopping to regain his breath.

" Who—Grandmother ? " and Mrs. Nye seemed petrified, grasping a plate in one hand and the dish-towel in the other.

" Oh yes," said the boy, beginning to dance insanely about the room. " Grandmother, with her bandbox and hair-trunk ! They must be lifting the trunk down now. Why don't I go out to meet her ? Because I'm so glad—no, so sorry, I mean ! Don't go to the window ; wait till she comes in."

" Philip, you mustn't act so. Do let me go."

" No, mother," but as he seized her apron, the door opened and a voice, not Grandmother's, said, " Where are you ? Why don't you come to meet me ? "

" Why, it's the child herself ! it's Elizabeth ! " and Sam Peters stood patiently by, waiting to be paid, while the three kissed in unrestrained delight. Sam thought, himself, that such goings-on were a little foolish. His wife kissed the children, to be sure, but they were little ones, and were expected to outgrow the ceremony with their pinafores.

" Well, how did you get away ? " asked Mrs. Nye, when Elizabeth was at the supper table.

" Mother," said Elizabeth, laughing a little hysterically. " I begin to think I ran away."

" Heroic Betty ! " cried Philip. " Brave young woman, who took her life in her hand and lowered her-

self from the window! Say, Elizabeth, what will
Grandmother think of your stripping up the sheets
when she finds the shreds and tatters hanging?"

"Seriously," giving Philip's hand a caressing pat, on
her way to the sugar-bowl, "I was astonished at myself for insisting that I must do any thing when Grandmother said 'No,' but I was quite desperate. You
know all the days had been just alike." Her voice
quivered a little; now that the first excitement was
over, they noticed how pale and thin she had grown.
"I didn't mind it so much when Aunt Mercy was alive,
because I knew to-morrow wouldn't be worse than to-
day; but just as soon as there was a change, I found
I hadn't the courage to stay. It took less to face
Grandmother. You don't think I was wrong?"

"No, dear. Why no, I guess I don't!" said Mrs.
Nye, moving nearer Elizabeth in an excess of motherly
fondness, while Philip, with beaming face, sat opposite,
resting both elbows on the table. "Is Hannah going
to stay with her?"

"Yes, she is glad to do it. Grandmother really
didn't need me, not even for company, and I did need
to come home."

"Tell some more, Betty," said Philip, as she turned
to her plate again.

"You must tell now. How you've grown in these
months, Philip! And how about the new Academy
teacher? I hoped you would tell me why he left.
Grandmother said he was an atheist, and was drummed
out of town."

"It was the meanest thing that ever was done!"
said Philip, his eyes flashing. "Yes, I know what

Grandmother thought. She was just like all the rest of them. But he helped me with my Latin, and I have begun Greek."

"I shall want to hear it all," said Elizabeth, her eyes resting on him with a pleased, motherly delight. "It will take days and days to talk it all over. Mother, I don't feel as if I should ever want to do any thing again. Any one might think I had had enough of being quiet, but it seems almost as if I'd been sick, and must give myself time to get well."

"And so you shall, dear. There isn't a thing to think of but having a good time, now."

The mother was as good as her word. Elizabeth slept late, and lay down in the middle of the forenoon if she chose. The neighbors shook their heads with raven-like omen, and said that "'Lizabeth was goin' the same way as all the family did, sooner or later. They thought 'twould ha' been Philip; he had a consumptive look, but 'Lizabeth was so peaked that they guessed it would end that way for her." Some one gave a like melancholy hint to Mrs. Nye, and she watched Elizabeth jealously, trying so hard not to annoy her by anxiety that the girl never suspected its existence, wandered dreamily about, helping with the housework, and giving herself up to the enjoyment of peace at other times.

Elizabeth had been starved of the food which youth demands, and will have, if it break over boundaries to crop forbidden herbage. Her home life had been one of repression rather than growth ; the home atmosphere close and deadening, and the medium through which she looked at her narrow world a dense and lead-colored one. There had once been relief in lavishing affection on Philip, infusing the freshness of her own life into his hopes, without stopping to con-- sider that such an indirect channel was not the legiti- mate one. Even that failed of effect now. Her grow- ing nature demanded nourishment. She felt vaguely the need of something life had not yet supplied ; an unknown quantity, too, for she could not even specify it. She wondered if books or activity would satisfy her. It seemed not. Her mind felt unequal to the task of opening its doors to intellectual truth. The very thought of effort tired her as much as that of new people. There was a question in her mind whether there were people really worth knowing—ex- cept the standard wise man and woman, who must be exceedingly fatiguing—and she clung all the more closely to Philip and her mother. They would take affection for granted without worrying her. Elizabeth had not, as happens with so many women, grown to the point at which definite work becomes a necessity. I am inclined to think her one of those whose whole strength runs to the expansion and intensifying of character. All the mental food she could digest would go towards broadening her sympathies rather than the making of a book or picture. She would more natur- ally become a moving impulse in the lives of others, than a worker of tangible deeds herself. Such women are among the mothers of thought.

.   .   .   .

It was a warm April morning, one on which you saw the face of May, as in a glass, peering over the shoulder of her fickle mother. Oswald Craig, hat in hand, stepped in at the open door of the kitchen, where Mrs. Nye was beating eggs for a custard.

" Si said you wouldn't, but I was sure you would," he said, including the three in a sweeping bow, his eyes dancing with laughter. " I have come down for a visit, and the Sea View doesn't look inviting. My own house did very well for a few nights in the fall, but not for more, and I want you to take me to board."

Mrs. Nye saw Philip's eager face, and Elizabeth's glance with more interest in it than there had been for months.

" I'm not sure. Perhaps we could for a few weeks."

" In that time I shall have had my taste of the sea and gone home," said Oswald, promptly. " I eat plain things and not much of them. I shall be out of doors most of the time, and I'll sleep any where. Please let me come."

Mrs. Nye succumbed to the suddenness of the attack.

" Well, if you're sure you'll be suited—"

" Quite sure ; I'll have my trunk sent over immediately."

CHAPTER XI

THE previous winter had been like any one of Oswald's last half-dozen, though various social events which had been wont to involve excitement had now grown stale from long acquaintance. He was a man of much intellectual brilliancy, without any one predominating talent, whose growth would have bent his life to a purpose. His mind, versatile and apprecia· tive, held always a critical attitude.

It was a finely-tempered blade, and chipped away at whatever came within reach, for the master-will which should have wielded it provided no legitimate material for its strokes. His position in relation to other people was full of power and influence. On familiar terms with actor, poet and artist, he could and did, from time to time, with a careless word, lay bare a defect or emphasize a meaning, the hint bearing fruit in the other's work.

His own thoughts, had he possessed the power or will of expression, might have placed him among the men upon whom he fed and whose best he digested. It would seem unlike a shrewd and ambitious business man to educate his son without reference to a profession, but this was what his father had done. There' was a strong reason for it. John Craig had no ancestors to speak of ; none of his boyish days were bright enough to recall. Unlike most self-made men, he was not fond of suggesting the contrast between his present prosperity and the unpleasantly noisome soil from which it had sprung.

It is safe to conclude that his mind was a far-reaching one in social matters as well as in stocks, grasping distant combinations and making definite moves toward ends whose disposal most men leave to circumstances. He knew that in the succeeding waves of American society, the servants of this generation, hewers of wood and drawers of water, are likely to become the social rulers of the next. As a first step toward enrolling his own name among the new aristocracy, he married a Southern woman who would not need to exert herself unnaturally in playing the lady. He may have loved her, and certainly had a vivid appreciation of her beauty and elegant ease. She died soon after the birth of her child. John Craig gave the boy every advantage of study, and, with a steady disregard of any claim of his own, sent him to the relatives in the South. The few who were left there admired Oswald's bright beauty, and seeing his dead mother's eyes in his, petted him for her sake. Southern society and a few years of Bohemian life in Europe developed in him certain traits which the average American does not give himself time to cultivate, and at the death of his father he was left with his trained mind and a fortune.

Since that time he had lived like a Sybarite who demands mental luxury as well as material rose leaves. No epicure ever planned his sauces and jelly with more earnestness than Oswald gave to tickling his emotional palate with new sensations.

Not only had the winter been monotonous, but the spring found him sluggish and unwilling to taste the accustomed fare. He remembered with positive relish the few days at Stratford in the fall, the bare house, the gray sky and sea. Stratford might act as a tonic, and with that possibility he would give it a chance to do what it might for his mental quickening. The next day found him there, installed in Mrs. Nye's "best chamber."

.   .   .   .

" I never had the country in the early spring before," he was saying. He stood on the bank outside, talking to Elizabeth, who was washing dishes near the window. There was much fine ladyhood in her touch of common things. " I go out from Boston for an occasional day in the suburbs, when the hepaticas and anemones are ready, but all that is quite unlike having country days and nights."

" It would be better to take the city in patches, you think ? I should think so, too, for of course you can begin things where you leave off, there—the music and seeing pictures. And if you're away from the woods one day, some dear little bud you've been watching opens, and you lose its first sweetness."

" Yes, that is true ; and haven't you felt, don't you feel always, the pleasure of a discoverer in chancing upon a flower for the first time ? It may be common as grass to a botanist, labeled by Solomon, but you are as triumphant as if you could name it for yourself."

" Do you know botany well ? If you are very learned I sha'n't dare to talk with you."

"A premium for lying, if I were! But I'm not. I haven't the slightest interest in naming plants, though there are a few like orchids, which, you know, are quite as much bird as blossom, that I should like to analyze down to their last atom! But here's a theory,— analyze as you might, you'd find nothing ultimate in an orchid."

"I don't understand what you mean," said Elizabeth, honestly, the little horizontal lines coming between her brows.

"I'm not sure that I do, either," said Oswald, lightly. "You know there's a temptation to say things that sound epigrammatic. That's the way the poets earn their bread. Mrs. Nye, I'm tiring your family with nonsense." For Philip had come up and was listening, too. "Oh, I guess not," said the mother, cheerfully. The sound of young voices not employed on any very sensible or practical subject seemed like ab·solute gayety and did her good. "Young folks ought to enjoy themselves. They never will have a better chance."

"So everybody says, except the young folks themselves. But here is a proposal. Philip knows a hundred places in the woods where the buds have begun to swell. No? is it too early? Well, there must be spaces where the pine needles are dry, and we can look up to the branches. Will you go?"

"Yes, of course!" said the boy, delighted. Oswald had noticed him so little this morning that he was disappointed and sorry. He had been carrying in his heart an admiration for the young man which was all ready to break out into flame. To arouse the

enthusiasm of a young soul inclined to hero-worship
it is necessary to provide very little combustible material and no tinder, for itself is always ready to fur-
nish the spark. " I never can find the hepatica place.
You know where it is, Betty ; see if you can tell us."

" Follow the old wall till you come to the little
white stone—you remember that ?—then branch off
to the right and go down the bank near the four pines.
Isn't that plain enough ? "

" Better still," said Oswald, " won't you go with us ?
I am sure you ought," he went on, as Elizabeth hesitated. "I came here because I was hungry for the
woods and sea, and I find somebody who looks as if
she had been more starved than I, without knowing it.
May she go, Mrs. Nye ? "

" Why yes, but you mustn't wet your feet, Elizabeth;
you'd better wear rubber boots."

" Yes, I will go," said Elizabeth, her face brightening as the note of a bluebird came like an added persuasion.

" This isn't the first time you and I have set out together, is it, Philip ? " began Oswald when they were
making their way rather slowly across the spongy
fields. " By the way, what a young scamp you were
to steal that boat ! Did he ever settle with you for
it ? "

" Yes," said Philip, laughing, and glancing at Elizabeth with prospective enjoyment of her disapproval.
" He began and forgot to finish. Yes, Betty, I know
I never told you, but I will now. I ran away, eloped
with the Mary Ann, because that was the only way I
could get her."

"I don't think that was funny or nice! Did mother know it?"

"Of course not. There wasn't any fun in telling." Philip had changed greatly in Elizabeth's absence. He had become more like other boys, careless in answer, given to whistling rather than brooding, and fonder of nonsense. She felt a vague, selfish disappointment, perhaps because he depended less on her sympathy and companionship, now that his manner of living had become healthier.

"Men with an object can't be scrupulous, can they?" said Oswald. "Like all great conquerors, you looked at the end and not the means."

·"If Mr. Lunt heard you say that, he would begin an argument with you," said Elizabeth.

"Who is Mr. Lunt, and what would he say?"

"He kept a sort of private boarding school, and I was there three years. We studied moral philosophy, and had long arguments about right and wrong."

"So you think he would have enticed me into a discussion? Well, he couldn't, you know," said Oswald, brightly, "because I should only say, My dear sir, no doubt you know best. It's a heavenly spring day and I smell the sea. I don't need to theorize."

Elizabeth could not help wondering if glibness of tongue and capacity for making smooth sentences always accompanied a high culture. She began to be a little ashamed of her own literal definitions. It seemed finer to think in parentheses.

"Here's the old wall," called out Philip, as they entered the woods and came to a straggling line of rocks. "I'll run ahead and see if I can find it first."

"The bit of acquaintance I have with flowers,"
Oswald went on as Philip disappeared among the
pines, "I owe to Julian, an artist. I used to tell him
another grain of some unknown element in his composition would have made him a naturalist, for there
isn't a bud or stick or stone that he did not love."

"Why was he an artist then ? "

"Yes, you would say that such strong tastes should
have drawn him away from painting, but if I may express it so blindly, he had only the artistic love of nature.
He didn't care about classifying and analyzing, as he
did about taking things to his heart. Do you see? "

"I think so," said Elizabeth, slowly. "You mean
he would have cared just as much about a violet if he
did not know what family it belonged to ? "

"Exactly. Thank you for seeing what I couldn't
put in words. Well, he did some exquisite water-
colors. Every one of his pictures held a thought."

"Were they landscapes? "

"Some of them, but his genius was of the micro-
scopic order. Now look through the opening between
these trees. You have just a vista of light, broken by
one pine and the charred remnant of another,—that,
we'll say, split by lightning,—the patch of blue sky
visible above. You see it all ? "

"Yes, but I shouldn't have seen any thing if you had
not shown it to me."

"Wait till you go out sketching with an artist and
you will learn to look for points. Now some painters
would give a canvas full of trees and a sweep of sky,
but Julian made one suggestion and let you fill it out
with what your mind saw above and beyond."

" Please go on." Elizabeth felt a keen delight in
the air, and a sense of having been awakened from
sleep in a close atmosphere, where she had wandered
in dreams through a world of pygmies.

"Well, this is one of Julian's masterpieces in little ;—a bare branch with one or two fluttering, dead
leaves, and, in a fork, one poor solitary nest, the lining
torn and hanging. Better, you see, than a great picture
of grain-stacks, laden trees and busy men, labeled
Autumn in the catalogue. Don't you think so ? "

" It is all very new to me, and I'm afraid I don't
think at all, yet. There's Philip calling. Please tell
me more about your friend."

"Better than that, I'll send for a portfolio of his
sketches, and we'll look them over together."

" Thank you, only it would be taking too much
trouble. Where is he now ? "

" He died six months ago, in Florence."

"Oh, I'm so sorry I asked you ! " said Elizabeth,
hurriedly. " I was blundering to ask questions. It
was kind of you to speak of him at all."

" What a soft little heart, and a voice to match it ! "
thought Oswald, rather amused. He did not think it
necessary to mention the slightness of the comradeship
that had existed between himself and Julian ; neither
did he enlarge on the only feeling the artist's death had
roused in him ; a regret that any maker of beauty
should have lost his power of creating. He had not
taken the trouble of deceiving Elizabeth, but, as she
had arrived at her own conclusions that the memory
was something deep and tender, neither would he convince her to the contrary. The tone of his answer

held a pathos instinctively thrown there to meet hers.

"It is not because I am kind, but because I was sure you would understand."

They came out on a bank where Philip was on his knees, pushing away the damp leaves the fall had left.

"I don't believe we shall find any blossoms, but here are some buds. Betty, you used to say they were like babies' heads."

"And I am sure they're much prettier," said Oswald, holding a leaf between his eye and the light to enjoy the outline. "There's nothing so funny and fuzzy in nature, except the pussy-willows."

"But I am disappointed," said Elizabeth, "I did want to see one of the little blue faces."

"Just as you will, in a few days. See, this is what I shall do. Philip, lend me your knife. I know you have one, because you are at the jack-knife age. Now I shall cut carefully round the root, take it up with ever so much black earth, and carry it home in my hand."

"And then what?" asked Philip, for whom Oswald's half soliloquizing speech held great charm.

"Well, as I said, I shall carry it home tenderly, making a nest of my hand, and I shall say to Mrs. Nye, Will you please give me a little glass or even an earthen dish? For this flower is to sit in the window at Miss Elizabeth's side, and by Wednesday it wont be able to resist her and the sun, and must peep out."

While he talked, he was busily cutting down into the earth, and by the time the words were ended, had the plant in his hand, holding it up with an air of boyish triumph. It was a matter of course to be on easy terms with him ; they found themselves talking and laughing freely, as if he were an acquaintance of years.

Elizabeth looked at herself in surprise when she shook down her hair before the glass that night.

"You're taking an interest in things once more," she said. "I am glad, for you were getting into a grumbling, discontented, moody sort of way. Go to bed at once, and get up early to help about breakfast ! "

CHAPTER XII.

THE spring came slowly, but was full of surprises. It did not yield at once to the sweetness of its nature, but advancing timidly, threw down a cluster of violets only to retreat and delay again, until the fra-grant gift should be quite forgotten.

Oswald was not the man he had been three months before. Under differing circumstances his nature itself changed, chameleon-like. It had always shifting gleams, responsive to varying rays of light, but some-times its whole surface altered so completely in reflect-ing a new surrounding that he himself forgot the existence of the unalterable core of self beneath. There are men—and let us be thankful that they exist only like rare fungi!—who feel within themselves a haunting consciousness of their lack of earnestness. Shifting like the tide, but without its rhythmic flow, drawn by any malarial swamp-light as well as by the moon, they may be constantly oppressed by this sense of a changing identity. Any human soul defies analysis ; we may classify it broadly, dispose of it with general epithets, but depth beyond depth are coruscations of light, blots of shade, which are never revealed to us because we cannot bring to the search a superhuman fineness of intelligence. If that be true of the coarsest and most literal of men, what shall be said of

those who elude even their own observation by light-
ning-like flashes of mental change ? Oswald was conscious that he should be broadly classified as fickle ;
he knew how many facts could be brought to the front
to prove it. If fickleness lay in having made more
than one woman love him, and finding the incense sweet
only while it was new ; in touching lightly upon flowers
,of art and science, demanding but a sip from each, and
not enough to necessitate the construction of a comb
of careful cells, he was guilty. But there was more
behind it. He felt within himself a moral weakness,
a defect of nature more radically lamentable than its
outward expressions. If his exquisitely susceptible
emotions demanded certain food, should he starve them
because there chanced to exist social prejudices which
were contrary to his view of the subject ? He was
simply an intemperate man, with the soul of a poet,
easily fanned aglow by a suggestion of beauty, but
lacking, God knows what element needed in human
souls, to make them capable of bending toward noble
and unselfish ends.

It was not strange that Stratford could fill his heart
as it had his expectations. The low level, the study of
a rural New England type of man and woman, struck
him with a peculiar freshness after his late conventional
days among conventional people. Elizabeth was as
truly a part of the scene as if she had stood, her slight
figure outlined against the light, in a picture where a
quiet sea touched a monotonous sky. Her grace
pleased him ; her simplicity and gravity appealed to
him as nothing except the new had the power of doing.
He had not lived among many people without meet-

ing earnestness in women, but here it was undisguised
by any fashionable mask. It was like an abstraction ;
she was the ideal Una, and as such to be drawn out
with delicacy, lest the value of the study be lost.

.   .   .   .

" Why do you ask me so much about theaters and
actors?" said Oswald, one day when he and Philip
were down on the shore engaged in skipping stones
with an absorbing interest.

" Because I'm going to write plays, sometime," answered Philip, coming out suddenly and boldly with
an explanation he had only dared hint at before,
and feeling immediately that he had committed himself
to something stupendous.

Oswald skipped another stone and laughed. " Four!
I said a charm over that one. Going to write a play,
are you ? Well, you have my blessing."

Philip's eyes filled with tears, and his next pebble
fell ingloriously. It is neither pleasant nor easy to
realize that one's own cherished plan does not affect
the universe at large as something important.

" You seem to think it isn't such a very great thing,"
he said at last, in a tone so low that the hurt feeling
scarcely betrayed itself. " Does every body write
plays ? "

" No, I might safely say nobody writes them nowadays," answered Oswald, smiling at his retort and
without the least thought of its effect on his listener.

" Why, I thought there must be ever so many new
plays! "

" So there are ; bits of comedy, fragments of farce
and attempts at tragedy, but I answered you as if you

were speaking of the real drama. Why, the boy is going to cry! "

"I'm not!" said Philip, dashing the back of his hand across his eyes and laughing feebly. "You think I can't do it because I'm only a boy,—but I can! Tell me why not."

"Now here is an anomaly for which nature's whims must account," said Oswald to himself. "A boy with no suggestion from circumstances, devotes himself to the drama. Let's walk awhile and talk about it," putting his hand on Philip's shoulder. "You may be a genius for all I know, but even that isn't sufficient. You need a thousand advantages ; years, knowing and studying a hundred classes of people, and, though that isn't necessary, going into different scenes and learning other countries by heart. Do you ever write—verses, for instance ?"

"Yes," said Philip, with rather a shamefaced air. "I've begun a tragedy."

"So, a tragedy! That's good ; the orthodox beginning, too! What is it about?"

"Helen in Troy. After she's there, you know ; while her husband and Paris are fighting about her."

"Rather a tremendous subject, but never mind that. It's quite suited to your years. Are you going to bring in a host of fighting Greeks and Trojans ?"

"No, there's no need of that. All the play is between the beautiful woman and the men that are in love with her. You see, she loved Menelaus always, and then when Paris came, she fell in love with him. She did not really care about him, but he was handsome and young and she wasn't used to him."

"Exactly ; he dazzled her by his fine hair and eyes and armor."

"Yes," cried Philip, delighted beyond measure. "Oh, I knew you'd understand ! I haven't told Betty, because she isn't to know till it's finished. Well, when Helen gets to Troy she's sorry, and falls in love with her husband over again. Because she can't see him, she imagines he's handsomer and braver than he really is, and she finds Paris is only a common man."

"A Trojan dandy ; I see."

"So while the armies are fighting, she sends one of her women—or hires a traitor—any way, she sends somebody to Menelaus to tell him she loves him and wants to meet him outside the city walls and talk with him. He sends back word that there's something better still ; if she can creep out to him, he'll take her away in his ships before Paris can help himself. So it's all arranged. Menelaus lets the Trojans think he's tired of fighting, and the ships set sail one after another, all but the king's. They go out slowly, one by one, so that if the king's is going to be the last it will be dark before he can start. Helen creeps out to the place where Menelaus is waiting, but the traitor that carried the messages runs to tell Paris, because he thinks he shall be rewarded. Paris hurries out with a band of Trojans, and just as Helen has reached her husband and puts up her face to kiss him, Paris brings his battle-ax down with a crash through his skull. And Helen turns and sees who it is, and stands there looking at him for a whole minute as if she was turned to stone—think, the most beautiful statue in the world !—and they look at each other. Then she screams and stabs herself with Menelaus' dagger. Some of the Greeks have waited for their chief, and when he doesn't come they go up to the city walls to find him. They meet the Trojans, and after the battle not one Greek is left alive."

" Have you read the Greek ? "

" No, Mr. Kewe began to teach me, but I don't know any thing about it. I read his translation. I don't see why I need to follow that. It wouldn't make a play."

" Well, you're a very young boy, and as crude as you can be. Still, you're wildly original enough for a genius, if nothing more. Stranger things have happened than for a fellow with more drawbacks than you have, to succeed."

" You think I shall ? I knew you'd understand ! " cried Philip, wildly. " But the other things, the world, people, books—where am I going to get them ? " Just then, a slender figure appeared in the foot-path above them—Elizabeth, straight and well-defined, against the sky, unconscious of them at her feet. Oswald's eyes followed her mechanically for a moment before he said, "Come back to town with me ! I'll give you a taste of life, if you want it."

Elizabeth was in her chamber when Philip rushed up there and began an incoherent account of Mr. Craig's having promised to take him away. " Tell me what you mean," she said, turning from the glass and letting her heavy hair fall. " Don't talk so fast, Philip. Don't be beside yourself."

" He said I had genius—at any rate, it was as good as saying so, and all I needed was to see people and the world. Nothing about college, Betty, as Mr. Kewe did ! and this is so much easier ! and he said I should go with him if I wanted to. Think of it, Elizabeth ! It would be beautiful to go any way, but when it's with him, for he knows so much, and sees what you mean and cares for what you like—Oh, I never was so happy ! "

" But how will you pay him ? "

Elizabeth's more literal mind could see in the word money an indefinite number of dollars, while to Philip's vision it represented only some hazy medium through which forbidden pleasures were more clearly visible. " Will he lend you or ——— "

"Betty, don't ! you make me cross. When I'm all fire, you're so slow and have to understand ! You used to talk about my plans, and now, when there's something real coming, you stand back and look it all over. Why, I don't know about the money ! I suppose he means to invite me to stay with him. Of course any body like him wouldn't think of money at all."

" I'm sorry to be stupid," said Elizabeth, her lips quivering a little, while she turned to the glass and began brushing her hair again. " But you see I can't jump at things and understand them all at once."

" I was cross, Betty ; I'm sorry, too," and Philip began dancing about the room, nervously moving an article here and there. " But I did want you to be glad. And I know he's seen ever so many great people and read wonderful books ; so if he says I'm to be famous, I shall."

Running, as usual, far ahead of words, with his vividness of imagination, he would have been able to assert with the utmost honesty that Oswald had promised him fame.

His spirits were too high for finding much relief in an overflow of words, and he ran down into the garden, where, to the surprise of his mother, watching from the window, he began hoeing with astonishing vigor. When Elizabeth went down she found Oswald in the little sitting room.

"I wish you would tell me what Philip means. Has he been telling you how much he wants to go away?"

Oswald was holding a book which he made no pretense of reading. It gave him an added sense of indolent ease to have at hand some means of amusement which he did not need.

"You are going to scold me for encouraging him? I did, I confess, but it was because I thought I found talent in him, or, at least, originality and ambition. Are you angry?"

"No, oh no; it is good of you to talk with him, and I am as thankful as I can be to any body who helps him. But when it is more than words! he said—"

"He said," put in Oswald, with an easy smile, helping her out of her difficulty. "He said I offered him a bite from my apple, schoolboy fashion."

"But there would be so many things to consider. Encouragement means a great deal to Philip; perhaps it means more than you intend it should, and I can't bear to have him disappointed."

Oswald was always charmed with the intentness of her manner. Just now, he told himself she was a sufficiently unusual woman to be a very fascinating one, and it was due to this fascination that he said in earnest what half an hour ago he would have pronounced wildly erratic.

"I don't see why he need underestimate my words. Why shouldn't I even educate him if I choose, for his sake and——yours?"

Elizabeth had been looking at him quietly ; his eyes still held hers for a moment. Then surprise hurried in and frightened away all other expression, before her glance fell and she turned away. Some one came in at the moment, and so the conversation was dropped without awkwardness.

CHAPTER XIII.

THERE were no fancies in Elizabeth's mind relative to falling in love with Oswald, but he had gained a power of making her uneasily happy. She had felt, from the first, the charm of his personal grace and quickness of thought, but since his looks and tones had acquired a meaning for her alone—since, by a thousand signs imperceptible to an observer and tantalizingly incapable of analysis, he had made her sure that neither sea nor sky was the center of his interest in Stratford, she was only conscious of a trembling desire to escape. There is nothing very unusual in that. Many a woman closes the doors of her reserve and retreats to the innermost recess of her castle, just before showing the white flag in a half reluctant grasp, and yielding unconditionally.

Perhaps there is a merciful provision in this trembling advance of the spring. If love should grasp a heart so that it could not flutter, I question whether the poor thing would ever beat afterwards.

There was for Oswald a peculiar pleasure in stirring the consciousness of one so fine, so entirely inexperienced, and in spite of that, so self-contained as Elizabeth. She had not been through half a dozen flirtations, which leave girls with no deeper knowledge of the world nor larger field of vision than she, keen observers of the emotions, sage in noting effects and prophesying results. She never doubted sincerity, having no occasion for doing so, and would have said that an unswerving line separated honest men from liars, as if a moral leprosy must inevitably be visible on the surface. Sometimes she wished, with an exhibition of pettishness quite new to her, that Oswald would go away, and on seeing him half an hour after, blushed at herself for having been either childish or a prude. And running through all, like a silver thread, the spring brightened her reveries in spite of their waywardness.

One morning Oswald brought her a letter in Grandmother's cramped handwriting. Elizabeth had been carrying potted geraniums out of doors to accustom them to the strong sunshine and fresh winds, before they should take up their summer residence in the garden. She held the letter an instant without speaking, put it in the pocket of her gingham apron and then, with an access of resolution, took it out and broke the seal. A sigh of relief accompanied the reading of the first half page.

"Shall I tell you why you hesitated in opening that ?" asked Oswald, laughing saucily.

The air from the sea had awakened in him an abundant vitality ; how could he work it off better than by amusing himself with the first person at hand ?

"Yes, if you can," said Elizabeth, trying properly to be serious, but yielding to the mischievous suggestion of his eyes.

"The postmark is Stowe. I found that out on the way home, having nothing else to do till I reached the point where you get a glimpse of the sea. Madam Nye is there. Your fear to read the letter said, 'I'm afraid she's coming home.' Your sigh of relief, ' She isn't coming, and I'm glad.' Am I a seer, or not ? "

" How long have you been a detective ? " said Elizabeth. " If you are so very wise, you might have saved me from opening my letter at all."

" Right, then ? I knew I was! Mrs. Nye," as she appeared in the midst of a flock of hungry chickens, some, more clamorous than the rest, flying up to her shoulder, and one gaunt creature with long legs perching on the dish of dough, " I am glad to inform you that the crisis is past."

Mrs. Nye looked up inquiringly, ceasing for the moment to repel her feathered assailants, and thereby giving them an advantage.

" A letter from Stowe states that Madam Nye will not return for—how long, Miss Elizabeth ? "

" Not for a month or six weeks," answered Elizabeth, smiling at her mother, in whose face an answering gladness at once appeared.

" But I think Mr. Craig ought to be scolded. He pilfered the news from my face, or my mind—it doesn't make much difference which."

Oswald looked from one to the other with a face of such innocent vacuity that the two broke into a laugh, in which he joined. He had, with almost all people, the privileges of a child or other irresponsible being, and Elizabeth was often annoyed in remembering that he had made her laugh against her will.

Mrs. Nye and her feathered train passed on.

" Don't go, Miss Elizabeth," said Oswald. " Oh,

no, you haven't finished your gardening, yet ! Stay till
you've picked all the dead leaves off those geraniums.
That will take long enough for me to air my morning's
reflections."

" I am anxious to hear," said Elizabeth, throwing off
her hat as she went further into the shade of the house
and began examining the plants. " This sounds quite
like something to be put down in your journal, and
published after your death."

" Doesn't it ? But there lies the point. I've resolved
not to die."

" Have you found the elixir of life ? "

" Yes, in this divine air, the blueness of the heavens,
and the exquisite simplicity of your people. No, you
needn't laugh. It is quite true that these homely,
rough men strike me like powerful character sketches
in great novels."

"But they are nothing but rough and homely men,
just as you say. I always thought we must be the
most common sort of people in the world, and when
you pretend to admire us I'm afraid you're making
fun."

" On my soul, no ! "

Oswald was sitting in an open window, his body
bent forward at an uncomfortable angle, and his feet
dangling, and the attitude came as near being tolerable
as it would have been ridiculous for most men.

" Now, I'm not learned, but I'm tired of books. I
believe their best purpose is to force a man into finding out how to do without them. Of what use are
novels but to give you artificial sketches of life, that
you might take at first hand ? "

"But histories and works on science," put in Elizabeth. "They do good."

"If you call it good. Science only increases our craving after appliances for economizing time and labor, and we have so much to do to keep pace with the age that, after all, we haven't any time or strength either. Elizabeth, did you ever imagine the perfectly natural man and think how happy he must be?"

"No," she said, not even noticing his use of her name.

"He will grow up with a sound body. Every sense will be so perfect that ordinary uses of life, which we only count means to its preservation, will be sweet as our first spring days—the perfect ones when we sleep soundly till dawn, and wake to be glad we are alive. Haven't you seen such days?"

"Never till this spring." It was an unguarded slip. How should she have realized yet whether her pulses' quickening depended on the new budding of the world, or on some miraculous spiritual change of her own?

"Then you know what it is to be happy without help from any thing but a fostering earth-mother, a beneficent universe, a pure soul and clear conscience. This perfect man will know it even better. He will have no ambition; he will eat the fruits of the earth thankfully, sleep on her bosom and live at peace with every animal. Then, when his heart beats high with youth, he will set out to complete his life, led on by that vague longing every man feels, when he seeks the object of his possible love. Perhaps, some day in his wanderings, he will meet a young creature innocent as

himself. Her glances are soft where his are piercing,
but the shafts from his ardent eyes melt into hers and
are not quenched, but wake a gentle glow. Their lips
meet, in the simplicity of their hearts, and he says,
Fair, soft creature, will you make your home in some
corner of this great forest, wherever we chance to be ?
I have been years looking for you. There has been
in my heart a little ache, though I have not known why,
and now I see it was because life did me a wrong, in
half creating me and leaving me to find the other part
of my nature."

When his voice ceased, with a beseeching modulation,
Elizabeth felt her own heart beat quickly. A rapturous
bluebird, carrying a straw to finish the bridal home,
chirped from the gate. Oswald went on.

" Well, she will say 'Yes,' or there will be no need
of saying any thing, because in such a world, there are
no doubts or denials. They wander wherever they
choose in the shade of the protecting forest, stop beside some friendly stream until they know its banks
well enough, and then leave it for still unfamiliar nooks.
Each day is new ; and when the man and woman, full
of days, but never acquainted with ache or sorrow, die
sweetly and happily, as a red, ripe leaf flutters down
and decays, only.to enrich the earth and autumn air,
their children cover them over with a fold of their
earth-mother's dress, and above them live happy lives in
their turn. Elizabeth, is the picture worth painting? "

" Yes, but it isn't possible," she said, in a voice almost inaudible. Her hands had long ago left their
task, and her eyes turned seaward.

" No, think a minute. Couldn't a man and woman,

—so young, remember, that there would be no ghosts to haunt them—loving each other, make such a home and such an ideal life in this land of work and day of steam-power? Are you sure it isn't barely possible?"

"I can't be sure, because I don't know much about other people's lives," she answered, in a voice that had not relaxed from its tension of excitement. "But life is very hard. There are cares for other people, and trouble about them, so that it seems to me nobody could be perfectly happy, for he would always be seeing misery and hearing of it."

"Then you don't understand me. More than that, you haven't understood love." He had taken his stand near her, and now one of his hands touched hers, trembling at her side. His eyes, stirred by the momentary feeling, sought and held hers.

"Love blots out the world beyond its border. It does not wrong the people standing outside, because it never need shirk a duty to them. It simply does not need them. They are forgotten, as soon as the eyes of the man and woman who love find oblivion in each other's depths. Suppose a woman like you loved." Elizabeth shivered. So a violin vibrates when the strings are touched suddenly, with intent only to wake a sound, proving music or discord as it happens.

"Suppose she loved so that she could say to the man who made her destiny, 'Behold me, fine and pure, a gift to you from the immortals.' Do you think they, finding all delight in each other, would or could be made unhappy by the grief felt by some man or woman who had not reached such blissful heights? Psyche could not die after she had drunk immortality." The sun-

light was hot above her ; she was helpless under its intensity and the torrent of his voice. Neither wishing
to be there, nor able to break the spell, she stood
swayed by a personal magnetism far stronger than her
will.

"Elizabeth," his voice softening to a caressing tenderness, "we have every right to be happy. Look at
the sky, its delicious depth of blue, drink one breath of
this sunlight, and tell me if man ought to see bliss
without grasping it. Come, you haven't given the day
half the welcome it deserves. There is so much beauty
that the sky almost cracks. Come out with me and
help drink the sweetness up. Only a walk in the fields,
where it is all fragrant and still." She turned, half
dreamily, with a childlike obedience. Even at that instant, he noted, with a thrill of admiration, the grace of
the gesture, and the contour of her bowed head.
Then, as if recovering herself with an effort, she said
brokenly,

"Not to-day. I must go in. I have wasted my
morning." And, as much to Oswald's surprise as
triumph, she sobbed a little hysterically, as she hurried away. He did not see her again that day, but
overheard Mrs. Nye tell Philip that Elizabeth had a
bad headache.

Was Oswald in earnest, or had he played on Elizabeth's sensibilities for the mere triumph of moving them?
Neither, wholly ; here, as usual in human affairs, was a
complication of motives. The beauty of the day
working on his own perfect physical condition had
roused in him a kind of mental ecstasy that might
have come from an intoxicant.

His rhapsody had begun in more than half earnest, and as it went on, he gathered sincerity from being himself affected by the moment. Elizabeth had always seemed very fine and sweet, and now that she showed possibilities of being stirred to more intense emotion than if she carried her feelings nearer the surface, he began to excite himself as much as her by his poetic train of thought. Oswald was not insincere ; he only failed to compare the sincerity of his present with that of his past. Consequently, there were enormous discrepancies between the thoughts and desires of the man of to-day, and the man of yesterday. He was pleased with himself,—more, delighted,—and wandering down to the shore after Elizabeth had left him, he blessed his bubble-like temperament that had not become incapable of rising at a breath.

His last play at love had left him surfeited and deeply wearied over the monotonous round of emotions the boy-god had at hand. The woman who had acted, for a time, the part of the " incomparable she " had been of languid and matured beauty. She had warmth of coloring, vibrating tones, and her glances were charged with steady electric fire more deadly far than the flash. With such exquisite physical organization, it disgusted Oswald that there should have been no corresponding fineness of perception. Mrs. Tyrrell drew far more from Oswald's devotion than he meant to imply. Baskets of royal red roses, carelessly tied bunches of opening buds, more passionate in their dead whiteness than any flower that can call the blood from its heart long enough to blush, told her more than that an idle young man was busying himself in worship of

Venus, embodied, for the present, in the form of Mrs.
Tyrrell. Mr. Craig wished, of course, to marry her;
he must not be impatient, but who knew what she might
say when, some fine morning, he told his hopes and
despair? Oswald would have opened his eyes at the
thought, in a surprise as real as scornful. He had intentions, certainly, though they were scarcely formu-
lated in his own heart, for a design too distinctly recognized would have spoiled the delicious aroma of the
experience. His wishes would have been amply satisfied by an intimacy made up of lover-like devotion on
his side and a properly feminine susceptibility on hers.
When the play should end, as it would suddenly, nothing
need be said in the way of farewells nor explanations.
To attempt a renewal of the amusement, when its
climax was once passed, would be like visiting the
scene of a revel where crowned Bacchus himself had
presided, to find wine-dregs standing flat and stale in
rare glasses, and the ashes of the weed that had
steeped the guests in languor scattered over the table.
Mrs. Tyrrell had put an end to this sickly sort of dream,
by plainly showing him that he was not to taste the
flavor of courtship without taking, during the 'rest of
his life, the non-intoxicant of matrimony for breakfast,
dinner and tea. So, at odds with awkward circumstances, he fled before the last act, and had since
abjured love.

As he went along shore that day he found Si wheel-
ing up seaweed by the barrowful, slowly, as was his
ponderous manner of doing things, except when a bird
came over unexpectedly; that was an incident capable
of rousing a temporary animation.

"Spring seems to be comin' on, don't it?" he said, putting his wheelbarrow down and his foot upon its side, in order to assume his favorite conversational attitude of resting both elbows on his knees. "Time for it, too. Summer 'll be here 'fore we know it."

"It's been rather a late spring, hasn't it?" said Oswald, trying, with the aid of a piece of timber, to assume the same attitude.

"Master back'ard. But some folks don't care. They come to spend the summer 'fore the warm weather does."

This with a slow wink of the sharp blue eye and hint of a smile about the mouth, signs which indicated the fact that Si had propounded a witticism and was unwilling it should pass without appreciation.

"What do you mean?" asked Oswald, quite in the dark.

"Oh, boarders don't come here 'thout they hev somethin' to come for. In the fall it's loon and in the spring —why, it does seem as if there wa'n't much to bring a young chap out so fur into the country in the spring. So I was goin' to say to 'Lizabeth yesterday, but she's so slow you can't tell how she might take things."

Light had dawned on Oswald. "I think I wouldn't say any thing of the kind to her," he answered carelessly, but with a good deal of meaning. "Sometimes jokes aren't as pleasant as you mean them to be."

He walked on, while Si took up his wheelbarrow and pursued the little path leading to his house, a broad smile illuminating his face at the success of his shaft.

"Master touchy young fellar," he said to himself. "Wouldn't ha' fluttered so if he hadn't been hit."

"She is going to be an unusual sort of woman," thought Oswald, "and if one tried to wake her heart, he might end by finding himself in love with her. If a man wanted to marry, a man who would hang or drown rather than take a woman with a set of ideas and an experience of the world, he couldn't do better than to marry a young creature like this. Her mind is like a white page ; he could put whatever characters he chose there. She isn't too decided either, nor likely to demand a great deal and hamper one's freedom. If a man wanted to marry, he couldn't do better."

CHAPTER XIV.

IT is always most likely that a day on the heights will be followed by a commonplace morrow. When Elizabeth and Oswald next met, it was at the tea-table to which he came late, after a long walk.

"Oh, they are delicious!" he cried, "those fishermen. I met the famous Jim Bolton this afternoon. Si had given me an analysis of his qualities before I ever talked with him, and when I met the man, the description all came back. He was standing in his garden with a hoe, and seemed not to have had the slightest previous acquaintance with it."

"And wasn't he willing to talk?" asked Philip.

"Jim is glad of any thing that stops his work."

"Yes, he began to question me with the utmost cordiality, as soon as I was within hailing distance; and his interest was so warm, his manner so gently sympathetic, that I'm sure if I had a story, I should have button-holed him adhesively and given him my unreserved confidence. The subject of button-holes also reminds me that there was but one button on his blue shirt. His attire was otherwise disheveled. I fear Mrs. Jim is not a careful wife."

"She has a good deal to do," answered Mrs. Nye, anxious to give her neighbor all the credit she benevolently could. "Though I know she don't do it. There are so many children, and all of an age, too! You

haven't touched your tea, Mr. Craig! won't you have a
glass of milk? Elizabeth, get it for him."

"Thank you," said Oswald, looking up with a glance
which might have been translated, "Won't you forgive
me? And after all what did I say? Did not your
rebellious consciousness supply what made you blush?"
But Elizabeth did not meet his eyes.

"Please go on, Mr. Oswald, about Jim, you know,"
said Philip, who never had enough of the young man's
gay descriptions.

"Well, I didn't confide in him because there was
nothing to say. It would take a tale of horror to stir
that gently phlegmatic nature. So I led him on, by a
judicious question now and then, to talk of himself.
It seems he has religious doubts. Has every body
religious doubts, I wonder?"

"Oh, Jim is a sad case," said Mrs. Nye, shaking her
head. "He gets converted every time there is a
revival, and then in three weeks he backslides again.
We all know what Jim is."

"Well, he didn't refer to his own shortcomings, of
course. I notice that only a few ill-advised people do.
But he considered the hackneyed questions of Jonah
and the whale, the miracles and a few kindred subjects."

"Don't you believe in them, Mr. Craig?" asked
Philip, boldly.

"Oh, never mind what I believe," said Oswald, instantly interpreting the quick flush on Mrs. Nye's face.
He knew the timid woman would suffer conscientious
agonies at hearing him decry Scriptural lore, without
having the courage to reprove him. "Let's talk about

Jim, first. What amused me most was his good-
natured manner of weighing all subjects, spiritual and
temporal. It was as if he tossed them up, caught,
estimated, and laid them in a pile, not disposed of
finally, but left until another passer should stop to talk
them over. He described, with a very keen relish, some
young fellow who, I should say, tried to suppress the
revival."

"Mr. Kewe," said Philip, his face aglow at once.
"But he only tried to do more good than the revival.
Every body was solemn. The boys at school were
afraid they should die before they had time to be converted, and he told us there wasn't any use in such a
fuss. But the school-committee were old fools—yes,
they were, mother, and I know you think so, too."

"And what did Miss Elizabeth think?" said Oswald,
turning to her with his brightest smile. "Were you
one of the disciples of the new leader?"

"I was away all the time," she said, quietly. "At
Stowe. My aunt was ill."

"Philip, I don't think it's quite right for you to say
so much," said his mother, as they rose from the table.
"Mr. Kewe meant well, I'm sure, and he was a real
nice young man, but the Evangelists expected to do
good, too."

"Yes, mother, but—" Leaving the discussion,
which was chiefly on Philip's side, with an occasional
denial or assent from his mother, Oswald went out to
look in at the sitting-room window and say to Elizabeth, "The sky is a rose. Won't you come down to
the sea? I'm sure the waves are like opals."

"I think not, to-night," said Elizabeth, trying to

make her voice unconstrained, and succeeding poorly. "Philip is going to the store, and I'd better sit with mother."

"Why are you offended?" said Oswald, in a softly pleading tone which made her heart at once beat faster. "Now you are beginning to say you are not, but that isn't true. You wouldn't look at me at supper ; you were not interested ; you didn't even smile when I was trying to be funny. Why was it ? I've made as poor jokes when you have laughed and inspired me to fresh attempts."

"I am afraid the way you amused yourself with Jim is only a specimen of the way you are studying us all. We all amuse you. Perhaps I don't care to have you make a study of my character. Besides you would waste time. It isn't deep enough."

"Now you are cruel. Have you any right to hurt me?" His eyes were very dark and pleading. She caught the pained expression of his glance in her one look, and was instantly ashamed.

"I'm sorry—yes, it was small of me to say that, because it wasn't true." His sunshiny smile broke out instantly.

"But you're not going to get away with an apology. You shall do penance. Are you willing to make amends for having been unjust to me? For you were, you know. Then give me your hand and ask to be forgiven."

Elizabeth hesitated only a second, and then with an instinctive desire of making as light of it all as possible, put her hand in his and repeated the formula.

" Now say—no, don't take your hand away for an
instant. I shall keep it as a hostage—say, ' I want to
punish myself by going to walk with you.' "

Elizabeth laughed, as she drew away her hand. " It
proves I am very penitent, for I do exactly as you
say. Will you tell mother, please, while I run up-
stairs for a shawl ? "

" The sky is two shades fainter than when I called
you first," he said, as they took the path to the sea.
" That is the penalty of delay ; you lose the first flush
of twilight. Now tell me," turning squarely upon
her, " why I shouldn't study your character if I
choose, without your being angry. You would say,
would you not, that a woman with a beautiful profile
was niggard enough, if she grudged a stranger his
glance of admiration ? "

" Yes, perhaps so, but the two things are different.
If I had a beautiful face, you might admire it without
disturbing me, but to study my character you must
work your way into my thoughts and feelings. And
all for your amusement ! It is like—I can't say exactly what I mean—like giving a stranger your confidence."

" Is that true ? Am I to be put with strangers ? "
There was no forced meaning in his tone. For the
time being, he was as earnest as she. This was the
one woman in the world who was engaging his
thoughts. " Elizabeth, you are even more unjust than
I accused you of being awhile ago."

" Then I am sorry again," she cried, in the futile
perplexity we have all felt in trying to explain some
slight thing which has magnified itself enormously,

until we are quite sure its proportions are over-drawn, but are by no means able to estimate them correctly. "And let us not talk about it. I'm sure I had a meaning when we began, but I can't find it. I must have made a fuss out of very little material."

"No, I am sure you had a reason for what you said, though you are too generous to hurt me again by confessing it. What you say would be right and just, if you did not apply it to me. Do you think I have so little fineness as to try to penetrate your reserve, if I had no object beyond amusing myself ? Tell me."

"Then why should you—no, perhaps you have not ; I only spoke hastily when I accused you of it. Mr. Craig, let us not talk of it. I am more and more convinced that there is nothing to say."

"But I must defend myself," said Oswald, impetuously. The process of breaking down her defense of timidity and scruples was delightful. It was a piece of fine, artistic work ; he was unwilling to cut it short. "Let me confess. I have studied you, but it was because I cared to do it ; because you are the rarest, finest creature I ever found."

There was a silence of a moment that seemed longer. He had expected her to flush at least, if she should give no other sign of confusion, but she was quite pale, though there was a troubled look in her eyes.

"I am sorry to hear you say so, because it doesn't seem to me you can mean it. Either that, or you are greatly deceived in me. I am an ordinary girl. I have seen nobody. I am not brilliant. Why do you give me credit for so much ?"

" No, I know you do not see, and I am glad I am the
first man—for I know I am—to teach you your charm.
Don't you know that with your slender figure, your
heavy hair and drooping wrists "— Elizabeth involun-
tarily looked down at them—" you would always be
distinguished, in that plain, black dress ! You pin a
cluster of violets at your throat as nobody else ever
did."

" But I never try, I—" began Elizabeth, helplessly,
overwhelmed by his impetuous argument.

" No, I know you never do, because you haven't realized your possibilities. But that is only your grace of
face and figure."

" Please don't, Mr. Craig," she said, stopping short,
her hands folded tightly and the shawl wrapped closely
about her shoulders. " I beg of you not to go on, if
you think there is any more to say."

" Ah, but there is, and you must know why I say it
all. Tell me, are your thoughts any thing but child's
thoughts ? You have had a bare, uninteresting sort of
life, but there has been no tragedy in it. Love is a
name to you. Ambition, jealousy, a dozen other passions are abstractions. Am I not right ? "

He had taken off his hat and passed his fingers
through his hair. Elizabeth noticed, in the glance she
seemed forced to keep fixed on him, that his eyes were
like two stars. It was an instinct of preservation in
her to keep her lids raised ; if they should once fall she
might tremble.

" Have you thought what it would be," he said with
a quick change of tone to one of such persuasive meaning that she shrank perceptibly, " for a man who has

scen gay and brilliant and beautiful women, and found them made after some half dozen patterns but of one monotonous type, to teach you to love?"

"You have no right to say such things to me," she cried, "I will not listen to them." Her eyes still met his bravely. He saw that if she yielded it would be after a long resistance. It was best to carry the fortress by storm.

"I claim the right of the man who loves you." Then her eyelids fell, after one wide glance. "Elizabeth, you must have seen I love you. Little foolish child, you have been drinking in love all this wonderful spring, without knowing it. Are you going to let me love you?"

"No," came quickly. "I was quiet enough before; not happy but not miserable. Why do you try to trouble my life, and fill it with questions and excitement?"

"It was not my fault nor yours; say the fault of the gods for making you woman and me man. Being a woman you cannot help being found, nor can I resist my need of you. What sweet wind blew me here to Stratford but one of fate? The breath of a divine whisper sent me to find you. You cannot resist fate."

"But I can resist this," lifting her head with a momentary pride. "I will resist it all. I only want to be left to my old dull life."

"Ah, no, I am sure you don't. Will you sit here?" She shook her head and they both remained standing, she looking out to sea. "Listen a minute longer. You want to run away from me now and never see me again. No, you can't deny it. Shall I tell you why?

Because you love me. No, don't start, though I like
to see you do it. It gives your head an erectness it
sometimes lacks. No woman ever loved without with-
drawing a pace, knowing her lover will pursue—as I
shall, Elizabeth."

"But you are mistaken. I don't care for you. I have
never thought of you in that way, in my life."

"I dare say not. You are shy even with yourself.
That is a part of your fineness. But stop to think.
Are you not happy this spring? Did your blood ever
flow so quickly, and has not all your delight in life
been connected with a thought of me? You can't say
no; Elizabeth, give me your hand." She did it quickly, as if to prove the act an easy one, though the hand
shook visibly. "See, when I hold it close in mine,
every drop of blood coursing though my palm so near
yours is warm with love of you. Is there no answer in
your own heart?"

"Oh please don't talk so to me!" she cried passionately. "I can't bear it! I—" and then, with a sudden
transition to a child's trembling and beseeching tone,
"Mr. Craig, do you think it is so? Do you think I
love you?"

She had thrown herself on his mercy, and another
man—one capable of coarser passions, perhaps, but
not actuated by an artistic delight in their counter-
feits—might have been too honorable to lead her
further.

But Oswald could not separate his appreciation of
the machinery of the play from his own part as
actor. For the time being, he loved her.

"I know you love me. A woman of your truth will

let me say so without false coquetry.   I told you before it was your fate that you were struggling against.
Stop beating your wings against destiny, dear wild
bird.   Rest here in my arms." His voice was soft and
pleading.   Every thing called her, but she fought back
the impulse to yield.

"You must let me think.   You have had time to
reason it out.   It is all new to me.   I can't reason.   I
am only bewildered."

"Yes, love crowds words to my tongue, and he
makes you silent.   Do not demand too much of him,
Elizabeth ; he makes me eloquent to persuade, and
chokes the words on your lips, to force your yielding.
Let me tell you what is in your mind and heart." His
breath was on her cheek, and his voice a whisper at
her ear.   "You hear only my voice ;   it shuts out
every thing, even the sea.   You know the darkness is
coming, but it is soft as down and says, 'I shut you in
a world where there is no one but your lover.'   And
the universe throbs like one great heart.   Your own
heart—ah, I know how it beats !   It sends out wave
after wave of tumultuous blood in blushes.   How I
wish for the dawn instead of the darkness, that I might
see them !   Every wave drives you gently toward
your lover's arms.   See, Elizabeth, here he stands ;
shall he wait ? "

She could see the outline of the slender, supple figure through the darkness.   He was right ; he had
taken possession of her mind and senses, and in her
world there was nothing but himself.   One half undecided step, and she was sobbing in excitement, with
his lips touching hers.

CHAPTER XV.

NOT only has the sea its ebb and flow on every shore, but waves lying motionless under a tropic sky may rise and dash themselves white on New England rocks. And the rocks, no matter how firm they stand from necessity of nature, might gladly shrink from the encroaching sea. Elizabeth had the Puritanic spirit, a gift of inheritance. That always pointed first to a repression of natural impulses. Yet in spite of it, she felt herself roused, through an instant of emotion, into a new and intense life. They had walked home in silence and parted without a word. Oswald was content, like one who has followed a melody sung by a climbing voice, which stopped on a rapturous note, not caring to follow its descent. Elizabeth's thoughts, too, lingered with the one moment that had stricken them dumb.

She answered her mother's questions quietly, and listened to Philip's story of seeing Mrs. Potter and hearing from Felix through her. The new life was so strong within her that it could wait. It need not yet burst the thinnest veil of habit to show its shining face. She went to her room without a light, and knelt by the window, not searching the heavens, but closing her eyes to breathe in the sweetness of the night. The air was prodigal of it, as if there were to be no more Junes

and nature knew it.   Does a man or woman feel in the
distinct lines which can be put into thought, after a
tidal wave or the blossoming of a flower in the heart ?
I doubt it.

This girl was conscious only of a living world ; her
breath came in sobs and her very face drank in the night
breezes. The pæans of a soul after such baptism might
read, " Oh, dead and inert mass of earth, and sea which
was once a waste of water, you are become full of a
living mystery ! Earth, I am no longer a woman of
flesh only ; my soul wakes and lies on the bosom of
yours as my body treads your solid frame ! Are not
my love and I immortal ? Then you, who have fed
and blessed us until we were worthy to be offered the
divine drink, are divine too." The pure feminine only
lived in Elizabeth that night, the woman as unconscious of conventional rules and inherited principles,
as Eve walked naked in Eden. Hour after hour went
by as she knelt there, until the dews grew heavy and the
seabreezes chill ; her pulses took on their wonted
slowness and she crept to bed, exhausted by her delirium. A few hours' sleep, and then, waking with the
ill-defined dread of some gigantic shape which had
haunted her dream, and which might prove either rosy
cloud or one dense and black, she blushed to find herself face to face with the recollection of the woman who
had given a lover her lips and heart. Was it her heart ?
Was she sure ? There was in her mind no tradition of
any such rapturous emotion. People married, but she
had never thought they were carried away by a flood
to the altar. There ought, said her literal mind, to be
a certainty of love in marriage, not a delirium of emo-

tion which shuts the ears to reason. Where was reason last night? "His heart spoke and my heart answered. Was I wrong to yield?" So, as the morning came, and the objects in the room put on their
every-day guise, Elizabeth felt an undefined shrinking toward retreat. She could only translate it into
the certainty that she had made a mistake. Condi-
tional love could not be real.

It seemed that Oswald had risen before her, for it
was half an hour before he came in from the sea.

"Breakfast is all ready, Mr. Craig," said Mrs. Nye,
cheerily, bringing in the coffee-pot. "You got up
bright and early this morning."

"Yes," he said, with a glance for Elizabeth. "Such
fine weather makes one too happy to sleep."

"Not healthy people," persisted Mrs. Nye, with a
smile. "When I was young it was a great hardship to
be called before day, and I went to bed at nine, too."

"Oh, well, in spite of your generation's good habits,
we have managed to cultivate a troublesome set of
nerves. Philip, what news? Your eyes dance like
will-o'-the-wisps."

"Everybody's going out fishing but me," said Philip.
"Si's got a boat load engaged to take over to Scone.
They start from there. I want to go awfully, but
mother says I can't. Mr. Craig, go and take me
with you! Then you wouldn't mind, would you,
mother?"

"Yes, Philip, I suppose I should. Strange that I
should be afraid of the sea when we've lived here so
long, isn't it?" she said, turning to Oswald. "But
perhaps it's because our men-folks were all farmers. I

don't suppose you're used to it, either. Do you feel afraid ? "

" Never a bit. I should like a home afloat. When I'm ready to settle, perhaps I shall live in a yacht. Well, my lady," he said softly, as Mrs. Nye went into the dairy with her shell for skimming milk, and Philip disappeared, hurrying down the road for news of Si's movements. " Haven't you a word for me this morn-ing ? "

" Yes, I want to see you," said Elizabeth, hurriedly. " I want to tell you I am sure it was all a mistake last night, and ask your forgiveness."

This was a conclusion on which Oswald had not counted.

" A mistake ? Not that you care for me. I know you do."

Elizabeth was too entirely bent on convincing him for resentment at his tone of assurance. " You excited and frightened me. I wasn't myself. That is not— caring."

" What do you expect me to do, then ? " asked Oswald, in his softest voice. " Give up the memory that you believed you did ? Give up the hope——"

" Yes, every thing," said Elizabeth, looking up at him beseechingly and with pain. " Forget it all. I wish I could, but I am sorry—oh, how sorry I am ! You know I told you I was an ordinary girl. Now you will think I am a stupid one, and you will be quite right. I suppose there isn't another woman in the world who wouldn't have known, but I didn't, till I had time to think. Oh, if you must ask me, why didn't you give me time ? "

"Love doesn't need consideration," said Oswald, still softly. "Well, we will not speak of it again."

"How kind you are to me!" she said, her eyes filling with tears. "And will you try to forget it?"

"Perhaps you will learn some time that it isn't easy to forget. No, don't look pained. I will do my best. I will go away."

"Will you?" she caught at the suggestion. "Then I am sure I can be comfortable again. If you staid you would make me troubled and undecided. I haven't been any thing else since you came."

A flash of triumph came into his eyes. "Do you mean that I have caused strange moods, such as you are not used to? Aren't you your old self when I am with you?"

"Every thing is changed. It must be because you are a stranger and have had such a different life from mine. It is like looking into another world to think of yours. It makes me discontented. I didn't know I was such a weak girl!"

"Then it shall be good-by. I will join the Scone fishermen, and you will be relieved of my presence, in a few hours."

The sadness of his voice reproached her. Besides, she had no means of knowing that he had arranged with Si to take him to Scone an hour before she saw him that morning.

"Please don't think I am rude or unkind," she said, earnestly. "It has been so pleasant to have you here! Mother and Philip will want you to stay, and so should I, if seeing you wouldn't remind me to be ashamed."

Oswald's eyes grew beautifully soft, when there was

a demand on them. That liquid glance might have
been sorrow or tenderness. "Will you give me your
hand now, so that we may have our good-by before I
say it to your mother?" It was a friendly and cordial
grasp. "Thank you for happy weeks. Don't regret
having been kind to me." And he went up to his own
room.

Elizabeth longed to call him back, but she checked
herself with a timely remembrance that impulse might
only lead her again into repentance. She did not want
him to stay ; she wished never to see him again, but
it was a pity that he should be hurt. Kindliness and
indecision are alone sufficient to make the truest woman a coquette, for the time being. Impatient at her
varying impulses, she took her hat and called to her
mother, "I am going to return Mrs. Crane's soda. If
·I wait a day longer, I shall forget it."

"All right," came her mother's voice, in hollow res-
onance from the dairy. That good woman spent the
next few minutes in reflections as to the general flighti-
ness of youth, which could alone prompt a girl to leave
the dishes unwashed and the work "up in arms" for
the sudden freak of doing an errand.

.   .   .   .   .   .

A week of brooding clouds and steady, continuous
rain settled down on Stratford. Every one of the
Nye household missed Oswald, and two of the family
at least did not hesitate to say so, Mrs. Nye heartily
calling on Elizabeth to share her regret, and Philip
complaining in his most injured manner that if his
mother had been willing, Oswald would surely have
taken him.

"And what did he mean, Betty?" asked the boy one day, as Elizabeth sat by the window struggling with the complications of making over a dress. "I asked him if he supposed I should ever see him again, and he said, 'Ask your sister.' Did he tell you something about it?"

"No, not a word," said Elizabeth, a little pink flush coming into her cheeks, which made her so impatient that she held her needle up to the light and tested her coolness by threading it with hands that did not tremble.

"But it must have been something," he insisted. "Elizabeth, you didn't make him promise not to invite me to Boston, did you?"

"No; but then we seldom talked about you. You were almost always with us."

The weather is to be held responsible for nine catastrophes out of ten. The victorious army fights with its back to the sun; a comet strikes terror to the heart of the barbarian. Had the sea been blue and the earth warm in the steeping sunshine during those first days of Oswald's absence, Elizabeth might have adhered to her resolution of forgetting him. But no one had ever created such a disturbance in her life, and she was not old enough to wait patiently for the ripples to subside. As one day followed another, and she fell asleep thinking of him and awoke with the happy expectancy of a day in his presence, only to be followed by a throb of disappointment when the next moment told her he had gone, she began to wonder if he had not been right in declaring she must love him. This was more than friendship. Friends could

clasp hands and part, with regret, but without this passion of loss. And deep down in her heart was a germ
of pity, which spread its rootlets further and further,
day by day, and bade fair to grow into a mighty tree.
"Could he be suffering?" Elizabeth as yet took the
world at its word. If a man had told her she was responsible for breaking his heart, though amazed at the
statement, she would have believed it implicitly.
Marvelous as it might be, it was not on that account
to be rejected, any more than the miracle of the loaves
and fishes.

.   .   .   .   .   .

Would the rain never stop? When it had poured
incessantly for four days, there came a day when the
sky, though still leaden, withheld its showers.

"May clear, at three," said Si, as he passed the
house, where Elizabeth stood near the open door,
searching the heavens for signs of a patch of blue.
"Reg'lar no'th-easter, ain't it? An' ther's no use lookin' for fair weather till the wind changes. Lost your
boarder, ain't ye?"

"Yes ; he went with the Verbena crew," said Elizabeth, out of patience that even such mention as this
was by no means commonplace to her.

"Guess them fellars 'll have a putty rough time, if
they started. Said they didn't care, but, Lord! I'm
willin' to bet they've had enough on't. Ain't thet th'
old lady comin' in Crane's buggy?"

Elizabeth's heart beat hard. There was no mis-
taking that square, upright figure in the black shawl ;
it was Grandmother, beyond doubt. The Sea View
driver, having been again forced to consign his whip

· to the bottom of the wagon, held the reins loosely, and sulkily allowed the all-too-willing animal to choose its own pace.

" Yes, it's Grandmother," she said, faintly, and opened the door of the sitting-room to break the news to her mother. She was not there, and Elizabeth went through to the shed, where Mrs. Nye stood talking to Philip, while he piled wood.

" Grandmother has come," she said, whereupon the three looked blankly at one another for a second. Then Philip went on with his work, and Mrs. Nye, with an immediate return of the caution she had not needed for weeks, hurried into the kitchen, saying : " How near is she ? We must go out to meet her, or she'll think strange."

But it was too late. The trunk had been deposited in the hall, and the front door shut with decision, before the two reached the sitting-room, where Grandmother was standing before the fire, awful in her array of large bonnet and veil. So seldom were they worn, that, upon the eye accustomed only to her household presence, they had all the effect of armor. She seemed more unlike other people than ever.

" How do you do, Eliza ? How do you do, Elizabeth ? " She had reached the stage of taking off her bonnet. " Did you see me coming ? Who stood in the door ? " ˙

" I, Grandmother. I went to tell mother, and didn't find her in time to go out and meet you. May I put your things away ? "

" Lay them on the bed in my bed-room. Don't try to put the shawl away. I know where it goes. Well,

Eliza, have you kept things as they ought to be ?
How much lard was there ? "

" The two firkins full and the little pint pail," said
Mrs. Nye, glad the first question was no more difficult.
" I've begun to use what's in the little pail, for pies."

By this time Grandmother had taken off her rubbers,
and was seated in her old chair, looking as if she had
never been away from it.

"When did you leave Hannah ? " asked Elizabeth,
coming back. " We haven't heard from you for so
long that I didn't know what you meant to do."

" Hannah's brother came home from the West, and
he's taken the farm.   She's going to live with him.
They're going to work it on shares.   I never meant to
leave it that way to any body that might cheat my eye-
teeth out, but Susan Fitts showed me pretty plainly I'd
better be in Stratford."

"Susan   Fitts?"   echoed Elizabeth.   "Where did
you see her, and what did she mean ? "

"She said," began Grandmother, turning her gaze
from the fire to apprehensive Mrs. Nye.   " She said
you were taking boarders, Eliza, she thought very
likely for nothing, and that the boarders had pretty
much the run of the house."

"Susan Fitts is forever making mischief," said Mrs.
Nye, roused to a just indignation.   "To say there
were boarders, when there was only one° young man !
And he paid me a good price, too ; enough to buy all
the meat we needed and get a new oil-cloth for the
kitchen."

"Yes.   Susan does make mischief, but when she
tells all she knows there's liable to be some truth in it.

After she'd emptied her budget, I told her she'd better give her mind to her dressmaking, instead of fetching and carrying what nobody'd thank her for. But I was much obliged to her, after all. She told me what you never did in your letters, Elizabeth."

"I didn't mean to keep any thing from you, Grandmother," said Elizabeth, honestly, trying to make her voice even. "I knew you wouldn't like our taking any one unless you had it explained to you, and I didn't want to do that in a letter. I thought it was better to wait."

"Did you mean to tell the whole of it, then?" asked Madam Nye, watching her narrowly. "Susan had a deal more to say—about your walking on the beach and round the pastures, with the man. She said she guessed you thought you might get him."

"Grandmother, you're going too far," said Elizabeth, her face flushing scarlet.

"I'm older than you are, Elizabeth," said Grandmother, stiffening slightly. "In this house I guess nobody can stop me from saying what I've a mind to. After all my telling you, did you forget that man's father had cheated you? Don't you know that's the reason you haven't got a cent to call your own, except what I give you?"

"It is a foolish thing to remember that," said Elizabeth, steadily, passing over the last reminder. "Mr. Craig is finer than any body I know. I should be proud of his friendship, if I knew his father was a thief."

"He seems to be a good principled young man," put in Mrs. Nye, feebly, hoping to stem the tide, and

listening for Philip's step with apprehension. If he
should come in and add the blaze of his inflammable
temper to Elizabeth's suddenly developed fire, she
trembled for the result.

"You'd better explain about his fineness," said
Grandmother, coldly, taking out her knitting and un-
rolling the yarn. "That might be some excuse for
the neighbors' saying you were after him."

"Grandmother, you do wrong to listen to gossip
and repeat it for the truth. I can tell you how he was
fine. He cared for beautiful things, pictures and books
and flowers ; he was kind, he—"

"Perhaps," said Grandmother, looking up suddenly,
and fixing her eyes on Elizabeth. "Perhaps, now
you're so willing to talk about him, you won't deny
you're in love with him."

There are moments when the greatness of an action
seems measured by its foolhardiness. Elizabeth felt a
quick impulse to contrast her courage with her Grandmother's suspicion. "I don't wish to deny it," she
said, lifting her head with pride. "I'm perfectly willing to tell you I made a mistake when I denied it to
him."

If she had been gifted with a stronger sense of the
ludicrous she must have laughed, even at the moment,
at the effect of her bombshell. Grandmother had very
evidently received a check from an entirely unimag-
ined turn of affairs, while Mrs. Nye sat quite dazed
by a development as unheard of as a summer fall of
snow.

CHAPTER XVI.

A N accomplished victory or defeat is liable to induce in the parties concerned a broader view of what preceded it, perhaps a less zealous partisanship. Before the next day, Elizabeth became aware that she had exposed a flaw in her armor and that she was liable to suffer gnat stings for the rest of her life, or at least while the memory of her unlucky admission was still green. She had astonished her mother beyond all precedent, and though Mrs. Nye did not refer to the conversation of the day before, her face did not once lose its disturbed expression. There are, unfortunately, some mothers who have learned non-interference in their daughters' affairs through long experience of the advisability of such a course ; but Mrs. Nye's forbearance had no such origin. There was a large surface of real delicacy beneath her usual show of hesitation, and this counseled her to wait for Elizabeth to speak. And then, too, interviewing her daughter on the subject of love would have been an ordeal she would not willingly have accepted. Elizabeth could see that Grandmother considered her to have fallen into a disgraceful and unholy frame of mind. As to Philip, he was too absorbed in his own thoughts to spend much time over the change in the family atmosphere ; of course it was to be ascribed, as usual, to

Grandmother. She had greeted him coolly on her return, but that was to be expected.

"Mother," he burst out suddenly at breakfast, "did Mr. Craig say he might come back here?"

"Yes, not to stay, but to get his trunk," said Mrs. Nye, praying in her heart that something might turn the conversation away from the unlucky subject.

"Oh, I didn't think of the trunk. But won't he stay? Won't he, Elizabeth?"

"I think not," she said, coldly, conscious that Grandmother was watching her.

"I should like to talk to him," said Madam Nye, with ponderous emphasis. "Perhaps he'd like to know just how much his father cheated, here and there. I should like to tell him what I know about it." ·

"Grandmother," said Philip, audaciously, "I can't see, if my father owed his father some money, why Mr. Craig hadn't the right to take the land to pay it. I don't see—— "

"Be quiet, Philip," said Grandmother, with more of a flash than usual. "When you can do something more than talk about money, it will be time enough for you to put your oar in. In my day you would have waited till you were spoken to."

"Si is bringing home the ax, Philip," said Elizabeth. "Hadn't you better go out and take it?" Which had the effect of ending the encounter, though the boy went with flashing eyes and lips trembling. The growing manhood in him was almost at the point of rebellion.

Elizabeth had not the very natural instinct which makes one, gratuitously presented with a bad reputation, wish to deserve it. Innate sincerity vetoed her assuming a bravado she did not feel. By nature, as well as training, she was obedient to authority, and having defied precedent, she had an attendant fear of being in the wrong. It was a very confused state of mind which she carried about, and it became every day more burdensome. Was it any wonder that her thoughts turned to Oswald as the bright spot in the midst of her perplexities? The very looks of the people at home questioned and wearied her ; the thought of him offered a vision of some one who had been always cheerful, at times radiantly so, who evidently understood her inmost self ; for had he not known her mind, when she herself was ignorant of it? It was a relief to reach the conclusion that he was right and she loved him. There are minds to which uncertainty is more harassing than acceptance of the hardest facts. Putting a peg here and there, comforts them. To fix on one central fact, simplified Elizabeth's war of emotion. So she caught rather eagerly at the suggestion that she had made an irrevocable mistake in sending him away; and bearing the consequences became easier, when she could refer them to a fault distinctly her own.

There was more general discomfort than ever at home. Grandmother assumed a dictatorial sway which she evidently thought necessitated by the anarchy that had prevailed during her absence, and Elizabeth felt the galling misery of a money dependence without love. A wild desire of escape grew up in her, and culminated in the idea of earning money. There was but one way of doing it, that open to the average American woman who cannot or will not work

with her hands—school-teaching. Without much
thought of the chances involved, and telling no one
her purpose, she walked to the Centre, one afternoon,
and asked if she might teach in her own district, the
next term.

"Never knew you thought o' such a thing. Allers
wondered why th' old ma'am didn't put you t' it, she's
so nigh," said Cyrus Pearson, with admirable candor.
"But the school's engaged. Hannah Blake asked for
it a fortnight ago. Spoke for any o' the other dees-
tricks ? "

"No," said Elizabeth, unreasonably disappointed.
"I haven't been thinking of it long."

Walking home, she took a longer road than was
necessary, in order to go down to the beach on the
way.

She had not been there since the night when Oswald
had forced upon her the most exciting scene of her
life. The sky was not yet clear of clouds, and the sea
still showed traces of the storm, but there was a wind
from the west which promised to blow in fair weather.
Elizabeth had not gone there for sentimental reflections;
she stood looking at the sea absently, not thinking
connectedly of the last few days with their discom-
forts, but vaguely conscious of trouble somewhere.
Some one was stepping over the round stones of the
rocky beach behind her. It was Oswald. Hat in
hand as soon as she turned, his face flushed and hair
matted and damp in the moist wind, he was a picture
of eager gladness. Elizabeth was not surprised, only
at once most thankful, as if a delivering angel had
come to smooth the way out of her difficulties.

" Are you glad to see me ? " he cried, reaching her in
a second more. " Why don't you give me your hand ? "

A fit of uncontrollable shyness had overtaken her,
but she was conscious that her face was brimming over
with delight. His eyes still sought hers with a merry
question in them.

" Are you glad ? Tell me."

" Yes."

" Then don't be in such a hurry to pull away your
hand. It's so cold, too—poor little fingers ! There,
I didn't mean to do that. I won't again, till you tell
me I may." After he had kissed them.

Elizabeth jealously covered the fingers, released at
last, with those of the other hand. It was impossible
to help a great throb of delight at this proof that he
had not forgotten.

" Why don't you ask me why I came back ? " said
Oswald.

" I knew—that is I thought it was—to get your
trunk ! " Seizing on the explanation with triumph.

" You didn't think any thing of the kind. You dis-
appoint me, Elizabeth. I thought you were clear as
crystal, above a subterfuge."

The girl was too used to seriousness to take the
badinage for what it was worth, and fell into the trap.
" No, it wasn't true," she said with a fine honesty in
which there was no trace of shyness, though she did
not lift her eyes. " I thought you wanted to see me
again. I had wanted to see you."

" Why ? "

" Because—oh, it is not generous to make me tell it
alone ! "

"No, sweetheart. Shall I help you? You found
you did love me. No, don't answer, look at me."
The brown eyes were obedient. The steadfast look
told Oswald more than he had expected of their
capacity for speech.

Mingled with the love there was what he did not see,
an appeal to the noblest part of his nature to sustain
and strengthen hers. As, after the advent of a blessing, a devout heart feels the instinctive desire of sacrificing to some god, so the sacrament of love is seldom
touched by lips which feel its holiness, without causing
them to owe devotion to an ideal purpose. As much
in Elizabeth's heart at that moment as could be translated ran : "I will be good. Help me, and be my
best."

"You are chilly. Let us go home," said Oswald,
drawing her hand under his arm. "And on the way I
shall catechise you."

"Oh, but Grandmother has come!" exclaimed Elizabeth, stopping short.

"Well, what of that? She seemed to be a very
amiable old lady when I saw her last winter, in spite of
being somewhat unapproachable," said Oswald, with a
laugh at the recollection. "I dare say she'll fall easy
prey to my graces of manner."

"No, you don't know Grandmother. The more you
tried to please her, the more she'd despise you for not
being above politeness and liveliness. And if you were
stiff, she might not like you either. I wish you were
a minister." Looking up at him with a satisfied pride.

"No, you don't, little girl. I know better. You've
had enough of the ministerial view of life. That's

why my general lightness and worthlessness are not quite distasteful to you."

"But it isn't because you are not serious," said Elizabeth, wrinkling her brow with extreme earnestness. "Yes, I might as well tell you ; but do be charitable in thinking about it, won't you ? Grandmother thinks she has a particular reason for not liking you."

"In the name of mystery, what ? She never heard of me before last winter, and the story of my misdeeds can't have traveled here this summer."

"No, not that ; I'll tell you. Let's walk back across the beach to keep warm. You know your father had the land and house, down here, from my father. He took it to pay a debt. My great-aunt Susan had left it to father, so he could do what he pleased with it, in spite of Grandmother."

"I didn't know who owned the old shell, originally, and I never thought myself very lucky to inherit it. Though it seems it's brought me luck after all. Little maid, you do love me, don't you ? "

"I love you very much," said Elizabeth, quietly, but with a thrill in her voice. "But I want to hurry over this. It's so hard to tell ! Grandmother can't bear to remember that my father lost his money in speculating, and, from knowing your father advised him, she thinks he drew him into it and ruined him. She thinks it wasn't honest." Her voice choked here. It seemed a cruelly indelicate thing to breathe such a suspicion ; she was prepared for his indignation. But Oswald only whistled. "I see, an old feud. Well, I confess I don't know any thing about my father's business transactions. They might not have been further

above board than any other man's, though he had a
good name when he died. That's all I can tell her."

It seemed a fine justice and integrity to say no more.
Elizabeth admired him for it. "So you see she won't
treat you very pleasantly," she went on. "If I
didn't know Grandmother so well I should think she
couldn't help liking you. But I know she could."

"See, here's our programme," said Oswald, after a
minute's thought. "I'll go to the Sea View to-night.
If you think best, I won't even walk home with you,
and to-morrow I'll come round and lay siege to the
Grandmother's heart. Will that do?"

"Yes, I think so, better than any thing. And don't
come any further with me, please. We are so near
home."

There were minutes of whispered words and fond
looks. Elizabeth's hair curled in rings about her face;
her cheeks were flushed, and her eyes alive from surface to depth. Oswald confided to himself, as he
turned away, that she was an exceptional girl of rare
possibilities, and that he was very much in love with
her.

There is no doubt that he was, and that circumstances had conspired to make him realize the fact.
He had put out from Scone with the fishermen, but,
warned by the persistent rain, they had come back to
port the same day. Oswald took a room at the little
hotel there, and spent his days over the fire, reading a
week-old paper and the almanac, waiting for fair
weather. It seemed easier to do that than to make
the exertion necessary for reaching another place, in
the storm.

The summer stir of life had not begun there. Only two boarders were at the hotel, an old lady and her niece, who came early every year and staid late. They and Oswald had the house very much to themselves, and as they were not disposed to enter his field of vision, he found not the slightest difficulty in the way of becoming desperately bored. With plenty of time for thought, Elizabeth's charm for him was not broken by absence. It grew as, in the lack of other employment, he endeavored to analyze it, until he found it impossible to wait for fair weather before going back to her. And now, this finding her willing to own she loved him had all the sweetness anticipation had promised, which was, for him, something remarkable.

The next morning, with the pleasant sense of a victory to be won, he went to make his call on Madam Nye. She was alone, and knitting. Elizabeth had told her mother how it had happened, and Mrs. Nye, with the true maternal gladness of a woman who had been happy in her own married life, showed a deeper tenderness than Elizabeth had ever seen in her. She had no thought yet of that sweet selfishness which will not let a mother give up her child without a pang.

" If he's coming to-morrow, we'd better keep out of the way," she said. " I should rather he'd see Grandmother alone. I'm sure I can't imagine what she'll say ! "

But Elizabeth, quite at rest now that Oswald had come back, did not care. A great love seemed omnipotent, its shelter second only to that of the heavenly powers. So, while her mother was pale and nervous, she felt only a proud joyousness.

Qswald's manner showed a quiet gravity when he
came in at the open door, and, without knocking, entered the sitting-room.

" I hoped to find you alone, Madam Nye," he began,
with not too great an effusion of cordiality. " My call
was intended for you, in fact."

Grandmother, who was apparently quite unconscious
of his entrance, unwound some yarn from her ball, and
put her needle in, before looking up.

" Well, what is it ? " she asked monotonously.

" You remember me, perhaps ? " said Oswald, venturing to take a chair, and drawing it near her. " I had
the pleasure of seeing you last winter."

Madam Nye would waste no time in vague plati-
tudes ; they were always frivolous, and, from Oswald
especially, not to be borne.

" Did you say you wanted to see me ? " she asked,
the click of her needles growing more steady. "If it's
about your clothes, I believe they're where you left
'em. Philip 'll help you fetch the trunk down stairs."

Oswald realized that a circuitous mode of attack
would not do. " No, it is not my trunk. I came to ask
your consent to my marrying your granddaughter."
Then, indeed, Grandmother laid down her work.

" I've no time to talk nonsense," she said. " Elizabeth never will marry a man like you. What have you
got to support her on ?   Where did the money come
from ? "

Oswald went on, with unmoved fluency. " I can't
give you the precise figure of my income, at such short
notice, but I assure you it is a comfortable one. As
for the cleanness of the money, my father gave it to me

unconditionally and without explanation. Can I say more than that ? "

" Yes," said Grandmother, a faint flush appearing high on her cheeks. " You can tell me whether you've got the name of an honest man to offer. Like father, like son. I wouldn't have trusted your father, and I won't see you Elizabeth's husband."

The most successful diplomacy sometimes demands a bold push.

" Elizabeth has promised to marry me," said Oswald, in his quietest voice. " I know she wont break her word. If you think there's any thing questionable about my right to the house opposite, I shall be very glad to give my wife the deed of it."

With such great issues at stake, the offer seemed lightening the load of her aversion by a straw's weight only, and yet, she felt that it was not a bad thing to say. But she loved Elizabeth with all the hidden strength of her heart ; better, now, than any thing except the memory of her dead son. She could not see her sacrificed in a marriage founded on wrong.

" Elizabeth, come here," she called, hearing a step in the kitchen, and as the girl appeared, she cried with real feeling, " Elizabeth, you'll do what I tell you, wont you ? I know what will be best. You can't marry him." But she noted with a sinking heart how, when Elizabeth turned to her lover, a flush rose in her face, and the tenderest of slight smiles came. The two did not speak, but Oswald rose and kept her hand while she answered: "I told you I cared for him, Grandmother. I do care very much. It is best for me to do what he says." Oswald flashed such a glad smile at her that

Elizabeth could not remember to be troubled at having disappointed some one else. Madam Nye took up her knitting.

" That's all, then," in her ordinary, even voice, which held, moreover, a trace of bitterness. " You've taken your own road. Do as you please."

" But do say something pleasant, Grandmother," going forward and standing close by her chair, made bold by the childish longing to see every body happy because she was.

" I haven't got any thing to say that would be heeded. Take care, you'll snarl my yarn."

And Elizabeth, disappointed in her turn, left the room with Oswald.

But, in spite of such a beginning, the days of court-ship were not unhappy. Elizabeth went about in such a dream of contentment that she hardly knew whether Grandmother was angry or not. She was particularly gentle both to her and to Mrs. Nye ; her own happiness made it seem impossible to be any thing but kind. Grandmother had neither eyes nor ears for conciliatory measures. She never spoke to Oswald, beyond returning his good-morning or good-by. He spent a part of every day there, but never came to the table, though Mrs. Nye courageously invited him. At first, it seemed rather an entertaining campaign to win the regard of such a belligerent old lady, but, after some days, the monotony of the warfare became tedious, and he preferred giving his whole time to watching the woman develop from Elizabeth's crude girlhood. It was such an absolutely new thing for her to be sure some one cared whether she wore daisies or blue ribbon at her throat, cared because her hands were white and supple and her hair full of bewitching golden lights at the temple, that she began to take a curious and delighted sort of interest in herself. First love is a mirror such as the first clear pool might have been for the newly born Eve. "Am I really all this?" asks the maiden of her glass. "But if I am this to him, it is quite enough." Elizabeth was conscious that she had begun to live.

Philip took it all with an exultation not to be concealed. "And now you will let me go to Boston and visit you, wont you, Mr. Oswald?" he said. "Elizabeth can't say a word, can she? because she'll have to do what you tell her, and you'll take me to the theater and concerts—oh, I think it was beautiful of you to fall in love with Betty!" at which the others could not help laughing, though Elizabeth, in her heart, was conscious of echoing the boy's unwise frankness.

"But perhaps I sha'n't be there, this winter," said Oswald, letting a stream of sand run through his fingers on Elizabeth's lap. "I shall have to be down here a great deal if Elsie doesn't make up her mind to go back with me."

"Why, of course she will, wont you, Betty? She'll be glad enough to do it, and I'll coax her. There's Si coming in with the lobsters. I'm going down to see him."

"Well, sweetheart," said Oswald, covering her hand with his, and looking at her with the smile that had not lost its power of bringing a blush. "Shall it be? Am I to have my wife this fall?"

"Oh no," said Elizabeth hurriedly. "That is, if you

please not ; we're so happy, and there's no need of changing."

" No need of being happier ? Dearest, come."

" I haven't had time to think of it ; a woman ought to make up her mind before such a great step."

" You can have all your life to reflect on it afterwards and as to making up your mind, aren't you quite sure you want to be my wife ? " But Elizabeth shook her head with a sweet willfulness that was quite unusual and made her all the more charming, so that Oswald vowed even the denial to have been worth the pleading. Circumstances did what he could not.

" I've been thinking what we're going to do with Philip," said Grandmother, when she and Mrs. Nye sat alone one morning, paring apples. " He seems to have his mind all made up not to go to school."

" It's only his thinking he hadn't ought to be a minister," said the mother, hoping to make some impression. " He does want to go to school ; no boy ever wanted learning more."

" That means he's willing to be supported all his life, and read foolish novels. That never'll be done with my money, so you needn't mention it again. I've always meant to do something for him,—nobody else will, if I don't—and I've made up my mind he'd better go into a store, at Stowe." Mrs. Nye's heart sank. She knew how Philip would receive the news.

" Do you mean for a clerk ? "

" Yes, to tend behind the counter. If he's got any smartness, it'll come out there, and if he hasn't, I don't know what will become of him. You know he's got no strength to work on the farm, if he wanted to.

He's always been pindling." Mrs. Nye said no more,
but took occasion to break the news carefully to
Philip, that, it not being entirely unexpected, he might
bear it the more coolly from Grandmother. His passion of grief astonished her.

"O Elizabeth, you are to blame!" he cried. "Mr.
Oswald says you are, for if you'd go to Boston with him
this winter, he'd surely invite me to stay with you.
And if I've got to be sent to Stowe, I might as well
give up."

"But, Philip, think, there's mother," said Elizabeth,
distressed. "You wouldn't have me leave her, this
winter, if she isn't to have me again, would you?
Think how lonesome she'll be."

"You mustn't think about me," said Mrs. Nye. "If
I knew you and Philip were comfortable, I should be
twice as well off. And this can't last forever." It was
the first time a relief from the burden had been mentioned, and Elizabeth realized how grievous the trial
must have been, to bring her mother to such a pass.
"You see something ought to be done for Philip," said
Mrs. Nye, "and if Mr. Craig will do it, I think you
ought to let him."

Such an outside pressure had its effect on Elizabeth,
and, when Oswald came, she told him the state of things.
"I wish you would tell me what to do. You know I
didn't say I wanted to stay away from you this winter
because I wasn't willing to come. But now when other
people are concerned, it almost seems as if I cared for
their sakes and not yours."

"Is that true?" asked Oswald, holding her at arm's
length and looking at her till the inevitable blush

came. "Dear little Puritan, always trying to do things with a moral end in view, be a little more selfish and a little less anxious. Shall I settle things for you?"

"Yes, I'm tired of deciding."

"Then we shall be married the last day of August, go immediately to the mountains for a breath of wonderful air, stay for a glimpse of gorgeous color, go to our own home in November, and invite Philip up for the winter."

And so it was. The marriage was a quiet one with no guests—indeed, there were none to have—and though Grandmother's face showed a swift shadow of feeling when she said good-by, Elizabeth felt sure she had not forgiven them.

CHAPTER XVII.

PROFESSOR GRIMWALD began to tell me about hearing the Seventh Symphony, in New York," said Elizabeth, turning from the glass to Oswald, who lay luxuriously, with pillows crushed beneath him.

" How did you receive the dissertation ? "

" I said I never had heard a symphony. I didn't know what it was."

" Was he petrified, or voluble ? " said Oswald, with a low laugh of enjoyment.

" He looked at me. I think he was very much shocked. What shall I do? People will find out how ignorant I am. Do you want me to keep quiet and learn things to say, to patch up with ? " The tone was a laughing one, but it held an anxious meaning. Elizabeth seated herself on the arm of the sofa and passed her fingers through her husband's hair, a stroking he liked well.

" Never that, Priscilla. Your charm lies in your wild-flower nature. Really, Elizabeth, if you should take on the air of know-nothing comment, if you dabbled in colors and practiced scales weakly, I'm afraid you'd be insupportable." Elizabeth laughed, and looked critically at the effect of laying her finger in a brown wave of hair. " But I should like to know something, Oswald. It makes me feel so insignificant,

like a country school-girl—and that's just what I am,
you know !—to hear those people talk. It's a comfort
to think you are willing to be ashamed of me ; or do
you only say so to make me happy ? "

" No, child ; when you've been here longer you'll see
what I mean. Though I pray you wont get to analyzing people enough to find out the difference between
you and them ! See, Elsie, you are precisely what these
cultivated people try to seem. They talk about character, and sincerity, and what not, but they're not even
sincere in the talking. You have the flavor they adore
but can't assume,—pine, resinous, with a touch of
sweetness. I'm very much in love with you, sweetheart ! "

Elizabeth sank quickly on her knees, and kissed him
with an impetuosity she was just learning. After the
kiss, she blushed ; the girl had not been quite trans-
formed into the wife, yet.

" There is a difference in life, isn't there ? " said Oswald, taking her hands and holding her when she
would have risen. " You thought you loved me before.
You thought we were going to have pleasant, friendly
living together, but you didn't even guess how much
happiness there could be in life. Isn't it so ? "

" Yes," said Elizabeth, her eyes dwelling on
him fondly. " I certainly didn't have a happy life,
and I begin to believe I never dreamt of one."

It was true, her fancy had never suggested this.
How could it, from an outlook on the same sky and
sea, an interest in no wilder emotions than the storms
and ocean-upheavals ? "

Set down at once in the midst of luxury and beauty,

absolutely unacquainted with music and other art except by hearsay, she was bewildered, awed, but not
overwhelmed, because her mind had not yet expanded
enough to take in the wonder of it all. So far, Elizabeth was rubbing her eyes awake. Pictures were little
more than canvas and color, and the winter's music
had not begun.

Oswald could not love by halves. He kept her rooms
smothered in flowers ; he made her feel her every motion to be a charm. Elizabeth sometimes paused in
her toilet, to wonder at herself. Was this the staid and
quiet girl who had cared only to have her gowns whole
and her collars fresh, who had pinned arbutus at her
throat because it was sweet, and not for approval,
and who had now become the center of interest to
one who might be poet, painter or musician, if he
chose ?

"Your clothes are an inspiration," said Oswald, as
she came to him, ready for dinner, one night. "Now
that soft fabric,—I'll warrant it doesn't cost much a
yard, but it hangs in miraculous folds. I dare say
you'll set a fashion, and all the pillow and bolster
women will be trying to look like you."

"It is cashmere," said Elizabeth, demurely, stroking
the gathers with one hand, as if rather grateful to them
for being praiseworthy, but not quite understanding
how they had managed it. "Grandmother gave it to
me, and said I must have the skirt made full and gathered, to keep from cutting up the cloth. I felt dread-
fully about it, but when you came in as we were sewing
on it, and told me to put puffs on the sleeves, I was so
relieved ; it seemed as if it couldn't be wholly bad, or

you'd have told me to throw it away and get another.
Are you sure it's all right ? "

"Sure. You are—all I could wish you," kissing
her hand. Oswald liked to worship, perhaps from an
instinct that no one phase of passion would last long.
But his eyes were not deceived in Elizabeth. In her
plain black dress, with the white ruffle and amber at
her throat, and her heavy hair, she was a woman to
be looked at twice. Perhaps she really would set a
fashion. No one could tell. Her reception by Oswald's friends had in it something of the ridiculous.
He had coolly surveyed beauty and passed her by,
and mockingly given coquetry the attention for which
she angled. But now he had married. Who was she?
A fisherman's daughter, a lighthouse keeper's, a girl
who had lived on the coast all her life and written most
wonderful poetry, which would shortly be published ;
indeed, it was now in press. The rumors were various, and in the midst of them, Elizabeth came. It was
easy to see that she was not of their manner of life,
though her simple unconsciousness kept her from being too much abashed by their frequent discussion of
the world's affairs. And whatever was plainly unusual
in her they pieced out with the remarkable qualities
Oswald must surely have demanded in a wife, giving
even her commonplace little speeches a hidden and
mysterious meaning which would have surprised her.
Elizabeth saw nothing, but Oswald did, and enjoyed it
all. Her great charm for him lay in her sincerity and
youthfulness of heart, and he could but smile—
it would have been with bitterness had he been
earnest enough for that—to see his little world pass

the real attraction, supplying attributes which could be worshiped by the book.

In the meantime, Philip came for his promised visit. Oswald had proposed it again, after they had been home a few weeks, telling Elizabeth, with the good-nature which always characterized him when his sun shone brightly, to have the boy down at once. Thereupon she was smitten by remorse at finding in her heart a slight jealousy at the thought of any third person's entering her selfish Paradise, and wrote Philip at once, on receiving a particularly discouraged letter from him. The roads were freezing, and the first sprinkle of snow had come, for a threat. He had one of his colds and was sitting over the stove in flannels. Would Elizabeth write him every thing? And had Booth come yet?

Her answer brought the boy, the next day. He was pale from confinement to the house, and worn by a distressing cough, but his eyes grew large and eager over the wonders of the city.

Sometimes Elizabeth remembered, with a start, that Philip might be lonesome. When she was alone with her husband, and found him ready to talk or read to her, she could only think when he rose to leave her, that there was a world of people beyond him.

But Philip was usually in the library, taking down one book after another, reading here and there, never finishing a chapter even, but, in the first delight of riches, roaming about to count his treasures, sometimes accumulating a pile of volumes on the floor and sitting in their midst, dreaming dreams.

Felix was still at Cambridge, and wrote to say he

should be very glad if Philip would go out to see him
first, being a boy of leisure while he was a man at work.

"I must go right away," said the boy, when the letter was brought him at breakfast.   "Betty, can I go
to-day?"

"Yes, if you know how to find him.   You and I
are not city people yet, you know."

"Take the carriage and go for a drive while he makes
his call. It's like spring, to-day," said Oswald, putting
down his napkin.   "I've promised to see Hudson's
Venus, and you can use up the time while I'm gone.
Is this your reformer, your anti-revivalist, Philip?"

"He's the one I told you about, the one that was
sent away from Stratford," said Philip, his old hero-
worship reviving, at the prospect of seeing Felix. He
grew eager enough before they reached Cambridge.

"Elizabeth, do you suppose I shall ever do any thing
great?" with all his old enthusiasm. "I don't believe
Oswald thinks any thing about it, now,—but he likes
me, I know he does."

"I can't tell, Philip ; I hope so. It makes me sun-
blind to hear great things talked about as if people expected them to be perfect. Yes, Oswald likes you, but
he has seen so many people, that perhaps he wouldn't
think it would do to encourage you till you had shown
him whether you could do any thing or not."

"But I know I can," insisted the boy, "and I shall
die if I don't. Is this the house, and when will you
come back for me?"

"In half an hour, perhaps ; but find out whether
Mr. Kewe is at home, first, and don't stay if he doesn't
want you."   •

Mr. Kewe did want him. He was leaning over the banisters four flights up, when Philip heard his, "Ask him to come up."

It was rather a common lodging-house, with narrow stairs. Philip, after his one week's experience of luxurious living, thought it stuffy and bare, wondering, as he went up, if Felix minded being poor. Certainly he did not seem greatly out of patience with fortune. His grasp of Philip's hand was full of heart and vigor, and his face all sunshine.

"Isn't it strange for you to come and see me here? But isn't it jolly, too?" showing him into a large attic-room. " I am glad you're here."

"So am I glad, Mr. Kewe," said Philip, warming his hands, which were not at all cold, with a general sense of accepting hospitality. "And I can stay half an hour, if you want me. Do you?"

"I certainly do," said Felix, drawing forward two worn but deep and comfortable chairs. "Now, how are you, and how is Stratford?"

"Stratford?" said Philip, vaguely. It had already begun to assume the proportions of a mote in the distance. "Stratford's just the same and I—why, I'm here!" They both laughed.

"You think that tells the story. Well, perhaps it does for you, just now. Place is a good deal at times, though people make general remarks to the contrary. And what are you going to do?—or is that family business?"

"I don't know," said Philip, frowning. "They make a great fuss about my cold. I'm hoarse, you see. I always have a cold, but they've made me go to a doc-

tor and he says I must not go out every day to school.
But I shall make a fuss till I do."

"So," said Felix, thoughtfully. "No, I think I
wouldn't, if he says not.   There is so much irregular
work to be done, you see.   You can learn something
about pictures, and people, and books, without risking
any thing by study in school."

"But I must have that."

"Yes, I know, the old story.   You can't wait.   But
you wont come again if I preach.   How do you like
my room?"

"I like it," said Philip looking around curiously, as
he had been longing to do ever since he came in.   "It's
queer."

"Yes, I believe it is that, but I like it."   One side
of the roof sloped almost to the floor.   There
were two broad windows on that side, generous of
light, and just now the sun flooded the room, exposing
its bareness, but compensating for that in good cheer.

"You'd be surprised to know what a house furnish-
er I am," Felix went on.   "There was a carpet here
when I came, red and green, a complexion to make
one sick.   I took it up and painted the floor brown,
myself."

"Did you paint the hearth, too?"

"Yes, and wasn't it fortunate there were real bricks?
I was so enraptured with the first coat of this red, that
I sat on my knees adoring it some time, in artistic
frenzy."

"With the brush in your hand?"

"Yes, like a mermaid.   Indeed, I absently allowed
it to rest on my knee and thereby spoiled my trowsers."

Some one shouted up the stairs that a lady was waiting, and Philip took his leave.

"Come again soon," said Felix. "Next Wednesday afternoon, if you will."

"Mr. Kewe, come down and see my sister, please, and tell her you want me. Besides, I want you to see her."

Felix went out to the carriage, and was introduced to Elizabeth. He was bareheaded and she noted that his face was strong and perhaps fine. Still, she was disappointed. He was more like an athlete than a spiritual guide.

"How the faces differ," he thought, as they drove away after a few words. "The boy's is all restlessness, but hers is quite contented. She must be happily married."

Philip had not been made anytheless anxious to work, by seeing Felix. He attacked Elizabeth, in and out of season, to be told why he could not go to school. To say he had a cough was not enough. Plenty of boys had colds, and were allowed to go out when they pleased. Elizabeth, in her perplexity, went to Oswald and asked what could be done. He had just come in from a drive behind fast horses, and was in radiant good-humor.

"Why, let him have private lessons," he said, throwing himself down as far from the fire as possible. "Then he can study or not, as he pleases. There wont be any competition. Ask that Harvard man to give him lessons. Didn't you say he was a tutor?"

Elizabeth's anxiety seemed hardly lightened, though she did not speak.

"I like the boy, you know. I fancy he may have real talent. He's erratic enough."

"But private lessons! Don't they cost ever so much?"

"Now, my child," said Oswald, "you are never to hint that you don't want to spend money. Don't let me feel there's a bit of vulgar pride in your heart."

Elizabeth put her cheek softly down on the hand that rested on his chair and then looked up at him, with happy tears filling her eyes. "You are so good to me," she cried. "So generously good to help Philip, too! Don't you suppose I am grateful to you every day, when I see him so happy?"

"Foolish child," said Oswald, caressing her head with his other palm. He could not have endured much literal, outspoken gratitude, but a subtle trace of incense in the air was sweet savor to his nostrils. That the fragrance should rise suddenly, when the fire blazed higher on the altar, was exactly as he would have had it. "You forget, I never asked you for gratitude. I want the sweet look in your eyes and the blush that hasn't done rising yet, when I come near you. Why, it's coming now! Elizabeth, you're not quite used to your lover yet!"

He held up her face with one finger under her chin, and dropped his own laughing one to a level with it. Elizabeth was fast gaining a charming coquetry, which the simplest woman is easily taught. Since Oswald had told her the corners of her mouth held tiny dimples, and laughingly laid kisses there, bidding the dimples keep them till he came to take them away, she could not be unconscious that the lips quivered with remembrance, when he looked at them again. If he laughed at her blushes, how could she help their rising when there was no excuse for it? Oswald knew the alphabet of love, and read and discoursed fluently in its language. Elizabeth answered, in such eloquence of word and thought as astonished herself. "The dull, quiet girl of Stratford must be dead," she told herself in exultation, seeing her own face glad and awakened, as only a delight in life can make one. No inward peace, no philosophy of contentment ever approaches it.

So it was arranged that Felix should give Philip lessons, coming for them twice a week. It was of more value to the boy than any one estimated, then.

Felix's strong, calm nature balanced Philip's impetuosity and reduced some of his flights of fancy to reasonable proportions, often stopping ambitious fabrics in the building.

"Well, write me some verses," he said, one day, when Philip had been most extravagant in worship of the people who had seen themselves in print. "Take this fragment from Horace. I'll help you translate it, if you have any trouble, and then you may put it into English verse."

Philip trembled with delight and a sense of responsibility. It was a crisis for him; he had a wholesome respect for his master's opinion, and this seemed a test which might establish his claim as something beyond the ordinary. He was busy half an hour and then came to Felix, holding out the paper. Felix carefully read it aloud.

"Very good for a translation, very good indeed!

Your meter seems to be all right and you've kept the spirit of the original. Yes, Philip, you did well. Why, what's the matter?" noticing how white he had grown.

"I'm so glad. I was afraid it would be wrong and you would laugh," he said, trying to laugh at himself.

"Why, you mustn't take things in such deadly earnest," said Felix, kindly. "Suppose you had made a wretched botch of it all, what would it prove?—why, nothing final. You might fail and yet be a real poet. Don't you see?"

"Yes, but it was the first time. I didn't fail, did I?" with a flash of delight. As Felix was going, Philip called him back to say, "Mr. Kewe, guess what is going to happen next week!"

"I can't tell, I'm sure. By the way your eyes shine, I should say you were going to sit on a street corner and see Mr. Longfellow go by. You've bribed a policeman to let you put a camp-stool and foot-stove there."

"Now that's too bad, Mr. Kewe! I sha'n't tell you. Yes, I shall, too, it's so jolly. I'm going to the theater to see Victoria Landor, in Juliet."

"That's the new star, isn't it? I sha'n't see her yet, probably. I'd rather wait till the critics have labeled her. But if you're disappointed—oh yes, you may be, for you expect a miracle—don't blame Shakespeare!"

CHAPTER XVIII.

THERE were not only the usual announcements before Victoria Landor's appearance as Juliet, but
paragraphs had been finding their way into the newspapers for months, saying, in one form or another, that
Manager Rose had discovered in her the light of the
modern drama. All the excitement to be kindled by
judicious advertising had been called to the aid of the
problematic woman, and tickets sold rapidly. Even the
critics were as expectant as such a cool body politic
ever becomes over an uncertainty, and the house was
crowded, the first night. One item in her favor was the
well-known fact that Rose was cautious, and not prone
to lend his name to uncertain ventures. Even if she had
not been heard of before, it was safe to say she was no
raw girl animated by stage frenzy.

When she came on, that first night, the house was
silent, except for the efforts of a few irresponsible
young men animated by the tradition that the star
must invariably be applauded. But the grave, judicial
few on whose fiat her standing was to depend, kept
still and waited for the test. She understood that, it
seemed ; she had no eye for the audience, barely acknowledging the applause she had not earned.

This Juliet was pure Italian, red-lipped, with a cheek
of warm olive and masses of black hair. If her eyes

were not black, excitement had made them so, and
nature had given them a shape and fullness with which
art had no need to meddle. Her tone was full and
true as a bell. It could not have caught its trick of
liquid modulation from any teacher ; it was for speech
what a deep, sweet contralto is for song, one with no
masculine chord or bass heaviness. When she began
to speak, Oswald, who had been lounging and studying her carriage and drapery through his glass, sat up
to listen. Midway in the first scene he turned to Elizabeth and whispered, "She's well trained enough,
but there's no fire in her. Rose has made a mistake.
She won't make the sensation he expected."

"I suppose you know ; but I think she's beautiful.
Look at Philip ! "

He was bending forward, his hands clasped and his
eyes fixed on Juliet. There was no disappointment.
The stage was Wonderland ; nay, there was no stage
nor painted scenes. It was Italy, and this fair young
creature was the rose of love, blossoming for his fortunate eyes. Others might see her, too, but whether
others were affected with him, he never thought ; the
crowd of human beings had faded out.

To breathe in time with the lovers of that play, one
must either be a poet or have loved intensely. Philip,
the child, with his highly strung nature, had all a poet's
capacity for response to genius. That amply took the
place of experience. He felt, where he had neither
lived nor loved, as an improvisator pours forth music
of language, strung pearls of epithet which he can
neither analyze nor spell.

"Well, Mrs. Craig, how do you like her ? " asked

Jack Perham, coming over to them at the end of the second act. Jack was a good comrade, a hearty, impulsive fellow who was willing to get on in the law, but would probably never reach any more laudable consummation than lay in spending five comfortable hours a day at his office. Fortunately he had money, and after all, a man can be busy enough without maliciously interfering with the people who are exerting themselves to see the Charles River on fire. Jack read the papers luxuriously; he was always ready to talk or smoke with a friend, and sometimes it was a fact that he did half a day's work.

"I think she is wonderful," said Elizabeth, scarcely less enthusiastic than Philip. "She helps me with the play, too. I never could understand Juliet."

"Haven't I helped you?" whispered Oswald.

"I can't, either," said Jack, frankly. "You don't know how relieved I am to have you countenance me! I always thought her rather a brazen young woman. Oh, of course you're laughing, Craig. Mrs. Craig, your husband thinks I have no soul."

"Never mind, Jack, you're a most excellent fellow without one," said Oswald, adjusting his glass.

"I shall go, Mrs. Craig, I am offended," with a smile and bow, threading his way back to his place.

"I'm afraid you have hurt him," whispered Elizabeth to her husband.

"Kind of the gallery to wear bright green and orange feathers and red ribbons," he said, finishing his survey. "If you half close your eyes and blur the effect, the color is lovely. What was that about Jack? Oh, he isn't used to tender treatment. Sarcasm from

the tongue and a clap of good-fellowship on the back
suit him well enough."

" But I thought you liked him ! "

" Oh yes, so I do.   That is, I see more of him than
of any other man, because he's too good-natured to be
a bore.   I consider him rather a fool, but besides
never asking your confidence, as most fools do, if you
give them an excuse, he never seems to think of it.
Therefore, he's no strain on your intellect ; you don't
have to lie to him."

" But, Oswald, do you like him?" persisted Elizabeth, trying, in her straightforward fashion, to reconcile her own definitions with her husband's.

" Bless your heart, child, yes.   Why do you insist
so ? He's a good fellow enough, and as I told you, less
a nuisance than nine-tenths of people.   See Philip !
He looks like a sleep walker."

The curtain rose, and Juliet, desperate and at bay,
sent away the pandering nurse and cruel mother ;   she
looked the dead in the face, before joining them.   When
the death scene came, Elizabeth grasped her husband's
coat as it lay beneath her own drapery.   Did love and
death, then, come so near each other ;   walking on the
heights, might one stumble over some clump of fragrant
weeds, and falling, find the edge of a precipice with
death at its foot ?   Oswald laughed, as they rose to go.
" Juliet would be flattered if she could see you and
Philip ; after that, she wouldn't believe a score of newspapers, if they unanimously tore her to shreds.   Trembling, Philip ?   And you haven't spoken all the evening.
Well, I won't disturb you.   Go home in a dream, if
you like."

The dream did not break with the morning, even. Who does not remember such a first tasting a new brand of life's wine?

Elizabeth was too much absorbed by the drama of her own life to be lastingly affected by one from without. After the evening's excitement, she had only words for Juliet, but Philip had burning thoughts. He was late at breakfast, but came down just as Oswald was leaving the house for an hour at the club.

" I've written some verses about her," he said, excitedly, thrusting out a sheet of paper. " How can I get them to her? Would she read them?"

" Bless me!" said Oswald amused. " Who? Are you in love?"

" Juliet. Do you think she'd read them?"

" I dare say she'd be glad, if they were bad as advertising rhymes. She isn't likely to have much said about her. Let me see. 'Passion and pain,'—hackneyed—'Stain of thy cheek,' 'red wine of the lip!'—not bad. Lame but honest. Any body could see the writer was a boy, and daft. If you like, I'll pass it to Dobbs and see if he'll print it. He prints worse verses every day."

" Oh, will you?"

But the door closed, and Oswald walked away, leaving Philip to construe Latin so vilely that he threw his book into a corner, and sat vacantly by the window, half the forenoon.

Oswald met Manager Rose, half-way down the street.

" Well, what do you think of her?" asked that gentleman, stopping short and transfixing Oswald with his keenest glance.

"She isn't all you've claimed, but then, that isn't to
be expected, of course," said Oswald, indifferently.
"You must gull the public enough to draw an audience."

"But I didn't mean to gull the public," said Mr.
Rose, with warmth. "I believed she was all I said,
and more. I think so still, but how the devil to get it
out of her is more than I can tell."

"How has she been trained? Are you in a hurry?
Then come into the club if you feel like talking."
Seated in a window and half concealed by the full
curtains, Mr. Rose felt himself in a seclusion like that of
his private office, and was on his own ground at once.

"I'm willing to tell any body about her training,
now. I didn't want to, at first, because I thought it
was better, in a business way, you know, not to say
any thing about it. As long as you keep still, a dozen
stories will start up to help you along. No matter
whether you tell the lie or somebody's good enough
to tell it for you, the lie floats you. Some said she
had been at the Paris Conservatoire, and was too pa-
triotic to appear at the Théâter Française. Some
said she had appeared there. The Dawn had a paragraph that said she'd been on the boards ever since
she was old enough to walk,—born in Australia.
Some said she'd been educated for the stage and not
allowed to go on till she could star. Every word
helped us. See?"

"I see," said Oswald. "What happens to be the
truth,—or are you going to lie to me, too?"

"No, the last story is the one. I'll tell you more
than I should want repeated, for I want to know what

you think. There may be some intellectual quibble
I can't fathom, that's going to settle her success. She's
a New Hampshire girl, born up in Ridgeway, my
place. I knew her mother there, when she was Judge
Terry's daughter and I was a poor boy just making
my way in the world. Queer how things come round,
and how it's my turn to help the family that was at
the top of the heap then !"

"What was the family ? Does she inherit talent ?"

"Yes, that's the beauty of it ; that's why I should
have faith in her if she was to play a year like a stick.
Her great-grandmother was a French woman with a
passion for the stage.—Passion for it, sir ! I guess she
had. She led her husband a devil of a life because
he wouldn't let her go on. I don't know any thing
but what I've heard about the grandmother, but Victoria's mother married when she was pretty young. I
always thought she regretted it, too."

"Did she long for forbidden fruit, like the French
grandmother ?"

"Yes, and nobody knows better than I do how
much she longed for it," his face softening, and
growing a little abstracted. " Her husband died when
Victoria was a baby and left them all his money.
His wife was twenty-five then, and she came here to
Boston and asked my advice about going on the stage.
I told her, no. She hadn't any experience and she
wouldn't have been satisfied with common pickings.
And if she failed she would be twice as miserable as
she was before."

"How did she take that ?"

"She didn't take it. She engaged lessons of Fannie

Fallon, half an hour after I'd talked to her. Said she
was willing to begin low and work up to be leading
lady somewhere. But just as she was working herself
to death, Victoria had diphtheria and was ailing for
more than six months. No mother could stand that,
you see. She forgot every thing for the child, and
when Victoria got better, Mrs. Landor was sort of discouraged for herself, but made up her mind the girl
should have every thing she'd missed. And she began
there and gave twenty solid years to educating that
child, and training her up according to her own notions. Whether they're paying notions or not, has got
to be proved now."

"You kept track of them all this time?"

"Yes; we sort of kept track of each other. You
see, though she never'd had a very good time there,
Ridgeway was her native town, and she would have
been glad to see a dog that came from there. And I
could give her some insight behind the scenes, that nobody ever gets out of books. Well, I can't tell you
what a queer training that girl has had. Says her
mother to me, 'My daughter is going to be a scholar.'
She calculated the time her money was going to hold
out, and found there would be just about enough to
put Victoria through. So they took two rooms, got
their own meals, and carried out the programme just
as she made it. She wouldn't let the girl go to a public school, she wouldn't send her to boarding-school;
but they had masters and masters, and they've read
together ever since Victoria could talk plain. Kate
Leary taught her most of her stage business, and
they've spent a mine of money on Fixter."

" Where is the mother now ? "

" She died, a year ago. I knew she was failing, but I hadn't any idea it was so serious till a little while before she died. It was a cancer. When she found there was no help for it she told Victoria, and they talked it over and made up their minds what must be done after she was gone, as if it was—well, a trip across the water. Victoria behaved like a woman of fifty, after it, and kept right on with her studying. Now, do you know, I don't believe her mother would have done just as she did, if she'd been into society any. They just shut themselves up, and lost track of the wickedness in the world. Or, rather, I guess they never knew whether 'twas wicked or not, coming from Ridgeway here. Now you and I would see it wouldn't do for a girl like her to live alone in lodgings ; but she almost snapped my head off when I advised her to board, or get an elderly woman to stay with her."

" You surprise me, Rose. This is America, man, and women are supporting themselves and living alone, scores of them."

" Yes, I know all that, but you see I know Victoria, too. She's been brought up with extravagant ideas of the calling. I really believe the girl thinks she ought to thank the Lord every day, for letting her go on the stage, if she starves there. Now you know, to keep on carrying her head just as high as she does now, she hadn't ought to run the risk of suspicion, any where. That's why I wish she could be fenced in, so that even you young swells could see she is as much of a lady as your sisters. You didn't think much of her acting, now, did you ? "

"Well, I shouldn't go so far as to condemn her. She has possibilities, but so have dozens of people. It all depends on how they pan out. But her physique is splendid and so is her voice. I can't explain what I think she lacks. It seems to be that she doesn't move you. She isn't magnetic."

"That's what I tell myself," nodded Rose, approvingly. "I should like to introduce you to her. Come round any night and I will."

It was not long before Oswald found his way behind the scenes, but he delayed it until the curtain went down, and then looked in vain for Rose. Victoria went past him to her dressing-room, coming out presently with her cloak on. Rose appeared suddenly, performed the introduction, and hurried off with his hat under his arm to give some directions.

"Mr. Rose says you have come to criticise me," said Victoria, looking at him frankly, as far from boldness as embarrassment. "Please do it."

"I don't want to," closing his eyes a little to scan her, and speaking with a coolness that was half impertinence.

"But I wish you would," she said, earnestly, throwing a piece of lace over her head—which she might easily have done from a coquettish impulse. Her hair proved to be blonde, and was very bright through the black meshes. But this was not even an artistic suggestion. She was afraid of taking cold. "I don't mean to care for criticism usually. I'm not even reading the newspapers, because I always thought their critics hadn't much notion of art, and perhaps their little opinions would paralyze me as much as if they

were greater. Mr. Rose says you are more of a dramatic critic than all the newspaper men put together.
Tell me how I affect an audience."

"You will certainly have to ask the newspapers ;
that is, for your effect on the majority of people," said
Oswald, rather cruelly, watching her, "for you don't
move me at all."

"Really?" said the girl, looking at him with the
utmost gravity and intentness. "Oh, I'm so sorry ! I
don't believe I am conceited, but—I'm surprised,
too."

" It wasn't a gallant speech, but I thought you wanted
the truth. Why, your eyes are actually wet ? How
rude I must have been, and how sensitive you are ! "

"No, not very, but I am anxious," she said, not
minding her eyes in the least. " I feel doubtful
whether I'm going to be a success, and though I expect to work hard for years and years, I want to set
Mr. Rose's mind at ease now. He's been very good to
me, and has expectations of my deserving it. Can you
tell me what I lack?"

"No, not without thought. I think you do some
things admirably ; a good many stiffly. I should like
to talk with you and ask your reasons for some points.
If you would let me call to see you, with Rose, we
might understand each other better."

"Yes, please do," she said, with frank pleasure. "I
shall be glad to see you. And perhaps you'll bear me ·
out against him in some ideas he sets down to my
ignorance. Good-night." She nodded and smiled, and
was half way down the steps before he could follow
her. · When he came out at the stage-door her carriage

was just driving away.   Oswald was amused.   He was used to various styles of Bohemian—the girl who accepted an invitation to supper from a stranger, and drank her champagne like a man ; the one so severely proper as to need a chaperon on all occasions, except that of fainting in her lover's arms on the stage ; and the genuine lady—but he had never seen such a mixture of self-possession and childishness as this.   The simple straightforwardness with which she assumed that he knew something which would help her, and therefore depended on him to impart it, touched his self-love. It tempered the admiration he could not help feeling for her beauty by a half-patronizing flavor which added to his kindliness.   Elizabeth was waiting for him at home.   She had not known how long he would be gone ; there had been a dinner at the club, and dropping into the theater was an after impulse.   He was running up stairs when she opened the library door and called him   With a sudden thought of her, he wanted to see her.   It was a great addition to his present pleasure not to have thought of her all the afternoon.   She looked a little tired, but her face brightened too quickly for him to guess she had worried about his delay.

"Are you glad ? " holding her at arm's length, and waiting for a smile.   " And you've had a supper brought in here.   I smell it.   Elizabeth, if your forethought goes as far as that, you'll be the comfort of my declining years."   Elizabeth tried in vain to bring her face down to a demure seriousness.

"Come in.   Perhaps I can find you a crust, at least. Now, lie down there, and have the crimson pillows.

I know you like this better than a chair. Now, you're not to say a word, but watch and see what I do."

Oswald had a genius for accepting petting. He sank back on the sofa, with a sigh of delight, and looked hungrily at the table. It was a tiny table, covered with a cloth, and bearing delicious bread and butter, with a picturesque salad. Elizabeth took a napkin and lifted a small pot of chocolate from beside the grate.

"It was made half an hour ago," she said, pouring a cup. "I thought you would be home then, if you were at the theater. But it's hot, Oswald; so you wont mind?"

"It's delicious," said Oswald, sipping and adding sugar till it was a nectar of sweetness. "Elsie," as she drew up the table so that he need not leave his lounging position, even to use his fork, "you know exactly how to make me comfortable."

His wife laughed happily, sitting down on a hassock near him with her own cup. It was enough pay for this whole evening's anticipation of his comfort to see him pleased with the result.

"I've been talking to your wonder of an actress," he said, throwing his head back on the pillows, while she filled his cup again. "Rose introduced me."

"You have? Tell me about her. How I wish I could see her, too! But no, I shouldn't know what to say."

"There really isn't any thing to tell," beginning a second deliberate raid on the sugar-bowl. "Except that she's a beautiful creature and doesn't need much making up. She has a combination of features you seldom see in an American woman, full, very red lips,

white teeth and a clear complexion, added to a fine profile. She walks like an Indian. I should say that
what you would remark first in her, is her splendid
physical health."

"What did she say to you?"

"Asked me to criticise her, which there wasn't time
to do. Elsie, it's no end of comfort to find you here
when I come in."

Elizabeth brought her hassock closer and put her lips
to his hand. "Are you sure I shall make you happy?"

"Yes, on the whole, very sure," said Oswald, lightly.
"You haven't an obtrusive way about you; consequently, you please me. If you insisted on a frantic interest
in every breath and coming and going of mine, we
might get tired of each other. But you philosophically
don't."

Elizabeth was not conscious of having deserved
praise of just this nature. She had felt vaguely disturbed
in his absence, and now longed to draw nearer, to be
soothed and indulged, but his very tone good-naturedly
warned her to wait for an invitation.

CHAPTER XIX

I T was somewhat confusing to Elizabeth not to have become, with marriage, a busier woman. She found her husband's household in running order, as it had been for the past five years, and could suggest no improvements. Being a woman of good sense, she did not attempt innovations for the purpose of claiming her rights, but remained aloof from the field, penetrated with a sense of awe at Ward's generalship. Ward was the head of the establishment, an English man-servant, with the inherited tendencies of generations of service. American air had, as it unfortunately has a way of doing, given him a deep regard for his own personal importance, but that never became offensive. Ward had too nice a sense of the fitness of things to spoil a good servant, even if that servant chanced to be himself.

Life hurried its action with Oswald. His love for his wife had been an absorbing emotion. It had not yet spent itself, but he had reached a point where her presence in the room did not rouse him to mental ecstasy.

One night, Jack Perham came in, and, after a pleasant hour, went into the library with Oswald, to smoke. Thereupon Philip grew sleepy, and possibly a little cross, at not having been invited to witness that manly pastime, and grumbled up to his own room at ten.

Elizabeth made herself somnolently comfortable in a chair by the fire and settled down to thought. That was made up, nowadays, of two threads—a tender longing for her mother's comfort and rather an humble recognition of her own happiness. Soon she was only conscious that, healthfully tired after a long drive in the wind, she was sinking into a delicious doze. An hour after, she waked to wonder dreamily if she could have been asleep, and if her husband would be in soon, changed her position, and slept again. When she waked for the second time, the clock was striking nine— ten—it could not possibly be twelve ! But the strokes declared it, and she sat up hastily, winking sleep away. There was an eerie sense that she must be alone in the house, and, though by no means given to troublesome fears, she crossed the hall quickly and pushed open the library door. Oswald sat by the table reading, with that peculiarly alert, concentrated look which sometimes indicates the person intellectually alive at midnight as he never is before sunset. He held himself erect, as if too intently fixed on a train of thought to lounge at his ease. Jack had sunk forward, his head on the table, a deplorable caricature of his usual presence, and, unmerciful witness, a half-filled wine glass stood close to the helpless right hand. Elizabeth sickened at her first glance, though she would not confess to herself how well she understood. Oswald looked up : perhaps her glance drew him.

"You there, Elizabeth ? I'm sorry you waited up," he said, slightly annoyed. A pale, frightened woman breaking in on his train of thought was an unexpected apparition. "I shall be up-stairs, presently. Don't wait for me." He rose and put down his book, running his hand through his hair and glancing at Jack incidentally. But Elizabeth did not go.

"What is it? Is he ——," she asked, in a whisper of suppressed excitement.

"I'm afraid he is," said her husband, carelessly, touching the bell and looking at his watch in the second of waiting for the sleepy servant. "Get a carriage and take Mr. Perham home. You know the number—19. Now come, Elizabeth." With a polite decision she could not resist, he led her to the stairs and went up with her. She was only alive to a sense of sudden and awful calamity. Drunkenness was one of the vices, and not among those most tolerated in Stratford. The few people addicted to it were sweepingly, and therefore Pharisaically, condemned to a social region below notice. This had happened in her husband's presence. Consequently, there must be some way of explaining it. She sat down, leaning her arms on the table, without a thought for her white, shocked face, visible in the glass.

"Oswald, come here, please," she called, unable to wait longer for having her mind set at rest. "How did it happen?"

"What? Jack, do you mean? Why, he's fond of wine and he took too much, that's all."

"Was he ever so before—with you?"

"Scores of times. What have I to do with his drinking?"

"Oh, it is dreadful!"

"Elizabeth, don't do that. Don't fall into extreme, vulgar notions. Nothing annoys me more."

And nothing baffles like that sense of having at
heart a principle which, in the mind of another, repre-
sents nothing more serious than a whim. Elizabeth
began taking down her hair, without a word. For the
first time, she put her husband far enough away to
judge him by her own standards. But, in the morning,
few things seemed of more importance than making
sure there was not the slightest shadow of difference
between them.

"I am sorry if you thought I interfered last night,"
she said, touching his hand penitently, as they were
going down to breakfast. "I didn't mean to ; but it
seemed so wrong."

It was a proud humility ; her erect young conscience
would not yield a jot of protest against the deed,
though, in sweet loyalty, she repented of judgment.

"All right, dear," said Oswald, carelessly, putting
discussion by to kiss her hand. "Don't let us make
each other uncomfortable. That's morality enough for
the present."

And as Elizabeth said no more, the question was
dropped. Nevertheless, little consideration as he
allowed himself to give it, her evident opinion left a
bad taste in his mouth. It roused no uneasiness of
conscience, for, if brought to the point of thinking
about it at all, he would have seen no reason for not
helping Jack to wine, to the last point of hospitality.
The possible moral involved acted as an irritant to the
comfortably disposed mind ; for where is there not
latitude for such questions ? One might make it a point
of conscience to abstain from butter.

The morning was fine, and Oswald took his way along

the street, reaching a corner just as Victoria Landor rounded it. They recognized each other, and were, as it proved, going the same way. So it was the most natural thing to walk on together. Victoria had an almost audacious bloom of health. Some of you pale women might have slightly disapproved of her, because she was so brilliantly colored in hair and complexion, and because her teeth flashed so white.

"You are not walking for pleasure," said Oswald. "You don't dawdle."

"Yes, I am, but my pleasure is not to dawdle ; I can't mince "—with an excellent accompaniment of six little bridling steps, holding her hands primly clasped in front and her mouth pursed. Oswald laughed, whereat her eyes did also, without the aid of her mouth.

"You ought to carry a muff."

"I had one, twenty years ago or more, but I took it for a cap when I wanted to be drum-major. Then it fell into the gutter and Tike worried it."

"Who was Tike ?"

"My little dog. She died of dropsy."

"I am inclined to think you were making game of me the other night when you asked my advice so seriously," said Oswald.

Though the remark was intended chiefly to keep the conversation running, he had more than half a suspicion that it might be true. Her face instantly dismissed its childish gravity for one of real earnestness.

"Nothing is of more importance to me than help in my profession," she said, in a peculiarly full tone. "I want it so much that I haven't the least hesitation in asking for it."

"You talk as if I might have a treatise in my pocket, any time, 'The Full-fledged Actress, How to make Her.'"

"Not at all ; but you said I had no effect on you. I want to know why. I should ask the man, of all others, who says I fail, *how* I fail."

"Well, as I advised you before, read the newspapers."

"When they are wiser ! I will cross here, I think. Good-morning." And Oswald had lost his chance of finishing a conversation which opened well. He did not suspect Victoria's quick guess at the truth, that he was answering indirectly while she questioned honestly. He thought of her with keen pleasure. The day had begun with his wife's pallor and approach at explanation. Of two people, one would naturally muse over the more attractive, and Victoria looked like a beautiful animal with a joyful, healthy soul.

You could not conceive of such a complexion's going with too troublesome a conscience.

CHAPTER XX.

ONE day Elizabeth chanced to go into the room where Philip was reciting history, and, caught by a sentence, asked permission to stay. Then she dropped in again, and fell into the habit of doing it. Occasionally she did a little private tutoring of herself in Latin translation, in order to work with Philip when his master was not there. Their history reading interested her chiefly, for she had the kind of memory which is able to retain dates and relations of events, gaining a delight from its own accuracy which is as real as the pleasure of generalizing. Felix had very little to say to her beyond the commonplaces incident on coming and going ; he was too anxious about the success of his work to filch minutes from it. Still, he was glad to have her there and a little disappointed if she failed to appear.

She always brought sewing, and never interrupted, except by laying it down sometimes, forgetting that she was not a pupil, too. He discovered it to be a pleasure to tempt her to this. She was so studiously resolved against it, that her voluntarily expressed interest was a voucher for the success of his teaching.

"I think Cæsar was just like Napoleon," said Philip, one morning, breaking off his fluent account of Roman history.

"And why, if you please ? " asked Elizabeth, biting

her lip and blushing at having answered, while Felix
turned to her with a smile that excused the liberty.
Just then, a card was brought in, announcing Mrs. Tyrrell. Elizabeth had no idea who Mrs. Tyrrell was,
but was struck at once by her beauty and ease of
manner.

"I have known your husband so long that I wanted
to know you, too," she said, in a soft contralto, which
meant nothing in any of its tones, but had the power
of inspiring a great deal. "I know you sent me cards
to your Wednesdays, but I like to be informal."

"I am very glad to see you, I'm sure," said Elizabeth, and then thought how commonplace her own remark sounded.

"And I knew I should feel out of place on your
Wednesdays," said Mrs. Tyrrell, going on with the
train she had already laid, and placidly ignoring interruption, "because Mr. Craig knows so many celebrated
people—queer people, too—I hardly know how to talk
with them."

"They have so much to say themselves that it's
very easy to get on with them," said Elizabeth, quite
unconscious of any possible sarcasm in her words.
"I find it all interesting, even when it gets beyond
me."

Mrs. Tyrrell made a few more equally important remarks which, couched in exactly the right language,
seemed the only perfect things to say. Then she
gracefully added an ornamental flourish which she had
not previously prepared.

"How fine your husband's taste is, in flowers particularly ! He used to keep my little library—I like the

name, though there are no books there—filled with very fragrant, heavy ones."

" Did he ? "

"Yes, he said they suited me. I never see tube-roses without thinking of him."

She took her leave almost immediately, but Elizabeth did not return to the history. She felt slightly uneasy, as if life in general were more complicated than she had supposed.

"Your friend Mrs. Tyrrell called to-day, Oswald," she said, when they were alone at night. With no idea that there was any thing to conceal in his acquaintance with her, she felt that it would not be a delicate thing to remind him, in the presence of any one else, of a woman who had received his gifts, and to whom a flower could recall him.

" Did she ? I wonder why."

" She spoke as if she knew you very well," said Elizabeth, her heart beating faster.

" I dare say. Most women overrate an acquaintance. You don't ; you would know to a mathematical certainty, exactly how many times you'd seen a man and what he said. You're a clear-headed, cool, little piece," dropping a kiss on her hair. This was one reason for his satisfaction in her. Independent complications of emotions, in others, tired him ; if they must exist, he wished to excite them himself and clear the sky when he pleased. Elizabeth was beginning to learn that her husband was absolutely inscrutable where that was concerned which he did not care to explain. She was never suspicious of him ; her faith was quite as absolute as before she had any reason for caring about his

past ; but mysterious, non-committal innocence may be
as exasperating as the secrecy of guilt.   What placidly
evades, gives one an irritated sense of being baffled.
Perhaps one has never undertaken the solution in
question, but he has the consciousness that some time
he may wish to do it, and what then ?

CHAPTER XXI.

TO run forward some weeks from Victoria's engagement at the World will bring to light the fact that Oswald had seen her in her own home almost immediately after she began playing. He went into the theater at rehearsal one day, ostensibly to see Rose, and walked away with her when it was over. The large mold in which her thoughts were cast commanded his admiration. Evidently, he personally held no place in her consciousness, except as he was a man of trained intellect, and one who was liable to say something worth hearing of her profession. The simple frankness with which she asked him to talk embarrassed even him. This superb creature had the air of seating herself at your feet and saying, "I hear you have a theory of the way Rosalind should move and speak. Please tell me about it!"

On that particular day, they walked to Tremont street, where, at the top of a building, were her two rooms. When they reached the entrance, he was saying: "I have the more faith in your talent because Rose tells me it is inherited."

"Ah, then you know about Estelle?" she said, turning to him with an expression of frank pleasure. "I am glad, because I want every body to be interested in her, and sometimes I can't drag her into the con-

versation, though they say she was but a slight body.
Would you like to see her portrait ? "

" Very much."

" Come now, if you will, and be introduced. I am
proud of Estelle."

Up the various stairs, lined on either side with offices, to the very top, and there Victoria unlocked a
door and led the way into a peculiarly furnished room.
There were no little ornaments made by the fingers
in womanly leisure, though an abundance of homely
articles scattered about, here and there, gave evidence
of housewifely use. A piano was in one corner, and
over it the head of the one Apollo, in marble. On an
easel in another corner stood the portrait of the greatest living actor, and beneath it lay a pile of books in
careless order, all, as far as Oswald could see from a
title page here and there, Shakespeare commentaries
and dramatic criticism. A case, filled with books above
and below, held a middle shelf of odd china and
glasses. Victoria had excused herself and now reap-
peared, without her hat. " I hoped you would make
her acquaintance while I was gone," she said, turning
merrily to a picture behind him, which Oswald had
not noticed. " Why didn't you introduce yourself,
Estelle ? It would have been less embarrassing for the
gentleman."

Oswald turned, with a start which made her laugh ;
the genuineness of her tone had made him expect to
see the portrait flesh and blood. " Lady Estelle—Mr.
Craig," said Victoria, with an air. The picture looked
at him graciously. A young woman in a short-waisted
black dress ; with its dark background, the picture de-

pended on her brilliant tints of face and hair for its
only light. From the dusky shadows the face shone
out victoriously ; not a handsome face, but one holding a certain indomitable quality. The brown hair
was in great soft curls over the head, surmounted by a
piquant white muslin turban. The eyes were brown
and laughing, and the full red lips satirical.

"The Lady Estelle isn't easily deceived. She must
be an excellent friend and adviser," said Oswald,
gravely.

"Yes, I talk to her a great deal. We are very intimate. That is the reason she allows me to use her
Christian name, in spite of her being my great-grandmother. She led her husband's family a life of it,
I've been told. Didn't you, Estelle ? "

Oswald fancied the lips curved a little more. "Will
you tell me about her ? What did she do to shock
them ? "

"Nothing in the world ! " said Victoria, laughing ;
"only they were afraid she would. To be French
was to be radically bad and to have drawn in with the
very air the sins of court and people. So, whenever
she took her walks abroad, they felt obliged to watch
her and gossip about her. I like to think she looked
at them with those great brown eyes and made them
shiver for fear of what she might do next. But her
husband loved her."

"That probably added zest to her *diablerie*. She
knew she couldn't go too far."

"Yes, but there was one difference between them.
It was her great wish to go on the stage, and he
wouldn't let her. She might have done it in spite of

him ; she had daring enough, but unfortunately she loved him."

When Oswald went away, he asked leave to bring in a collection of photographs, and Victoria gave a hearty assent.

The American girl abroad, obtuse to social usage, is a type we are forced to acknowledge. The American girl not only unaccustomed to protection, but never needing it, is quite another person. She may make mistakes, and, in her frank dealing with the world, accept some very soiled cunning for truth equal to her own, but it will be done purely. Victoria liked and admired Oswald more than he guessed. Why should she not see him ? His social relations never caused her an instant's thought, partly because she was busy ; furthermore, because she had a theory that a friend's relations to other people did not affect those he bore to one's self. Inquisitiveness was a sort of indelicacy. Oswald made himself a part of the enjoyment of her little leisure. He was his brightest, most whimsical, and most intellectually earnest self all in one. He had no plan of action ; his mind had fixed on no definite result. As usual, the moment was all, and the moment favored him. Her only friend, the manager, was busy and preoccupied. He was about carrying out a project conceived years ago—that of building up the best stock company to be had for money, and putting on a succession of Shakespeare's plays. If it should prove a losing investment, there were, to balance it, the proceeds of the traveling companies, who were constantly on the road, giving some taking society dramas.

Victoria was steadily drawing larger and larger

houses. With the uncritical part of her audience she
was immensely popular. They yielded to her beauty
without a struggle, and thought they were in love with
her art. The few men whose opinion was really worth
hearing, paid her the compliment of consideration.
She had such evident possibilities, said they, that it
would be worth while to wait a couple of years before
giving a verdict. If she could but gain the fire which
it seemed she lacked, there would be no question of
her greatness.

Seeing her every day at the theater, Rose never
came to her home now. Perhaps the absence of her
mother, whom he had adored for years from a social
distance, affected him too strongly.

Oswald occasionally took Elizabeth and Philip to
see Victoria play, always excusing himself under pretense of an engagement, and returning for them after
the curtain was down. For, however indefinite his intentions might be, he preferred that the woman he
admired most should not see him with any other, and
draw inconvenient conclusions which might shake her
interest in him. Philip continued his adoration and
his sonnets, though none of the later verses found
their way into print. But his star-worship was ideal,
and easily satisfied. He only asked the privilege of
making his lady the Helen of his tragedy and dreaming of her, in the intervals of study.

When Oswald gave a light reason for absence from
home, Elizabeth schooled herself to accept it without
a question. Having once said to her that a curious
calling people to account was one of the forms of vul-
garity, she was genuinely ashamed whenever such

curiosity cropped out in her own mind, and made
haste to kill it as if it were the rankest weed. She had
many little confidences to give him which were never
offered. Joyfully as she would have responded to interest, she felt that only her own inability to reach a
high intellectual ground, like his, made her so pleased
with the slight, every-day blossoms of love.

Jack Perham, who, if he could have had his own
way with fate, would have done no man harm but
himself, was destined to become her guide into new
regions. When Jack had taken a certain amount of
wine, or kindred liquors, its effect was to rouse his
moral nature, making him didactic and argumentative
on the subject of right. One day, having spent
a few hilarious hours with some friends, who
coupled Oswald's name with Victoria's, already
toasted and tossed about, he gravely conceived
the idea of remonstrating with Oswald, and took his
way there accordingly. Oswald and Elizabeth were
together, he looking over papers impatiently, and occasionally at his watch. He meant to take Victoria
some Jacqueminot roses, and it was too early by an
hour. He had never offered her flowers. It was quite
natural that he should be absorbed in wondering how
she would receive them. Elizabeth held a book and
pretended to read, to avoid disturbing him. She
wished he would interrupt her, or even look up once
to smile.

Her reception of Jack was rather cool. She had not
seen him often since the evening which she was unable
to forget. In his present condition, Jack had no conception of the proper times and seasons for entering on

his mission, but began, with pompous gravity, interrupted by intervals for rest : " I've come to talk with
you, Craig. Some of the fellows have been talking, and
I thought I'd better come to you. About Victoria Landor, you know. I'll say this for her, she encourages
nobody but you."

" Damn you," said Oswald, quietly, with the air of
uttering an easy commonplace, but with very thin and
firm lips, " will you be quiet ? "

Elizabeth looked up at her husband with a start, and
then fixed her eyes on her book, not to take them away
again, while her hands trembled violently.

" No," said Jack, regretfully, but persistently. " I
can't be quiet. It's my duty to talk with you. You
walk with her and you visit her. Very likely she's no
better than the rest of them, though Rose says she is.
And if she is, you've no business to compromise her."
Oswald had thrown his head back, and resting it easily
on the chair, continued to look at Jack.

" Is that all ? " he asked, with an irony which did not
conceal his annoyance.

" No," said Jack, " not yet. I never have talked
with you before, seriously—morally—now, have I ?
Well, that shows great self-control in me, for you
know I've had an eye on all your love affairs. That
was before you were married—the devil !—you *are*
married ! " with a momentary glimpse of the truth
and a half-sobered look at Elizabeth, whose presence
he began to realize.

" I think," said Oswald, quietly, " that you'd better
go." And Jack, retaining his dignity to the last, thought
so too.

Oswald came back and took up a paper without looking at his wife, but Elizabeth had lost her self-control.
" How dare he say such things to you! " She began indignantly. Oswald laid down his paper, with
resigned abandonment to an annoying situation.

" To say nothing of his being drunk, you can excuse him by remembering that he is one of the people
who interpret every thing vulgarly," he said, looking at
his white hands, and then at her, rather indifferently.

" But what does he mean? What is there to interpret,
one way or the other ? " cried Elizabeth, worried at the
impossibility of seeing any clear way neither overhung
by a mist of sophistry nor darkened with lies. She
could only interpret what Jack said as the latter,
spoken out of some inconceivably malicious motive.

" Only that I have made a new friend in the person
of a fascinating woman, and, as I said, it is the part of
low minds to judge such a thing according to low
standards." He looked at her now with a certain interest in seeing how she took it. An undercurrent in
his thoughts was that of keen appreciation of one
feature in his life—the suddenness with which its de-
velopments came. With some men, events seem to lead
slowly and gradually up to tragic conclusions ; in his
own case, accidents fell upon him without warning.

" Do you need friends apart from me ? I thought—"
She was stung too deeply to dare go on.

" I know what you thought," said Oswald, coolly.
" You thought that, as my wife, your society would
absolutely content me. Now, are you a woman intellectually gifted and educated to such a point that a
man need not look beyond you ? "

Elizabeth looked at him with eyes that dilated as he went on. Her dry lips framed a "No," which was not audible.

"Certainly not. You know it as well as I do, and knowing it, you are selfish enough to covet the position of judge and jailer. You are not the first woman who has wanted to keep her husband on bread and water, however."

Elizabeth rose and went blindly toward the door. Reaching it, she turned and said in a broken voice : "One thing I want to know. You saw me at Stratford, and I didn't try to deceive you. You knew me, and— why did you marry me ?"

"That's nonsense," said Oswald, his good humor returning, as he looked at his watch and found it time to go. "A shallow question, child ! Why, because I loved you, of course. And I do now ; only I can't consent to regard you as a universal genius, and expect you to answer all my moods. Be sensible when I come back." He left a kiss on the hand which held the side of the door, and was gone. Elizabeth went slowly up to her room. There was no weeping to be done yet, though she felt oppressed by a great horror. One must in some measure realize a loss before he can actively despair over it. Her first conscious thought was spent in wondering what she should do—how she could most nearly put on the appearance of her old self. She was like one who has received a tingling blow from a beloved hand, and longs only to conceal the bruise.

When her husband came home to dinner he kissed her, as usual—a caress she took passively.

"Elizabeth, you are not going to be sulky," he said, looking at her keenly.

"I don't mean to be," she said, conscientiously making her words and tone void of offense. "But I don't understand you."

"Why?"

"Because either a thing is, or it isn't, to me. I don't understand the half-way sort of things you seem to bring into your life. I am afraid I don't understand just what I am to you, either. And I can't see things with any body's eyes but my own." Her lips quivered grievously.

"Now listen," said Oswald, drawing her down beside him on the sofa, with not only a praiseworthy desire to see her mind at rest, but to provide against such scenes in the future. "You know I've told you, again and again, that you're a little Puritan. Now, that quality in you is charming, so long as it keeps you to simplicity and singularity. But when it tempts you to sit in judgment on others, you get every body into hot water."

"But I don't mean to judge," said Elizabeth, struggling to be reasonable against her suffocating sense of an intangible wrong somewhere. "I only want to understand your life, Oswald, and how can I be your wife really, unless I am first in it?"

"So you are first—if any body can say that of any body else! I choose you to hold a certain relation to me. Now, not being a narrow nature myself, I can't help demanding other friendships. Many a man would deceive you. I don't; I take pains to tell you the truth, and if I didn't think you above taking coarse views, I should go to the point of assuring you that an intellectual friendship which you don't share may be, and is, perfectly justifiable."

"But if it is only having a friend, why should it be a secret? Why should it be kept from me?"

"I don't keep it from you. Haven't I told you all there is to know, as soon as there is the slightest necessity for it?"

"But if you admire any woman, why can't I admire her, too ; I'm not selfish enough to want to crowd your friends out, Oswald."

"Because you wouldn't assimilate. You haven't a thing in common. Bringing you together would be a bore for us all. Elizabeth, you don't mean to say that you suspect me of any coarse sort of unfaithfulness !"

"O Oswald, no ! no !" she cried, in genuine horror.

"I thought you couldn't be so different from the pure-minded little girl I kissed, down in Stratford." How long ago that time seemed ! She drew a quick sigh that was like a sob over the days of fearless love. _

"I am glad you are willing to talk it over with me," she said, with a hopeless sort of feeling that at least she need not fail in her duty through severity. She would meet kindness with kindness, though she understood her husband no better than before. "I will try not to annoy you, Oswald."

"Yes, that's the most welcome thing you can say. When people begin to nag and worry each other, they're much better apart."

Nothing was explained, and she began to see that, where Oswald was concerned, nothing was ever likely to be. Perhaps it was better so, for she could set down her lack of sympathy with his hazy motives to her own ignorance. It was far better to suffer from a limitation in herself than in him ; this was as a woman of common but generous fiber might feel in possessing a Goethe whom others appreciated, but for whom she could only cook.

There had been an unwilling listener to a part of Jack's unlucky remonstrance. Felix had asked permission to write a note in the library, across the hall, and had been forgotten. He could not help hearing a few sentences before he rose and closed the door. He knew Elizabeth was there, and felt a quick rush of shame and indignation. The subject of Oswald's intimacy with Victoria was not a new one to him. Tim Ellin, who was really bitten deeply with admiration of her, and was Felix's pupil, with the help of that detective instinct which seems to be a lover's sixth sense, managed to keep track of all her movements. He sent her flowers and notes, of which not the slightest notice was ever taken. Poor Nellie, as the College men called him, could have borne disdain patiently, but in an evil moment for his peace of mind, he found out that she was receiving Oswald's visits. Once, after that, he met them walking together, and went home to confide in Felix who laughed him almost into tears, until he himself was suddenly sobered at hearing the rival lover's name.

He and Oswald had conceived a dislike for each other, at their first meeting, a feeling which probably did not detract from his present cordial desire of exercising his muscular skill on a man who could compromise one woman's reputation in making another wretched. And yet it was not his business : there was a sort of indelicacy in this meddlesome sort of thinking. So he told himself, and at the same time, he could not help longing to be Elizabeth's champion.

CHAPTER XXII.

THE spring found Felix undecided as to his next step, but June brought a resolution. He would go to Stratford for the summer. The desolation of the place and the spiritual poverty of the people had appealed to him and he felt a strong inclination to begin his ministry there.

When he spoke of it, Elizabeth looked up in quick sympathy with any one who wanted the place. Dull and monotonous as life had been there, it still looked more like home from this distance than it had ever done nearer.

She had been down several times for short visits, and felt her mother's need of her more keenly after each. The visits might have been longer if she had chosen, but absence invariably gave her a longing to be back before Oswald should become used to doing without her.

"I suppose we shall go, soon," she said. "There is nothing to keep us, and my husband is fond of the place."

But Oswald proved not quite as desirous of it as she supposed.

"I may run down for a few days, later," he said, when she opened the subject. "First I want to take a little trip to the north, with Canning. He is going to Grand Manan and says it's the quietest, most genuinely pastoral place ever seen."

"O Oswald, I thought you cared for Stratford! Last summer was so beautiful," said Elizabeth, her eyes filling with tears.

"So it was ; so will this be when I'm there. You'll be all the more glad to see me, for absence.' She had learned too well how annoyed he could be at remonstrance, to say more. So the middle of June found her again in Stratford, sorely wanting some satisfactory ground-work for her coming life.

Mrs. Nye cried gently, when her two children came, thereby eliciting Grandmother's scornful disapproval, and making her severely indifferent in her own greeting, as a matter of example.

"How do you do, Elizabeth," she said, giving her large hand stiffly. "Is *he* coming?"

"No," said Elizabeth, trying to make the excuse a matter of course. "Oswald is at Grand Manan and wont come here till later in the summer."

Grandmother shut her lips tightly, in a manner which implied that she saw the state of the case as plainly as any one, but she only turned to Philip, to say, "You'd better go right up-stairs and put some old clothes on. Your mother's mended up a suit for you."

Felix was already settled at Mrs. Potter's, and came to call, in a few days.

Abstractly, Grandmother had the strongest reasons for disapproving of him. He had preached a counterblast to her own fundamental laws of faith, and she considered him a man not only bound to perdition but bent on drawing others after him. But, to the general surprise, she liked him at once.

"Are you down here to apply for the Academy

again ?" she asked, suddenly transfixing him with her keen eyes.

"No," said Felix smiling, "I couldn't very well, you know, when I was asked to leave, before."

Strange that there may be such phases of humor hidden under stolid exteriors ! It had never been known that Madame Nye possessed any sense of the ludicrous, but her grim features suddenly developed a slight smile.

"It seems as if that was a pretty sure sign that they didn't want you any more," she rejoined.

"There were a good many that did," said peacemaking Mrs. Nye. "Some folks thought the committee took too much into their hands."

Felix smiled brightly at her with a look which said that, although he didn't in the least care about the public opinion, he was just as grateful for her support. He had an undertaking in mind which he wanted to talk over with Elizabeth, as being the most likely to understand it. She and Philip fell into the habit of taking a walk to the sea every night, and once he joined them.

"I want to give a course of lectures here, Mrs. Craig," he said. "You see how I try to thrust myself before the public."

"A very good thing for the public," said Elizabeth, smiling at him. "And good for me as one of the public. I should like to hear them."

"You are kind to say so. Here are my reasons. If I try to hold any sort of religious service, I shall be ostracized. I do feel I have something to say. Now, why shouldn't I give a series of talks on great men some attempts at portraits of character ?"

"It is a fine idea. You make me ashamed because you are always thinking of other people."

"Thinking and talking, yes," said Felix. "Theories have a fatal attraction for me. But here's the rub. I want to be both politic and successful, and I don't know how. If I ask for the hall, they'll refuse it."

"That is true," said Elizabeth thoughtfully. "We must get into somebody's good graces. Here's Si, for instance," as they came in sight of his giant figure in bold contrast with Philip's slender one. "He has a great deal of influence among the men."

There was no time to say more, for Philip called out, ecstatically, "Si says he will take us out in his boat, if we want to go."

"No, not jestly thet," said Si, gravely, a twinkle in his keen eyes, "I asked *ef* you wanted to go."

"I am quite sure we shouldn't refuse, if you were to invite us," said Elizabeth, thinking this was their opportunity. "Do you think you will?"

"I shouldn't wonder a mite. You're considerable of a stranger, 'Lizabeth. The schoolmaster, too; I didn't think o' seein' him in these parts again."

They pushed out into the calm sea. There was a gorgeous sunset, and a rising moon.

"Lookin' 'round for a school?" asked Si, managing his oars as if they were merely extended arms.

"No. Your committee needn't be shy of me. But I do want to give a course of lectures. Do you think I could get the hall?"

"Could ef folks wanted to hear the lecters. What be they—religious?"

"Not exactly. Historical."

"I sh'd like it well enough myself. I s'pose you're doin' it for practice."

Philip laughed at this juncture, and Elizabeth shook her head at him.

"No. I'll tell you the real reason," she said. "Mr. Kewe thinks it will do us good to hear something besides town talk, and so do I. Do you think any body really would object to his giving them in the hall?"

"Like enuff," said Si, with large scorn. "Some of 'em acted like a passel o' fools, year ago last fall. I'll see to 't myself, 'f you want me to."

This was far more than Felix hoped, and he thanked Si warmly.

"Somebody ought to sing," said Philip, who found the moonlight conducive to dreaming, and knew by experience how charming Fancy could make herself when Music was by.

"Don't you sing?" asked Si. "What, neither on you? Wal, I'll sing myself."

The proposition seemed to please him so that he stopped to look at them in sheer enjoyment of its startling nature.

"All right, Si," said Philip, in high feather. "Go ahead."

"Now, I aint sung a note for forty year," Si went on, in a gently explanatory manner. "My woman would laugh masterly, ef she sh'd get hold on't. Don't you never say a word." And thereupon he began the following song, in an ambitiously loud, but not unmusical tone :

Gipsy come triplin' over the plain,
Gipsy sung most nobly.
Sung for to make the green-wood ring,
For to charm the heart of his lady.

"Go bring me out my red-roan steed,
My black is not so speedy.
I've rode all day and I'll ride all night
Till I overtake my lady."

He rode till he come to the broad water's side,
The water so black and so rily.
Tears came tricklin' down his cheeks
When he beheld his lady.

The effect of a chorus made up of syllables not to be expressed in print, and sung to a tune of rollicking ins and outs, was quite marvelous.

"Splendid, Si!" cried Philip, applauding. "But where was his lady?"

"Lord knows," said Si, briefly and conclusively. "I never did."

"In the water, of course," said Felix. "Another gipsy had kidnapped her, and when they were crossing the broad water, the bridge broke, the current carried him and his horse down the stream, and she, falling into a particularly soft, muddy place, staid there."

"Like enuff," said Si, gravely, not in the least resenting their laughter, though he saw no occasion for joining it.

He was as good as his word, for he engaged the hall on his own responsibility, and quietly constituted himself Felix's manager.

"It's spoke for," he said one night, suddenly appearing at Mrs. Potter's kitchen window, near which she and Felix sat at the tea table. Felix had been taken up so quickly that he hardly knew, for the moment, what he had proposed doing.

" When you goin' to begin ? "

" Any time ; next week, if you say so. What do you think of Mondays and Wednesdays ? "

" Thet'll do," said Si.   " How much admission ? "

" Nothing."

" Lord, you must be green ! " said Si, frankly. "Folks wont come 'thout payin'. Don't know 's they will then, but thet's the only way to make 'em think you 'mount to sumthin'."

But Felix was firm, and Si yielded, with a respect for his generosity which left none for his judgment.

The first lecture was upon Epictetus, and Elizabeth was a little afraid of its being far over the heads of the audience. But it was not ; I am quite sure you, dear sir, whatever your culture, might have found something to inspire you in that homely talk about a great man. If you have any love for human faces, however, you would have been far more absorbed in watching those listening ones than in the best lecture ever written. Si had talked the matter up at the Sea View, and to such purpose that his cronies laid their pipes on the shelf, put on their neckerchiefs, and, uncomfortably sacrificed to decorum, came to the hall. The lecture over, as Felix was going out, speaking to this one and that, Si stepped up to him and said, with a ponderous hand on his shoulder, " I want to know one thing. How much truth is ther' in what you've said ? "

" As far as we can find out, it's all true."

" Thet's all. Le's have another Wednesday."
That was worth a good deal. Felix's eyes met Elizabeth's and she smiled. Then he was satisfied, and mentally flagellated himself a little, on the way home, for caring more for her approbation than for that of the homely souls he wished to reach.

Elizabeth could only wonder at Madam Nye's unexpected toleration of Felix, which continued like a protracted thaw. One day, Grandmother launched a sudden shot at him over her knitting. " You're an atheist, I understand."

" No," said Felix, composedly. " I don't consider myself so."

" Hm ! " with a long drawn exclamation signifying a kind of satirical surprise. " Well, most of 'em don't have the grace to deny it." And she never objected to the large attendance at his lectures, though it invariably included her own family.

To understand the effect on Elizabeth of this contact with the greatest minds known to men, it is necessary to remember that she was wholly unsettled, trying in vain to reconcile her old conceptions of right with new, and what she could not choose but think, broader views. With all a woman's passion of earnestness where loyal affection is concerned, she was trying to cover the moral lack in her husband's character, which she could not help feeling, with the excuse that she was too narrow to understand him. She had to acknowledge that her married life had its ᴡ's and stains. Perfect happiness was shut out, but there was left the comfortable makeshift of declaring the fault hers. But Felix awoke in her a passion of longing

toward a higher ideal than she had known. He came
in one night, when she was alone in the sitting-room,
and she said at once, "You have made me think a
a good deal, lately, Mr. Kewe. Is it possible to be as
great as your great men, now?"

"Yes, men are; I have a very firm faith that they
are. Do you doubt it?"

"I don't know," said Elizabeth, slowly, "It is so
hard really to know people. They seem to have beautiful natures, but not unselfish nor true ones. They
may be more wise and educated than we, and yet do
things which we have always called wrong. It is so
hard to find out who is good!"

"There is one difficulty always in the way of our
finding out," said Felix, gently. "You know we never
are quite sure how diseased a person may be, morally.
We never can judge. We can only abhor sin and be
loving to people."

"But you don't think love ought to make us less
hard to sin? We ought not to change our standard?"

"Never that, except for a higher one." He realized
as she did not think he could, how personal her questions were. It was better that she should judge
her husband harshly than lose one iota of her belief in
an unchangeable right. "It is best to choose the
highest, if it makes us unhappy forever. Our standard
may be a narrow one, but after we have fixed it as high
as the law in our own hearts decrees, it is a base thing
to lower it to excuse the world."

With Elizabeth, to know was to do, and she set patiently about accepting her future as it showed under
the pitiless light held by her conscience. In the midst

of her pain, there was a flash of high joy that, after all, ideals were true. Her own life might fail, but beautiful and good lives were possible. The frenzy of jealousy with which she had brooded over her idea of Victoria, for the past few months, seemed quite gone.

Felix thought of this young creature, so harassed by doubts and so sure to be unhappy, with a great tenderness. The highest type of worship for the womanly nature had begun in him, but so abstract, so removed from any desire of possession, that he never thought of repressing it.

She had no letters from Oswald that summer. He had laughingly told her that she must not expect them, nor would he, in his turn. Letter-writing was a powerful draw back to human happiness ; nobody in his right mind would ever think of it, especially in summer. If any thing happened to him, he would telegraph her at once, but write he would not, and could not. After hearing Grandmother ask, week after week, if she had heard from *him*, (for she always refused to pronounce his name), Felix grew to be acutely sensitive whenever he heard letters mentioned, and, if he brought the mail, tried to deliver it outside the range of Madam's keen eyes. Once, after the stereotyped question, when Elizabeth had answered as usual, "Oh no, I don't expect to hear. Oswald doesn't like to write letters," her mother followed her into the kitchen and said, "Elizabeth, are you sure you're pretty happy ? "

" Dear little, foolish little woman ! because I made a bargain with Oswald that neither of us should write ? " And she smiled brightly enough to deceive the tender, careful soul.

CHAPTER XXIII.

OSWALD staid only a week at the Island, and, leaving Canning settled there, went back to Boston. He frankly acknowledged to himself that he wanted to see Victoria. She spoke once of spending summers with her mother at Marblehead and hoped she might be there this year. To Marblehead, accordingly, he went, engaged board at one of the cottages, and set about finding her. For several days, he made no inquiries, but traversed the town thoroughly, expecting at every turn to see her before him or meet her face to face.

Nothing of the kind happened ; and then he began a cautious search, not using her name but finding out, as far as possible, the owners and occupants of the cottages. She was not there, or was mysteriously hidden. In a fit of disgust, he went into Boston, one cool day, thinking it might be well to call at her rooms and see if the janitor had her address. To open the subject naturally, he asked : " Is Miss Landor in ! "

" Yes, I believe so," was the answer. " She went up half an hour ago."

Oswald's heart gave a bound surprising even to him who was so used to the freaks of that extraordinary organ. " I care more than I thought," he confided to himself on the way up. " I wonder if she'll be glad to see me ! "

He rapped at the door which led into her little parlor. Victoria opened it and stood looking at him for an instant, a smile and flush coming together.

"Why, it's you ! I didn't expect you."

The accent on the pronoun was delicate flattery. "She is glad," concluded Oswald.

"Well, may I come in ? " he asked, smiling at her, and then Victoria stepped back and held open the door.

"I expected a caller so little that I'm not polite."

Even Estelle seemed to smile on him. Oswald was glad he came.

"I wonder at finding you here," he said, taking his place in front of the picture. He had been there enough to have an accustomed seat. "I came with only a vestige of hope."

"I have been detained here on business," she said, briefly. "An acquaintance was in trouble and I was anxious." Oswald immediately felt the pang of jealousy which comes when we are first made to remember that a new friend may have other ties. There is perhaps no envy so deep and powerful as that felt by a new comer, over old associations.

He noticed quickly that she was paler than usual, and had a trace of violet under her eyes. Sitting by the window, dressed in some thin, flowing white with much drapery, her golden hair plainly knotted, and the only color about her a large pink fan which she held idly, she seemed a more glorious creature than when she walked the stage at her best. Oswald felt a thrill of delight in her perfection.

"I didn't know you had made friends. You said you had none but Rose."

"No ; and this is a new acquaintance in whom I've been greatly interested. But "—evidently changing the subject with a purpose—"I'm going away to-morrow."

"Then I wish you as charming a summer resort as mine," said Oswald, making a bold push. "I'm at Marblehead."

"My dear old place ! Are you really there ! " she cried. "Why, I know it by heart ! I meant Marble-head when I said I was going away."

"I am glad," said Oswald, disguising three-quarters of his pleasure in what seemed cordial interest. "You will let me see you there ? "

"Oh yes. I shall be with Dame Trot. Dear old lady, I believe her name is Hopkins, but I never use it."

Oswald staid until the waning light settled into a dusk, softened only by the gas in the next room.

"I wish you would play to me," he said, "or sing. I know you sing." So far in their acquaintance he could not help being a little piqued that she had shown no very strong inclination towards ministering to his moods.

"I only sing ballads, and with more emphasis than art. I can't play. You'll laugh when I tell you why I keep the piano here for nobody to use."

"Why ? "

"Because to me it's a beautiful instrument. Old Mr. Sangster, my teacher for the six months I took lessons, said I was a barbarian. It was only an ugly piece of furniture, he said, and the violin was a delicate lady. Better fall in love with the violin, if any thing ! But I clung to my fancy."

She would not sing, and Oswald went to the piano and played to her for two delicious hours.

.   .   .   .   .′   .

A man gifted with an uncomfortable memory might have found something unpleasantly suggestive of another summer, in this one at Marblehead. Oswald exerted a self in winning this woman's love which he had never been called upon to bring into full play. Delicately alive to her presence, he assumed no attitude of lover-like attention. He was simply his most brilliant self, finding her eagerly receptive of ideas. They talk down subjects of all degrees of weight. Their days on the rocks and sandy walks were not eloquently filled with romantic silences, but alive with repartee and discussion. And the further her devotion to her profession seemed to remove her from him, the more cunningly did he lay siege to her heart. Victoria was quite innocent of the fact that she was face to face with a crisis in her life. She felt herself near the top of the wave. Young, and with a growing fame, ambition pointed out broad and attainable fields beyond. She hardly stopped to think of Oswald apart from herself ; he was too near her for that. He seemed a child of beneficent fortune, cast on the same island with herself. They loved and hated the same things ; he was her friend.

" And I begin work in October," she said one day when they were sitting on Castle Rock, looking out to sea. " How near it seems ! "

" You have been my friend so long that I can't bear to give you up to the public. However did you manage to forgive me," he went on quickly, to prevent her answering the last sentence, "for saying, the first time I saw you, that your acting didn't affect me ? "

"I respected you for it," said Victoria, frankly. "I saw you had a high standard. Do you suppose I don't know what the trouble is with my acting, as well as you ? "

"But I don't know. Tell me."

"I can't abandon myself enough. I can make it studied, intellectually perfect, but there is a sort of New England restraint in me that holds me back. For instance, there is a certain something which fights against my giving way to emotion. I have the consciousness that if I wanted to cry I should go to my room and have it out. The footlights make me feel as if I had gone into the street to wring my hands."

"Then, if your individual nature has so much to do with it, you may need to be the heroine of a real tragedy."

"Very likely. If that is so, I should thank any body for breaking my heart." She looked so daringly beautiful that he felt like accepting the challenge as recklessly as she made it.

"And I can't adapt myself readily to a part I have no sympathy with," she went on. "My *repertoire* will always be limited."

"I should like to see you play Camille."

"There is a case where I think the emotion is all out of proportion to the necessity for it. How could I put dignity and pathos into her giving up her lover, when I consider it a childish sacrifice ? "

"You don't call it noble ?" he asked, his own heart beating faster.

"Noble, as all self-sacrifice must be, but it wasn't the noblest thing to do. Her love for him gave him a right to claim it. She had no business to deceive him."

"But she was his mistress. You forget social sanctions."

"She was not. She was his wife, for he loved her and was true to her."

"Suppose he married," said Oswald, with a feeling that this was the final test.

"Why then, of course," said Victoria, with cold dignity, "he had become a villain. I was considering him as the gentleman and ideal lover."

The conversation was carried no further then, though it was again suggested.

"I wish you would tell me something," he said once, moved by a somewhat rash desire to force himself nearer her.

"What is it ? I am quite sure I shall tell you."

"The night I called on you in Tremont street, before you came here, you spoke of being troubled. Will you tell me why ?"

"I'm afraid not,—yes, it can't harm any body. A little girl at the theater came to me for advice. She had fallen in love with some one who proved to be divorced, and her family declared she shouldn't marry him. They had worked on her feelings and conscience, so that the poor little thing was afraid it wouldn't be right for her to be his wife."

"What did you tell her ?"

"I told her that if she loved him and believed h̄ι̇
him, she'd no business to give him up for such a
reason ; that the fact of having been deceived in
another woman was his misfortune. And I saw the
family and reasoned till they yielded. The little
thing and her husband have gone West. They went
the day you came."

"Suppose his wife, the first one, had not been what
he thought, and was happier without him. In fact,
suppose the marriage to have been really null, though
for some reason they couldn't or wouldn't ask for a
divorce, would you advise her to love him then ? "

"Yes," said Victoria, gravely. "That is, if I were
sure they had large natures and could love greatly
enough to be true. Human sanctions would weigh
for nothing with me, either in marriage or divorce."

Oswald felt a glowing intoxication of triumph. So,
gaining her love was to be all !

Victoria was at the image-breaking period of a questioning mind. Her own large truth and purity of
heart made her intolerant of all bonds, but spiritual
ones. She was so young, too, that she scorned the
conventional aspect of great questions.

At the moment, Oswald had in his pocket an
unread letter from his wife. It was only as great a
drawback on his happiness as the coming of a bill may
be to a man who knows he shall be able to meet it
somehow and sometime. That night he read it, with
some admiration for Elizabeth's common-sense. She
wrote quietly, with solicitous interest in the happiness
of his summer, asking when he would be at home or
in Stratford. She should be very glad to see him

there ; the sky and sea were the same. It was a letter which would have driven a husband in love or still loving, to take the next train for Stratford, to woo his wife over again. But its tone seemed to Oswald deserving only of reward, and he wrote her a brightly affectionate answer, that very night.

CHAPTER XXIV.

FOLKS talks a good deal about 'Lizabeth Craig,"
said Mrs. Potter, looking up placidly from her
knitting, at Felix. "Too bad, ain't it?"

"Talk about her? How?"

"Oh, they say her husband wasn't good to her, and
she's left him, 'n' more things 'n' I can think of. But
there ain't a voice against 'Lizabeth."

"Well, I should think not! Nor her husband,
either," he added, with an impulse of diplomacy. "I
know him, and nobody could be brighter or more
entertaining than he is."

"There!" said the little widow, in her comfortable
voice. "To think there should be such things said!
But folks thinks it's strange she come home alone, and
Jerry says there don't no letters go between 'em."

"Jerry is far too communicative on the subject of
the mail, I should say. Why, Mrs. Potter, Craig
went to Grand Manan, with an artist, for sketching. It
will be a great benefit to him; think of the scenery
and climate and queer people!"

Felix could scarcely repress an inclination to call
her attention to his stroke of policy. A man who
seldom works with a purpose to deceive is likely to do
it by the wholesale, and frankly admire himself after the
effort.

"Do tell!" said Mrs. Potter, in benign appreciation. "Do they have all that up there? I should think board must be high."

Felix rose, feeling that any further enlargement on the subject might induce his hostess to tell the next comer that Mr. Craig had gone to hunt hippogriffs or convert anacondas. After that, he was careful to allude frequently and familiarly to Oswald, for the benefit of Stratford ears. This was somewhat to Elizabeth's wonder, but she understood it, finally. Susan Fitts came in, ostensibly to call, but it was fair to suppose she had an errand. All the family knew her well enough to be sure of that; nobody resented the fact as belligerently as did Grandmother.

"You goin' back this fall, 'Lizabeth?" with a suavity, the effect of which was quite counteracted by her small, watchful eyes.

"Oh yes, indeed, some time in the fall."

"I thought maybe you wa'n't, from somethin' that was said to me." Silence followed. Elizabeth looked up, politely attentive, and, with no idea that there was reason for her being uncomfortable, waited for some one to start up the conversation. She never could think of topics both agreeable and correct for discussion with Miss Fitts. Most subjects were unsafe, unless one wanted to hear scandal. But Susan went on unaided. "Somebody says to me this mornin', 'I guess 'Lizabeth didn't like Boston as well as she expected to.'" Then, indeed, poor Elizabeth scented the battle. Grandmother headed the charge to the rescue.

"Susan Fitts, didn't I tell you once that them that would fetch a bone would carry one? Now, here's one for you to carry. You can tell any body that's

anxious to know any thing about Elizabeth's husband,
to come to me. I'll settle 'em ! "

"Lor', Mis' Nye, how quick you be ! " said the at-
tacking force, in a conciliatory manner signifying
truce, though her eyes flashed a little and, a flush rose
to her cheek-bones. " I didn't mean a thing out o' the
way."

" No," said Grandmother. " I believe that. Gossip
has come to be your meat and drink. You don't know
when you do it any more than Job Haddon knows
when he's drunk ! "

" If you come to twittin' honest women of bein'
drunk, Mis' Nye, it's time somebody told you what's
bein' said about your own. They do say 'Lizabeth's
had to leave her husband. I don't know any thing about
it, on'y that's what I'm told." Having fired her broad-
side, and being conveniently near the door, she swept
out before there was a chance of reply.

Elizabeth felt her face scorched with shame. She-
looked steadily out of the window in the uncomfortable silence that followed. Philip came running in with
a letter.

" It's from Oswald ! " tossing it to her. "Read it,
quick, and find out where he is." She took it with a
trembling hand. The relief of feeling his kindness
again at the moment when she most needed it, was too
much. The tears rose, and she hurried out of the
room.

" Mother, what's the matter with Betty ? " said
Philip. " Has any body been saying any thing to her ? "

" Susan Fitts was here, and you know how she
talks."

"Well, she'd better let Elizabeth alone." He meant
to find out more by and by, but his present interest
was centered on a rejected manuscript in his pocket.
Of course the editor would tell his reasons for not
taking it, and so he retired to the seclusion of the barn
to read his printed refusal and nurse his injury.

Elizabeth's first thought was of gratitude that the
letter was so kind : the next, one of bitter disappointment, because she could not find it loving. Who has
not read such letters, praying with every line that the
old endearments may be waiting in the next. "He
does not care about me," she said, when the first glow
of pleasure was over. Strange to say, the question
whether her love for him was the same, had never risen
in her mind. Change seemed so allied to weakness
that she expected herself to be true. As her thoughts
reverted to Susan's hints, the explanation of Felix's
public indorsement of her husband came to her like a
flash. Her mind was sensitive and excited enough, for
the time being, to grasp at straws and fit them together. And again she was ashamed, this time of being pitied.

Her mother, sure something was wrong, came in before going to bed to say, "I wouldn't mind a thing
about it !"

"No sensible body would," trying to speak lightly.
"Mother, Oswald has come as far as Marblehead, and
hopes to be home in October."

"Well, I'm sure !" said Mrs. Nye, not venturing to
commit herself. "When will he expect you to come
back ?"

"As soon as he's in Boston himself, I suppose."

Before morning, she had fixed upon her own movements. One desire lay uppermost, above that of con-
cealing her hurt from Stratford—to make herself necessary to her husband. Why should she not go back before he returned? It might please him to find her in
the house exactly as he left them. Oswald hated the
trouble of preparations for living. In proportion as
she realized the daring of taking things into her own
hands, she felt sure it must succeed.

Felix's opening seemed to have come at last. Professor Ryder, his best friend, wrote to say that a wandering cousin of his had moved to Albaville, Iowa.
The town was a growing one, but it had neither church
nor library, as yet. If Felix chose to undertake his
former plan of building up a society without money or
influence, this might be his chance. Felix did believe
that to be quite possible. He had a theory concerning
the number of cents a day it was possible to live on,
and he did not at all object to depending on his hands
for support. Once in Iowa, without a penny, he would
ask no man a favor, but he had not even money
enough to take him there. He would be quite contented with a daily sum, sufficient only for the simplest
possible living. There was, no doubt, a fallacy in such
lack of selfish provision for the future. The possibility of his some time wanting a wife and children
never seemed to make a part of his plans; though perhaps he expected to depend on the ravens for their
support. He told Elizabeth the news, with all a boy's
enthusiasm.

" It will be a splendid thing to do," she said. " But
isn't it full of risk ? "

"No more so than trying to help a few people. There are certain ones for whom you think and live. I have nobody, and so I adopt a community."

"Yes, but at the same time, smaller duties are not so awful. There seems to be a kind of safety in being related to people. You feel bound to be something to them."

Elizabeth was growing into a spiritual dependence on him, in those quiet days. They talked little about subjects involving moral relations, but she always felt in him a high purpose. Faith in this held her head above water in many a season when she was doubtful of her future and intolerant of the past. It is somewhat strange that she never proved him less than he deserved to be thought, by comparison. Oswald's sophistry was as fair on the surface as Felix's truth, but the memory of that did not breed doubt.

Felix took her into his large heart and loved her quite without self-reproach, since the feeling seemed only the excess of his pity for a delicate creature condemned to suffer. The dreams in which he approached nearest any connection with her lot were always of sacrificing himself, in some way, to make her path smooth. He went back to Cambridge not knowing whether he should see her again. He might be on his way to Albaville before she should return.

It was the last week in September, when, hearing nothing from Oswald, she went home alone to wait for him there. She wanted Philip, but Oswald had not invited him, and she would not take the responsibility into her own hands. Philip was hurt and disappointed. He could not understand and she could not explain.

The week before Oswald came dragged itself away.
Elizabeth felt herself growing nervous. In his fas-
tidious avoidance of trouble, Oswald had the house
kept open and in readiness for him at any time when
he might choose to return. The servants had a wholesome fear of him, and consequently were as faithful in
his absence as could be expected. They were rather
glad to see Elizabeth ; she was reasonable and might
be trusted not to interfere. She was in the library one
day standing before a case of books and wondering
what to take out.

"Well, Mistress Elsie," said her husband's voice.

She turned with a start, and clasped her hands in
front of her, unable to speak.

"Well ? " said Oswald, smiling and coming forward
to kiss her, good-naturedly. "So you were here before
me."

"Do you care?" asked Elizabeth, quickly. "I
wanted to come ; I thought you wouldn't mind."

"On the contrary," said her husband, absently,
throwing himself into a chair, and still keeping her
hand. "Let's have a little lunch in here. Stay, I'll
ring." He was in a very gay humor. Life seemed
particularly good and entertaining, just then, and,
owing partly to that fact, he was not at all displeased
with Elizabeth for coming back. It took the responsibility of deciding about it from his shoulders. Moreover, it was rather pleasant to see her, since she must
come some time. But he neither asked her questions nor
volunteered a word about his own summer. Watching
him with her heart ready to rise in joy if he should
give a sign of his old interest, she ventured to tell him

some of the odd sayings and doings in Stratford. He
was carelessly polite, and, with a choking sensation
that hindered words, she ceased trying to force him
again into another summer's mood. He might be tired
as well as indifferent ; she must gain patience.

Victoria's season at the World began with great promise. Oswald was as much a part of her daily living as her
bread. He had grown clever in disguising the fact of
their intimacy, seeing her at her own rooms and seldom going to the theater. That was quite possible,
for she had no calling acquaintances. She mentioned
him to no one. Perhaps she was growing conscious of
love, and kept him in her heart rather than on her lips.

Oswald had still no plans. He knew he should tell
her he loved her. He had no doubt of her promising
to be his, if he vowed constancy to her. The fact of his
wife's existence proving a drawback was an ugly con-
tingency, for which he had not provided. He by no
means hated Elizabeth for being in his way. If she
did not interfere, he could be rather sorry for her ; if
she judged his actions or tried to frustrate their result,
then his coldest aversion might spring into life.

Elizabeth, with the persistency of a nature not easily
turned, was trying to make something real of her marriage. She had only seen Felix once, and then not
satisfactorily. He called when there were others whom
she was exerting herself to entertain. She had very
little to do, and falling into habits of nervous thought,
longed to be steadily busy. She would take German
lessons of Felix ; there was also the further inducement that the money she should pay him would further
his own hopes. Besides, she innocently told herself,

he would help her. Seeing him occasionally would give her strength. Her note, asking him to call and talk the matter over, written and despatched, she had no chance to tell Oswald until the next day. He was not in good-humor, nor need there be any wonder that he was excited by what seemed the great question of his life He loved Victoria, and he would not give her up. Strange that at the very time when he would have bartered any thing to possess her, the first moral scruples of his life held him back. His love came so near the height of a great passion, he understood so well that if she should cast aside social bonds, she would do it with the heart of an angel, that his own baseness in asking the sacrifice carried a perceptible sting. But compunction was secondary to desire, and was sure to be swallowed up by it in the end. At the moment when he was most absorbed in mentally discussing his own affairs, Elizabeth spoke of her German lessons. Perhaps Oswald spent his moral scruples on her.

" I won't have the fellow in the house !"

" You don't understand—"

"I do. He's a ministerial humbug. He's been hanging about you all summer. I'm not afraid of scandal, but I'd much rather you shouldn't provoke it."

" Oswald, you are very insulting to me," said Elizabeth, her color rising, and pure indignation getting the better of her. "You shall not speak so ! "

" Very well, I wont," regaining his coolness. " Only don't let the fellow come into my house." He went out, meeting Felix face to face, and his irritation had not yet spent itself.

"I must trouble you," he said with ceremony, "not
to go to my house. Platonic friendships are not to my
taste. I decline harboring one."

Felix's answer was without premeditation. "What a
contemptible fellow you are! I wonder if you're worth
knocking down!"

But Oswald only looked disgusted and Felix recov-
ered himself. They parted, and Felix went straight on
to Elizabeth, governed by an impulse which he was not
cool enough to recognize as insane.

She had not moved since Oswald left her. Her hands
were lying lightly clasped in her lap, her eyes bent
forward as if searching a future which answered no
questions. She rose to meet him with a pitiful attempt
at a smile. He noted the painful composure of her
face, and felt that it might passionately break up at
any moment. It was then that he began to repent his
foolishness in coming.

"You came in answer to my note," she said, immediately. "Shall you think me very fickle if I say I
have changed my mind?"

"Not at all," said Felix, pitying her so that he tried to
speak brightly, meaning to get away as soon as possible.

"I decided—that is "—said poor Elizabeth, trying to
deceive and giving up entirely when she found the tears
were running down her face. Felix walked to the door
and came back. What started to life in him, a giant
at its birth? Not compassion for her struggles and
the wish to end them, but a man's overmastering desire
to protect the woman he loves.

"My God!" he cried brokenly, "why can't I help
you, when I——"

"Hush," said Elizabeth, quickly, finding her voice. Swift emotions passed over her like a tide ; shame, for Oswald was right ; fear, lest Felix should say what would always lie like a stain in both their minds; and, greatest of all, a supreme pity for him. She must protect him in his moment of weakness. "You do help me. To think of your goodness will be my comfort as long as I live."

A flash of joy came over his face. There was a long look of solemn delight in each other, and he left her.

CHAPTER XXV.

IT shakes a man roughly into fellowship with his kind to realize his kinship with them suddenly, through sin of his own. Felix had thought himself humble enough ; he meant to offer help from no pedestal above the common stress of temptation and failure, but it was still true that there were some sins he had never dreamed he could commit. He meant to say, feeling it honestly, " I understand how your guilt has come about. Under the same circumstances, I might have been the sinner and you the helper."

And yet, almost unconscious of its own existence, there would have remained the proud belief that no real stain could come near him. Now, he loved another man's wife. The first glow of spiritual recognition had faded. They were guiltless in seeing each other for that last time ; they would not be guiltless if, by their own free will, they should meet again.

He took hasty leave of his friends, and was off to Iowa, with the speed of a man flying to save his honor. To the railroad station, at the last minute, came his pupil Ellin.

" Tell me where you're going," he said, without noticing Felix's outstretched hand. " Albaville ? Are there any changes ? Can you buy a through ticket ? All right."

He ran off and came back breathless, with ticket and

checks. "I'm going with you. No, it isn't devotion to you, wholly. I've seen her. She's talked to me like a mother, and Jove ! Kewe, I wouldn't compromise her by hanging round her as I've been doing, to save my miserable little life !"

Later in the day, he confided largely in Felix, having spent the first few hours of the journey in retirement against the car window, his hat drawn over his brows. Indeed, when he emerged from that temporary seclusion, his flushed face and red eyes were significant of the boyish pastime in which he had been indulging.

"You know I'd been writing her notes and sending her flowers, for months? Well, last week she sent me word she'd see me. Wasn't I a happy fellow that week ! But somehow, Kewe, I almost wished she hadn't done it. There wasn't a thing in the world I wanted so much as to see her, but when I found she was going to be like other women—well, I needn't have worried ! I went to the Saint John's. I don't believe I saw a thing in the room for ten minutes, my head swam so. She began to speak—Kewe, if her voice on the stage was one half what it is off !—well, she asked what I was dogging her for."

"Rather a leading question ! "

"Yes, and I suppose I said a lot of stuff. Don't you see what a hard place it was for a man ? Here was I adoring her so that I would have killed any body for using a disrespectful word to her, but I couldn't say, ' I want you to marry a little rat of a fellow like me.' I never thought of such a thing, you know. The best I could ask was to be allowed to give her every thing I own, and hope she'd look at me sometimes. Oh, you needn't think I don't know what sort of a fellow I am, as well as the rest of you ! Then she began to talk, and by the Lord, Kewe, I'll never see a fellow annoy a woman as I've bothered her, without knocking his head off ! Oh, she's an angel ! I can't tell you all she said,—but just let me go with you. Whether she ever sees me again or not, I'd like to be more of a man."

" Do you mean to go for the trip, or to go to stay ? "

" I don't know ; for a long time, if I can be contented. You're a good fellow, Kewe. I'd like to be with you, and see how you do it."

So Felix and the butt of the college set out together to win their spurs.

CHAPTER XXVI.

OSWALD did not go home again that day. He devoted it to making up his mind, as if what was tacitly decided needed some formal sanction. All the remonstrances offered by his conscience were easily met, and quite honestly, too. Victoria was a part of his life ; he could not give her up for the sake of a marriage relation which might or might not interfere with his liberty. He was so sure of this being the true passion that any sacrifice to it seemed small, especially a sacrifice which only wounded another. The day wore on, and he delayed going to see her, setting the cup aside to tantalize himself before tasting. At night, hungry for a sight of her, he went to Tremont street, half an hour before she was due at the theater. She expected him, it seemed. That subtle telegraphy of souls had begun between them, for all day she had responded to his need of her. She was to be Juliet that night, and the intensity of her earnestness had made her throw herself into the very dressing of the part. Her mood was that of a youth keeping his watch before knighthood. She opened the door and Oswald went in, breathing hard, like a man who has ridden far to tell what there is no time to prelude. The sight of her was suffocation. She held out her hand ; he grasped both her wrists. Her face grew paler, but she did not shrink.

"I love you," he whispered hoarsely, and without waiting for a look, drew her into his arms. After all, . he had feared a little ; would she free herself ? At the instant of that fearful holding of his breath, she turned her face and kissed his hand which lay on her shoulder. A rush of blinding tears came to his eyes. Then he released her, pushed her away and with his hands on her shoulders, and his blinded eyes bent on hers, cried in despair over his weakness, " My God ! how I do love you ! "

" But why does it trouble you ? " said Victoria, in her full voice, thrilled by something no man had heard in it before. "I am yours. I have belonged to you a great while."

When he possessed her why did the joy deepen into despair ?

"This is love," he cried, drawing her back to him with trembling eagerness. " You are not afraid to look into my eyes and tell me so. You are a great woman. Tell me what you would do for love."

" Every thing," said Victoria, looking at him with a joy equal to his own.

"Come and put your cheek close to mine," he said, with the same desperate delight.

"It is time to go," with a long breath, trying to recall herself. " Dear and dearest, help me to go. Make me go. Because, I tell you truly, I believe you could make me forget my play."

" I shall not leave you all the evening," said Oswald, kissing her cheeks and neck, while he wrapped her cloak about her. He stepped back to look at her.

"My goddess ! this evening will be like all my coming
life. I shall never leave you again."

He drove to the theater with her. No Juliet, except
one who-played that immortal tragedy of love and
death with her lover, ever went on the stage with her
pulses so set to the time of a heavenly music, her soul
at white heat in the flame of a divine ecstasy, as did
this woman. Her tones were liquid love ; her very
magnetism charged the air, and the audience caught
the charm.

Oswald stood at the wing. She felt his presence
and played like one inspired. I doubt if he remembered the crowd of people hanging on her words, but
she felt her triumph and grew stronger and more exultant at every step. He was only conscious, from time
to time, that she was coming to him, and then that her
eyes were meeting his heavy ones.

Some one who saw her that night, in the full summer
of her years, remembers it as an experience to be had
but once in two or three life-times : She was like
nobody in all the world but one—Juliet, a creature of
fire and air, born to a moment of passion before death.
Rose was behind the scenes, watching her in anxious
triumph. He noted how, like the swing of a pendulum,
she came to Oswald at each exit. Once he spoke to
Oswald, who answered him from a dream. The manager grew alarmed. There must be something between
the two. Even the actors noticed it, and whispered a
little together.

Rose was a man of the best intentions and very little
tact. He drew Victoria aside, when there was opportunity, saying : "I want to give you a hint. You're

being noticed. It will make talk if you have so much to say to Craig."

She was too happy for offense.

"Never mind the talk, Mr. Rose. I can afford that."

"You can't afford to flirt with a married man and expect to keep your reputation," said Rose, testily. Her cool disregard of caution sometimes put him out of patience. A flush swept over Juliet's face, like the insistence of blood denied its right of coming for love, in swift blushes. She walked up to Oswald.

"Mr. Rose tells me you are married," she said, quietly, with a smile that held only confidence in him. A lie would have saved him. Her faith in him was great enough to withstand any evidence but his word.

"I am," said Oswald, doggedly. She did not wince.

"Why did you deceive me?"

"Because I loved you." Waking to the fear of losing her, and speaking in an intense whisper, while his burning eyes besought mercy. "I am wretchedly married. I do not love my wife. She doesn't need me. You said once that in such a case a man might make his own divorce and be true to the woman he loved."

"So I did," she said, slowly, and without looking at him. "I suppose your wife is at home waiting for you, now," she went on, with that impulse of self-torture peculiar to women.

"Probably," sneered Oswald.

"Does she like to sit patiently at home while you make love to other women?"

"Why do you torment me?" cried Oswald, beside himself. "How much of this do you think a man can bear?"

The scene was set and Juliet called.

"I am not going," she said, indifferently, turning toward her dressing-room. "You can tell them."

"For heaven's sake, think," said Oswald, roused to the situation, and for the first time noting her deadly paleness and the lethargy shown by her whole yielding frame. "You'll stop the play."

"Yes, I suppose so—but I'm going home." She had been called twice, and now nobody seemed to dare approach her, save the nurse, who bustled up with a question only to be waved off. Oswald resorted to a cruelty kind as pricking a fainting person in a moment of peril. When he saw her weakness, his own courage rose ; perhaps he could even feel an interest in proving her theory of playing tragedy with her whole heart, if she once suffered acutely.

"Let me take you to my house if you are ill. My wife will be glad to attend you."

The shaft struck home. Her body straightened like a frame upheld by electric currents. Shaking off her torpor, she went on without a word or look to any one. When the stricken bride burst into lamentations, they were her own as well as Juliet's. Romeo was banished. Victoria was conscious only of burning pain ; a wounded creature, which does not speculate on the final issue of life and death, may writhe in throes quite as agonized as if he can judge whether they are to be fatal.

The last scene was over and the audience would not go. There was persistent applause and her name went up in hoarse roars from every part of the house. She had won her name. To whatever level of mediocrity

it might fall, to-night's work would never be quite forgotten. She had gone to her dressing-room, and
Oswald grew alarmed. How far would her insanity
carry her? But she came out, presently; her face was
still pale, her eyes burning. So might look the ghost
of the girl who had undergone the horrors of prison
and the tomb. The audience shouted again and went
home satisfied. Victoria beckoned, and Oswald joined
her eagerly.

" You said your wife did not care for you ! "

" Yes, before heaven ! "

" Are you going to forsake her for me ? " Her whole
face was malicious now.

" I want you for my true wife," said Oswald, fervent-
ly. " I thought you loved me enough to brave the
world for me."

" Yes, so I do, but first you must do something for
me. Take me to your house to-night and introduce me
to her."

" Have you quite lost your wits? Come away ! let
me get you home ! " cried Oswald, aghast.

" I dare say my wits are gone," she said, with the same
composure. " But you must do it, or I swear I never
will speak to you again. What harm can it do,—if you
have told me the truth ! "

For the time being, she was quite insane. Oswald
saw it, and felt hopeless of controlling her. A temptation shot through him. It was harder to win her
than he anticipated. Why not let her do this?
There were chances enough in his favor; Victoria
might find her senses before they should reach the
house ; Elizabeth might not be waiting for him. Or,

if he dared play at such an uncertain game, why not
bring the woman he loved into the presence of the
woman who was in his way, as an inducement for the
latter to take things into her own hands ? In any case,
it became very evident that Victoria could not be managed unless he should begin with concession.

"Well, come if you must," he said, doggedly, having
made his resolution. Victoria threw her cloak about
her and hurried down to the carriage.

"For heaven's sake, go back and change your dress,"
said Oswald. But she only laughed and ran on before
him. It was the soft white robe that had shrouded her
in the tomb. Her long hair had fallen in bright waves,
and her neck and arms were bare. Oswald gave the
order and they drove away. He was trusting himself
to fate and cursing unlucky chances, possibly by way
of a spell. Victoria laughed and talked in high
gayety.

"You can tell her I am eccentric, and prefer to call
at eleven of the clock. Tell her, that being an actress,
I am quite ignorant of social restrictions."

"I wish you wouldn't make me so unhappy," as a
last effort, attempting at the same time to take her hand,
which she snatched away.

"Never, sir, till you have your wife's permission.
Unhappy ? How foolish you are ! you might walk
through comedy, at least, with a gay heart."

The carriage stopped, and Oswald stepped out saying hurriedly, "Wait, please, till I make inquiries."

He was growing frightened ; the scene must be
ended, and that could only be done by diplomacy. He
opened the door with his latch-key, and was about

shutting it again to turn back and say his wife could
not receive her, when there was a light touch on his
arm. Victoria had followed him.

"You were going to deceive me again !" she said,
with a wicked reproachfulness. "I shall take matters
into my own hands."

James was waiting in the hall, and came forward.

"Is Mrs. Craig in?" asked Victoria, with careful
decorum.

"Yes'm. She said," turning to Oswald, "that you
was to go into the library."

"Yes," answered Victoria, for him. "She will see
me, of course. Show me the way, please. Ah, this
door at the right?"

That night Elizabeth was feeling only the weariness
that comes after struggling. She put the thought of
Felix away, but only as something holy. If his attitude
toward her was not that which any loyal wife might suffer, it was his supreme misfortune, a sin that had
stolen upon him like a thief. And the thought that
his saintly knighthood would be strong enough to con-
quer any danger, upheld her like sacramental wine.
That Oswald could suspect a vulgar attachment filled
her with aversion. She shrank from his suggestion, as
something base. Perhaps it was one step towards
shrinking from him ; she was afraid of that. She
had come to the point of promising herself to make one
more effort,—the harder because there would be no
heart in it. If she should win her husband's love
again, she began to be dimly conscious that her whole
life would be a struggle in keeping it. An extreme of
outside observance becomes the natural thing, when

the inward spirit has failed ; she fixed upon making preparations for his supper, just as she had done in the first days of their marriage. She had begun to dread his coming, wondering what she should say when he should come. A few minutes after eleven there was a light tap at the door, followed by its opening. She was in an easy-chair, one hand over her eyes. Looking up with a start, what strange and beautiful vision met her gaze ! Victoria stood there, still mocking and conscious of her beauty. Elizabeth bent forward, her heart in her eyes. She knew Victoria ; her coming seemed to involve some fresh calamity.

"Your husband will introduce us," said the actress, turning to bring Oswald into view, and sweeping the soft folds of her dress about her feet, where they clung, making her still more like a beautiful statue. It was the awkward moment of Oswald's life.

"Elizabeth, Miss Landor is anxious to know you." While Elizabeth was gravely acknowledging the words, the actress had taken in the whole scene with her quick eye for effect. The little table was all ready, with its delicate cups waiting for the chocolate by the fire. Elizabeth, in her gray wrapper, a simple ruffle about her throat, was excellently dressed for the domestic goddess, destined alike for homely cares and sweet, sacred offices. The mocking spirit died out in Victoria. She bitterly repented her coming. If, by clever acting, she could save the sweet woman of whom she was jealous, it must be done.

"Please sit down," said Elizabeth. "Let me give you some chocolate. I have been keeping it hot for my husband."

"I thank you, no," said Victoria, sweetly, not taking
the chair. "I must apologize before going. You
know we people of the stage—"she glanced at Oswald,
smiling with some bitterness, "have a taste for Bohemian adventure. Your husband was behind the
scenes to-night, and I begged him to take me here to
call on you. It was not in good taste, but I hope you
forgive it."

Her beauty and gentleness impressed Elizabeth.

"Please do not apologize," she said, still gravely.
"I wish to entertain my husband's friends."

"But if I tire you, it will be carrying my freak too
far. Good night. Thank you, Mr. Craig, you may
see me to my carriage. No further," she added stern-
ly, as they stepped out of Elizabeth's hearing.

"I am going home with you."

"You shall not," said Victoria, pausing on the last
step and turning to face him. "I will not enter the
carriage to-night, unless you leave me."

Oswald waited in stolid patience. The coachman
sat discreetly unobservant of their low tones.

"I promise to see or write to you to-morrow," said
Victoria, anxious only to escape.

"Very well," said Oswald, after a moment's thought.
"I shall call in the morning."

"Not in the morning; I will send you a message
first," and she was driven away. Oswald went slowly
back into the house, mentally cursing Elizabeth for
having assumed the air that balked his plans. He
actively hated only the things which stood in his way ;
consequently, as circumstances were usually kind to
him, he had, in his own mind, quite a reputation for

amiability. He went into the library and sat down opposite Elizabeth, who still stood. The masculine attitude, when one indulges in stretching out his feet and dropping his brows, does not invite remonstrance. It is to be doubted whether Elizabeth thought of that.

"Oswald, what did she come here for?" she said, trying to control her quivering voice.

"She told you."

"Yes, but why did you bring her here? Why did you look so? Oswald, are you in love with her?"

" Yes," said her husband, narrowing his gaze slightly, as he looked at her and wondered whatever led him into marriage with this plain and commonplace woman. Please remember that his answers were not meant to be cruel. Not being in love with her, it did not occur to him that he might still retain the power of wounding her.

"Oswald," cried Elizabeth, something sharp and vibrating in her voice. "I won't be exacting—I will try not to worry you—but remember we are married—"

" Yes, worse luck," said her husband, coldly disgusted. "You needn't remind me what a damned theatrical ass I made of myself, that year." He strode off up-stairs. Not to their own room; it seemed to him, in his irritation, that nothing could be worse than hearing her speak again.

Elizabeth carefully set the chocolate aside and turned off the gas. Then she crept back into the easy-chair.

CHAPTER XXVII.

THE early train to Stratford took Elizabeth with it, flying to cover where she could at least hide her wounds. Oswald had gone out early, without seeing her. She heard his step pass the library where she had lain all night, too negligent of herself to change her position, and where the morning light found her stiff and cramped. As soon as the door closed behind him, she ran up to her dressing-room, made her toilet and went down to breakfast. It was unnecessary to interest the servants in the fact that something unusual had happened. So she gave an order for Oswald's lunch, and told Ward she might be away some little time. Writing on a sheet of paper, "I have gone to Stratford," she left it in a sealed envelope on her husband's table. There was no need of reproaches or tragic farewells. Besides, she did not even know whether her present step was a final one or not, her only clear decision being that she must have rest and quiet, away from him. Her preparations made, she hurried away, with a feverish joy in action. How could she breathe, even, until miles lay between her and the place where she had been so wronged! Pride had no part in her great suffering. Gossip and prying eyes in Stratford seemed far less to bear than this mockery of attempting a duty where none existed. As she stepped from the car at Stowe, Si's face was the first to greet her.

"Lord! do they do it as quick as this!" was his awe-struck exclamation. "I ain't spoke to the girl even!"

Elizabeth bowed and smiled, and was about passing him, when Si placed himself in her way and went on, "Your mother sent me up here to telegraft."

"What?" said Elizabeth, a quick fear shooting into life. "What has happened?"

"Philip. He ain't very well. They thought you'd better come," answered Si, with the brevity that comes of evasion. "I've got the Sea View buggy. Climb right in."

So Elizabeth, alive with the instinct of haste, entered the demoralized vehicle.

"You must tell me just what it is," she said, when they were fairly on their rattling way. "Don't try to make me more comfortable by deceiving me."

"The doctor says it's only pneumony," said Si, soothingly, using the whip with emphasis. "You see, Philip's acted like a crazed one, lately. He got a master cold—coughin' and barkin' round for a week, he was—and then he took to stayin' out doors and hangin' round the shore till he got powerful bad. An' I guess he had a hard row to fetch his breath last night."

Elizabeth's came in one quick sob; all other sorrow was effaced, and nothing seemed real and vital but her old devotion to Philip, as it had been when there was no paramount affection to overshadow it. Her life rebounded a year, to the absorption of old ties.

Mrs. Nye, like most women who endure and are patient, was a marvel of self-possession in illness. The habit of silence helped her there. But the unexpected sight of Elizabeth broke up her calmness ; her face changed, convulsively.

"How is he, mother?" whispered Elizabeth, when they could both speak.

"Bad, very bad. You mustn't expect any thing." The girl felt her heart die within her at the hopeless tone. Taking off her hat, she went in to see him, and Philip, painfully struggling for breath, was at once radiant. A slight quiver passed over Grandmother's face. Older, her countenance more deeply lined, she sat by the bedside, slowly waving a large palm-leaf fan. She gave her place to Elizabeth, and the day's watching went on. Philip was not quite himself. The suffocation of the disease so oppressed him that he could not waste effort in speech or looks. Once he whispered, painfully, "Betty, my play is almost ready. Could you finish copying it?"

"Yes, dear," said Elizabeth, feeling her own throat aching with the tears that must not come.

The story of a sickness to death is always the same in substance, and need never be told. Philip died that night in an agony of struggle.

When it was over, and they looked into one another's eyes across the bed, the supreme cup of solemn grief seemed to have touched their lips. Elizabeth had suffered keenly, but how was that rage of jealous anger to affect her life like this sweet and solemn mystery? We step out of our earthly garments in the presence of death, and make holy resolves to live henceforth in the shadow of its wonder.

In her first calm moment, she repented that she had not meant to stay with her husband and be at her best,

in spite of the worst circumstances. How, she did not
know, but great things seem easy at great moments.
That lesson of tenderness taught always by the dead
prompted her to telegraph Oswald at once.

"Philip is dead. Will you come?"

Perhaps he would think she had been called home
by the event ; it might be better so. She was sorry
for even the just resentment of her life.

There were neighbors in the kitchen when Philip
died, sitting like mute statues of country life, now
and then exchanging a subdued whisper. That was a
custom in Stratford. It was the custom, too, at such
times, to throng the room of the dying, watching the
failing breath with mournful interest. But Elizabeth
had steadily kept them out. Nobody should enter
that inner circle who had not the right of love.

It was Mrs. Nye who first remembered to rise from
the watch no longer needed.

"Grandmother," Elizabeth said in a whisper, touching her shoulder. "Come."

The old lady looked up with a face carrying dread
to the two who had never before seen it moved, except
by anger.

"Thirty years ago," she said, in a moaning voice,
"Jeremiah died, and it's all brought back again."

Elizabeth led her away with a tenderness she did not
resent, perhaps because she saw nothing but shadows
from the past and heard only the echoes of their
voices.

"Sha'n't we send for Mr. Kewe?" asked Mrs. Nye,
when preparations were being made for the funeral.

"I think not, mother. He is very busy."

Oswald neither came nor wrote. There was much "thinking strange" of it in Stratford. People augured ill for Elizabeth's happiness. Grandmother asked no questions, and Mrs. Nye was roused to interest by no earthly circumstance. She seemed stricken, and leaned heavily on Elizabeth, who, it mercifully happened, had to think constantly of others.

CHAPTER XXVIII.

BEFORE Victoria was half way home she began to hate Elizabeth as much as she pitied her. Do not mistake her motive in denying Oswald, for one higher than it really was. It was nothing more than generosity. If she could have been convinced that he had made an unfortunate and mistaken marriage, one that his wife regretted as much as he, she would have said, in all honor and honesty, "Come with me and be true to me. You have been deluded by a show and a phantom. If there are reasons why the laws of your country will not release you—nay, if you choose not to ask their interposition—trust as I do in the legislation of our own souls. Choose, in the face of the world, what is higher than the world."

You may have known at least one instance of such arrogance of truth, of one to whom the spirit is so immeasurably superior to the letter of the law that this last is ignored. Face to face with her embodied theories, Victoria stopped, aghast. When Oswald said "Come !" her heart cried, "I follow." It would still own its allegiance, in spite of the sorely perplexed and tortured conscience, but in the way stood the pale, sweet woman whom she must wrong. And she would wrong no one. Nay, to do so was to destroy the very right she had of obeying her heart. In the first days that followed, she did not consider whether Oswald was to be blamed or not, for deceiving her. They both seemed so wretchedly unfortunate, that perhaps she tacitly allowed him, too, to have been deceived.

The night after she left him was first a blank staring of life in the face, then a haste of packing and making ready to be away in the morning, before he should come. She knew he would come, though she had forbidden it ; she shivered with fear at the thought of again having to withstand his entreaties. It was not dread of further suffering. Any thing would be easier to bear than silence and forgetfulness, but she feared herself. Instinctively, she knew that his voice and eyes could put a new construction on what she felt to be irrevocable, and she shrank from the unnecessary pain of having to cling to her convictions against his will and her own heart. She saw the barrier between them, and to deny him when he urged her to leap that barrier with him, would demand more strength than the poor young creature felt herself possessed of. Suppose fair Ellen's conscience had been inconveniently active, would young Lochinvar's telegraphic persuasion have proved an unmitigated relief to her ?

Early that morning, she went with her trunks to a hotel at the other end of the city, anxious to be as far as possible from the place where he would expect to find her. Then she wrote two notes, one to Mr. Rose, giving her present address, and, with no reason, charging him to keep it a secret. The shorter the word she had promised Oswald, the more easily could it be written. Pity and love begged to be heard, but she thrust them back.

" You must never come near me or write to me. I

cannot be changed, so do not trouble me. You must
make her happy. It hurts me most to think how we
have wronged her."

Oswald, as she had expected, did not wait for
a message, but was early at her rooms. Daylight
had simplified matters for him. Nothing looked
as tragic as it had, the night before. He did not
feel himself as hopelessly at the mercy of two
jealous women, and, as a result of having been so, he
was aware of a touch of provocation that acted as a
wonderful tonic. Victoria's delirium would have
cooled, as his own had done. And his wife? He had
not yet reached the point of deciding upon her disposal. He was in the habit of feeling that if a relation had ceased to be necessary to him, it had ceased
to exist. Inconvenient encumbrances always dropped
away of themselves, like dead leaves. He would not
waste thought on the manner of their going. The
morning was fine, and with the accompanying courage
which attends an access of keener animal vigor, he felt
himself master of the situation. He thought of Victoria and the strait she had put him in, with a half-
resentful pride in her. Fierce, beautiful creature ! Do
you, sir, think the worse of your horse because he cur-
vets and shies occasionally, if you are convinced that
his neck is thereby arched and his nostrils dilated,
even when you know your own bones are in some slight
danger? When Oswald reached the door on Tremont
Street, he found the janitor sweeping down the stairs.

" She's gone away," said that functionary, laconic-
ally, stooping for a paper that kept blowing beyond his
reach.

"Gone away?" echoed Oswald, stopping short, but only connecting the words with an absence of minutes. "Do you know when she will be in?"

"Not yet awhile, I guess. She took her trunks with her."

No questioning could elicit more. Did he know where her trunks had been sent? No, he hadn't heard. Oswald hurried away, with his belief in the general amiability of events somewhat shattered. So she meant to elude him! Too thoroughly alarmed for anger, he went home first, to see if any letters had been delivered. There were none, and as he only stopped to open the hall-door and ask the question, no one thought to mention his wife's going. He went to the theater to find Rose, who received him coolly. The manager had Victoria's note in his pocket, and, little as it told, he suspected much. Quite ignorant of the nature of the wrong, he knew it lay somewhere, and all his honest heart was alive with indignation. Victoria's general fearlessness put him out of patience. He had a strong desire to say, "I told you you'd come to grief," but remembered her mother, and the watch-dog instinct rose in him.

"Good morning, Rose," said Oswald, dropping into a saunter, and trying to assume the coolness that was never so far from his control as at the moment. "I called for Miss Landor's address. She neglected to give it me."

"Did she?" said the manager, looking at him steadily. "That isn't odd, for she told me nobody was to have it."

Oswald saw he was on the defensive. It annoyed

him to meet a counter-check from so insignificant a quarter.

" Ah ? But she would except me, I think. It will be safe with me."

" It's safer where it is."

"Has she gone out of town ? " asked Oswald, pleasantly.

"Yes," said the watch-dog, lying without the slightest compunction.

" And it's of no use—"

" No," said Rose, advancing ominously, though his intentions embraced nothing more serious than an encounter of words. " And I want to speak to you—"

" Another time, then," answered Oswald, lifting his hat and walking away. He had no idea of being called to account by a fellow who was generous with his negatives and sparing of various advantages afforded by the English language.

Going home again, he found the notes written by the two women. Victoria's was opened first. So she was likely to give him trouble enough, well worth it as she was ! Little sympathy as he had with her scruples, he felt, at every turn in the pursuit that hid her from him, an increasing admiration of her.

All the trouble she gave him only added to his growing bitterness against his wife, for having existed at all. But her written line seemed a solution. Courage ! she had taken herself away. The probabilities being against his inviting her back, she would doubtless have the good-sense not to come. When he left Rose that morning, it was with a smile on his face. Rose had betrayed himself. If Victoria were out of town it was at Rose's own house in Birchwood. Nothing was more simple. She had no other friend ; the manager's very glance showed that she had confided in him, and that he had constituted himself her guardian. It was quite evident that she feared pursuit. He smiled again at that and the thought that she would find herself mistaken. Oswald had reduced the subjugation of woman to a science. He knew that, under most trying circumstances, a judicious letting alone was a maneuver not to be despised. The most untamable easily succumbed after she had been left in the dark to sob herself sick. Victoria should have plenty of time for reflection. He would not entreat again, but await the rapture of seeing this proud creature creeping toward his arms. So he made himself busy that day, to avoid thought ; attended to some money matters which had been hanging on for weeks, invited Grimwald to lunch, trying to be amused by his rampant criticism on certain late music, and at night took the boat for New York. Arrived in that gay and busy city, he threw himself into its arms and said, " Entertain me." The first day passed and he went to the theater. The curtain, lights, even the indescribable smell of the place—musty, but delicious to the theater-goer—cast him back into Boston and before the stage where he had seen her walk so often. The comedy faded out. Other people about him laughed and applauded, but before his eyes moved only white vision. Her great worth, his great desire of possession, surged up again, and overthrew his interest in paltry tactics. Surely his only place was at her feet. The next night he was on his way home. Reading

Elizabeth's telegram, which he found there, awoke
only a mild interest, a little wonder, too, that she
should have sent for him. He had cut loose from
that phase of his life ; why should floating things
come up as impertinent reminders of a shore to
which he never could return ?

He meant to see Victoria that night at the theater,
but as the hours wore on, emotion grew to the limits
of endurance, urging him to seek her out before.
It made no vital difference, he told himself, whether
he saw her a few hours earlier or later. This, the
conviction born of passion, denied, making both their
lives seem to depend on it. Consequently, the early
afternoon found him at Birchwood, where he had little
trouble in locating the manager's house.

The servant who answered the bell was very genuinely surprised at his questions. No, Miss Landor
was not there. She had only been there once, a long
time ago, with her mother. There was nothing further
to be gained, and Oswald set off down the village
street, to kill time and his own disappointment.

In spite of probabilities, he half expected to meet
her. The street led into a country road, and he still
tramped on, thinking, with a smile, of the sudden and
accidental manner the events of life took, in dropping
down upon him. Led on by speculation, he walked further than he had intended, reaching the station again at
dark. He had not eaten since morning, and had been
played upon by one emotion after another until he
now felt most like a boy, longing to be once more with
the woman he loved, to be soothed and led back to
cheerfulness. It was inconceivable to him that she

could meet him coldly or with reproaches, he needed her so much. Once in the car, he found it impossible to stay there. Two people behind him were talking of going to the Museum that night. The woman hoped the play was funny, and the man assured her it was. Oswald went out on the platform. It was a relief to look into the darkness, a pleasure to feel the air, which had grown steadily chill. It would be the coldest night of the month. He tried to interest himself in shivering and turning up his coat-collar to guard against the wind, in wondering where he preferred to dine, and if Rose would object to his admittance behind the scenes. They were all superficial thoughts. The distance lessened ; the time shortened. His throat grew parched, and the painful choking of anticipation came. What fortunate accident would open the next act of his drama ? No emotion had ever before been so real as to become a pain to him.

He was beginning to live. He stepped back to let some one pass, and an express train shot by on the track he was facing. Another quick backward step, as the locomotive flashed across his glance, and balance and hold were lost. Some one had opened the door in time to see the lurch into darkness, and the train was stopped.

He was taken up quite dead. Falling squarely backward, his head struck the one sharp stone within yards. However cruel the wound, death left the face eager and beautiful. It was only one more accident. You probably thought so, when you saw it mentioned in the paper next morning. Perhaps, too, you read it at the same moment it came to the eyes of Victoria,

fortifying herself anew against the persuasions of a
tongue become silent.

.   .   .   .   .   .

When he was carried home, Ward was perhaps not
sorry that the mistress of the house was away and all
responsibility devolved on him. The servants were in
fluttering confusion, but there was little grief. They had
known their master too long to love him. Ward, among
other important items, remembered that he had not
Mrs. Craig's address. Then he thought of Mr. Perham, and went to his rooms. It almost seemed to
Ward that the solemnity of the occasion justified him
in sending a message asking Jack to come, but the
force of habit was too strong. He would have expected a reprimand from Oswald, for taking liberties
with a gentleman. Fortunately, Jack was in. He had
not heard the news and was shocked and excited.
There was genuine grief as well as surprise in his emotion. Jack was somewhat canine in his attachments;
once fixed, the unworthiness of the object did not
weaken his constancy. He had no idea where Mrs.
Craig had gone, but knew she was often at Stratford. It would be safe to telegraph there. So
he sent a cautious message, saying only that
she was needed immediately, and signing his own
name. As he did that, there rose to the surface
his dim recollection of having been unlucky in his
acquaintance with her—and Jack had some idea
why she had so little cause to tolerate him. But
having a genuine admiration for her, the more hearty,
perhaps, because she had never concealed her disapproval, he felt a shame in proportion. He wandered

about for half an hour after the telegram was sent, nervously unwilling to go to the house where Oswald lay. It seemed base to do nothing. Why not go down to Stratford and return with Elizabeth? He hurried away to consult a time-table and found it could not be done if she should catch the morning train, but he could meet her on the way and act as some shield against the possibility of her coming to the city quite alone. Again he thought angrily of his own folly in making himself so worthy the scorn of a woman that he could not expect her to be glad of his help.

The message need not have been obscurely worded. After one great blow, no other can very much surprise us. Elizabeth was sure her husband was dead. Stunned as she was, the only feeling of which she was conscious was that of great remorse. She had left him, and he had died. She made her preparations with intent earnestness, wildly anxious to be there as soon as possible, as the only small fulfillment of her marriage promises left her. She said hastily, at home, that she was sent for, and did not explain. She could not have her mother suffering for her grief, as long as it was possible to bear it alone. Jack entered the car at Havamill, and went through, hoping and dreading to find her. He had not imagined feeling so great a relief as it was when she turned to him and put out her hand.

" It was very kind of you to come," she said, making no attempt at civilities. " How did it happen? "

" Oh, then you know? " said Jack, with a long breath of relief.

" No, but I was sent for because something dreadful

had happened. Is he hurt—or has he died?" she
added in a low voice.

"He died last night. There was no pain. He fell
—from a car."

"I think I would like the window open a little," she
said, after a few moments. Then the two spoke no
more till they reached Boston. Jack watched her
anxiously, but she was quite still, her head resting on
the car window, and her eyes open. He had feared
her fainting. Afterwards, at least, an outbreak would
have been more easily understood than her calmness;
so Ward thought. Having expected hysterics, he felt
slightly disgusted at their non-occurrence. She asked
but one question. Passing up-stairs, she paused at the
door of a room adjoining her own, saying, with a slight
hesitation, "Is he in here?"

"Yes'm," said Ward, and she passed by. Most of
the day she spent in the library seeing no one, for all
necessary arrangements Jack took on his own shoulders.
At night, she was still there, and Jack constituted himself sentinel in the reception-room near. Once, near
midnight, he stole up to her door. It was open, the
light burning brightly and Elizabeth asleep in the great
chair where she had lain through that other wretched
night. He went softly in, turned the light down and
took up his watch again. At daybreak he heard her go
to her own room.

There were only the Southern cousins to inform, and
Elizabeth wrote the few necessary facts to her mother,
asking her not to come. It seemed to her that the
only way of living quietly through the strain, was to
undertake it alone.

When she was left in possession of the house, she
felt as if she had lived through a dream which yet led
to no clear awakening. She was a mystery to Ward,
the chief reason being that she only once entered the
room where her husband lay, and that for a few
minutes. In that little time, Elizabeth had stooped to
the dead man's ear to whisper : "If I was wrong, forgive me. And I forgive you. I meant to do right,
but it was so hard." She covered the face softly, glad
that death had left only his most beautiful self. Love
was dead in her, but remorse for some fancied duty
undone, unable as she had been to do it, would still
linger.

After the funeral, Jack felt himself to be rather
awkwardly placed. It was cruel to leave her alone,
and yet he had no right to stay. Whoever had the
right, was evidently not going to appear to claim it.
Before he had gone very far in the dilemma, Elizabeth
relieved him from it.

"I have been thinking what I can do," she said,
going into the library where he sat wondering if he
should take his hat and go. "Have I the care of this
house ? Can I close it and go away ?"

"Undoubtedly."

He was glad to see her look perplexed. Even this
little frown was more hopeful than the dead quiet her
face had worn. Yesterday, in the midst of his pity, he
had wondered that a man of just Oswald's tastes should
have married her. Now he noted the grace of the slender figure in black, the beauty of her hands.

"I want so much to go home," said Elizabeth, a little quiver touching the corners of her mouth. "We

have had trouble there. Did I tell you my brother had just died ? "

" No," said Jack, the tears coming into his eyes.

" I want to be there. I wish you would tell me ex-actly what I ought to do."

The appeal touched Jack to the heart.

" You want to get away and close the house," he said, settling to business. " But you mean to come back to it, by and by ? "

" Never ! " with a quick shudder that told its story. Afterwards he wondered if it could be possible that Mrs. Craig knew her husband too well.

" But you wouldn't sell the house ? "

" Yes, if it is mine to sell. And as soon as possi-ble."

" Then I should give the servants warning, or, if you choose, make them some compensation for that, and let them go away sooner."

" To-morrow," said Elizabeth, restlessly. " That will be best, and I will go to-morrow."

She was consumed by a feverish haste to be at home. The old associations had grown dear beyond words. She was sure that if she could have the old bleak days back, with her girlhood and Philip, it would all be paradise. " And all this business of taking care of things must be given to somebody. You are a lawyer, aren't you ; will you do it ? "

" Why, if you can trust me, Mrs. Craig," said Jack, with a blush. He was overwhelmed by her haste. " But there are plenty of men I know to be relia-ble——"

" You are going to refuse because I blamed you,"

said Elizabeth bravely, and very humbly. " I couldn't help that, but perhaps I was too hard. I don't seem to. see things or understand people!" she cried, bitterly.

"Mrs. Craig, no living woman ought to have forgiven it," said Jack, with a burst of shame. "If you'll let me work for you, I'll do it, and some time I may be fit to shake hands with you."

Elizabeth held out her hand quickly, with a smile, and Jack was her loyal adorer from that moment. He is married now, but he tells his wife that it was another woman, one with whom he never dared be in love, who was his salvation.

CHAPTER XXIX.

VICTORIA had known of Oswald's death from the papers, the morning after it occurred. There is a certain quality ready to be aroused in the womanly nature, which, for want of a better name, is referred to the fierceness of the tigress in defense of her young. In some women, this fierce loving is only called forth by maternity ; in others not at all. In the few, it lies sleeping side by side with love, to wake when that stirs. Victoria put down her newspaper, not overwhelmed by the shock, but emboldened. There filled and swelled her veins a flood whose every drop cried passionately for its own, making her long to stretch out her arms to the people who had a right to be near Oswald, and cry, " Give me my dead." She put on her hat mechanically, and then, as she was going out, remembered that she did not know where to find him. In the excitement of her escapade of a few nights before, street and number left no impression on her mind. She sank into a chair, her hand still on the door. The drive had been like a dream ; she did not know its direction. The house was the house of a dream. With every detail of the room she had entered photographed on her mind in a picture that stung the sensitive-plate, she had yet no conception of place. So she sat, her mind rather losing than gaining power of action, but always droning through it the insistent under-tone, " He needs me and I must go," to be met with and beaten back by the check, " I cannot find him."

The thought of rehearsal, coming from force of habit, suggested Rose. He would know. A woman of action again, she started up and hurried to the theater. He was standing near the stage-entrance when her carriage stopped. Rose had thought of her every second since he tasted his morning news. It solved a complication, to be sure, for Oswald to be so providentially removed before he had quite ruined the reputation of the World's star, but there would have to be a fine struggle with this particular gale of circumstance before Victoria could put out to sea again. He had not seen her under really tragic circumstances before that night of her first overwhelming success, and the workings of these events being inexplicable, they were none the less alarming. He was a little doubtful of the course she might take, and made up his mind if she should not be there promptly, to send for her, and at the same time make lightning arrangements for a change of programme. The Bells of Ballantyne was filling up the star's off nights, and could be resorted to.

Seeing her, he hastily quitted his companion, and went up to the carriage, with a smile that did him credit, though it left the upper half of his face inquiring and anxious.

" How early you are ! " holding the door open for her.

" I am not ready for rehearsal. I am going away first. I want to know Mr. Craig's address."

Then Rose knew he was not yet through deep waters.

"Victoria, you'd better listen to me. Do you know what has happened?"

"Yes, I am going to him. You must tell me where he is or——Good heavens, why didn't I think of it before! I can look in the directory."

She was about to rise, when the manager said quietly, "I'll tell you every thing you want me to, only you must listen a minute first. Victoria, you know I wouldn't cheat you?"

"Very well, don't try to manage me, then, and I'll hear you," she said, in a hard tone, folding her hands under her cloak. "But be quick. I'm in a hurry."

He stepped forward, and ordered the man to drive slowly back to the hotel, and then took a place beside her.

"There is one thing you must remember, before you go there. Craig's wife is the only woman with any right there, you know. You mustn't let yourself forget that."

A shiver passed over the girl, but she said proudly, "I know better than you, you see. I know who has the only right."

The carriage stopped before the Saint John's.

"Choose for yourself, then," said the manager. He had but one card that would count; there was no need of slowly dribbling out his hand in persuasions, before throwing down his trump. "I don't say any thing about your losing reputation in forcing yourself into a house where every living soul would turn the key on you. Probably that wouldn't affect you. But I should like to have you consider what sort of a thing it is to intrude on a woman when her husband has just been brought home dead. It strikes me as damned unmerciful. Shall I tell the man where to go?"

Victoria sat looking down into her lap. When she turned to him, Rose was shocked at the pinched look in her face, the work of the instant since the resolution had gone out of it.

"Back to the theater," she said, in a painful whisper. He bowed gravely, gave the order and walked away, feeling most like whistling. Now that the tide had really turned in his favor, he found he had not expected victory.

She went through her rehearsal painstakingly. Fortunately, it did not occur to her that there were critical eyes upon her, the same that had noticed her with Oswald and now cross-questioned her face for discovery of some effect of his death. Rose stopped her on her way out. His soft-heartedness had got the better of his generalship.

"If I could let you off a week or two, you know I would——" he began, when Victoria put up her head with a superb motion, and looked down on him, a smile on her lips.

"I am an actress, sir!" she rejoined.

"She'll get over it," thought the manager, and, expecting no more scenes, he thanked his particular divinities and gave himself up to business.

Victoria watched the papers feverishly, for further details. None were given. A second paragraph stated that the deceased had bought a ticket to Birchwood, but his business there had not been ascertained. Only two men knew why he was at Birchwood, and both had good reasons for silence. Rose had guessed the truth immediately, and lost no time in bribing his old servant to secrecy. It could help nobody to say Oswald had been seen, and would necessitate a lie if some one having a right to know should choose to be curious.

Victoria did not think much in those days. All the disturbance of her life forces found expression in her art. She played like one in a divine ecstasy, and seemed to take a fierce delight in seeing the city at her feet.

Outside the theater she kept a steady hold on herself and waited, she could not have told for what. Her very existence had been strained to so high a pitch of excitement that she felt the only natural occurrence to be some strange event crowding upon the heels of what had gone before. Expecting that, her breath held that she might not shriek, she had no eyes for looking closely at the ravages made in her domain of pleasure.

CHAPTER XXX.

WHEN she considered the tragedy that had overtaken her, Elizabeth had no distinct feeling
but one of longing to cast aside the memory and consequences of former mistakes, and throw herself at the
feet of old associations, crying, "I am not fit for
responsibilities and great tasks, but let me rest and be
comforted before I go on."

Yet what was the old life without Philip? Changed,
beyond measure. Side by side with the consciousness
that his absence made half her grief, was a rebellious insistence on happiness, that pictured him there, eager and
full of fancies as ever. In this stupor which came from
resting in the interval between two duties, she could not
be hurt beyond measure by reality, for, at present, its
outlines were far from being clear. They needed the
background of old associations, lacking now the one
object that made them most dear. The moment when
she stepped on the platform at Stowe began her acceptance of the truth. Here were familiar faces, and though
only those of the few loitering officials, they helped fix
the hard fact that the external aspect of her small world
had not changed. It would reflect no more sunshine
than before her life awoke to thought and suffering.
It is marvelous, this effect of a familar landscape, even,
in bringing a soul back to its bearings when it antici-

pates a hard task and yet hopes shrinkingly for some relief from it, through possible change of circumstance. Elizabeth found she had even expected that the overthrow of Grandmother's composure could only be followed by a permanent softening, so that it was a surprise to find her looking quite the same. Still, she herself could show no emotion at the sight of home faces. She was deeply wearied but not moved. Her keen anticipation of their grief, her eager resolve not to fail them in help, gave way to a kind of apathy when she was actually in their presence.

" Didn't you have any mourning made? " was Grandmother's first question.

" No, Grandmother."

" Don't you mean to wear any ? "

" I hadn't thought of it at all. But I am used to black, you know."

" And no crape veil ? And you've got the same hat on you wore away ! "

Elizabeth took it off, and turned it on her hand, looking curiously to see if some color she had not remembered could be a flagrant sin against social usage. It was a graceful hat, with a wide brim and long feather, all of black.

" I don't think any body can have been shocked by this, Grandmother," she said, putting it down and seating herself. " And there was nobody to mind what I wore. I have seen very few people."

" Didn't his folks come ?" asked Madam Nye, laying aside her knitting, in order to give her sole attention to details. So the facts were finally elicited, by means of a persistent cross-examination.

Elizabeth caught herself wishing she could be let alone and be allowed to rest, and then was remorseful at the thought. She was quite ready, in her despair and humility, to find all depravity in herself. Here was a new instance of it. She had come home fully resolved . to fulfill every duty toward the two people who had any claim upon her, and a few trivial questions made her irritable at the outset. Grandmother's curiosity was not satisfied in one day, however. The next morning, she was ready with a new list of questions, for which Elizabeth was better prepared. She had had a long talk with her mother, before they slept, one broken by weeping from the eldèr woman, who, after the strain of action was over, found herself all weakness. Elizabeth saw how she turned to her for support and comfort, and the knowledge gave her a delicious sense of having, af- ter all, one niche which she alone could fill. She could sleep now, not with the lassitude of utter weariness, but the repose of one who has something to wake for and must court the strength necessary for meeting a defin- ite duty. But irritating gad-flies were not to be intimi- dated by resolutions.

" Did he leave you well off?" asked Grandmother. Her remarks always had an explosive tendency ; they had accumulated such weight before delivery as to ap- parently jar the air.

" I don't know."

" Things seem to be carried on strangely. A fu- neral without one of your own folks there, and some not even notified ! Your mother's had her way about it, and I hope she won't repent it."

The amount of the matter was that Mrs. Nye, with a

firmness unknown in her previous history, had really
insisted on carrying out a course of action shocking in
the extreme, to Stratford minds. When Elizabeth's letter
came, Grandmother, in no sort of doubt that the orthodox custom was to be followed, began making out a list
of the cousins and second cousins who must be bidden to
the funeral. But Mrs. Nye flatly refused to have them
notified. It was shocking enough to her, too, poor soul,
this idea of burial without a concourse of relatives
and a funeral supper, but her love for Elizabeth had
risen in arms and boldly defied whatever threatened
her child's comfort.   This silent woman had keen insight concerning the hearts of the people she loved.
Her horizon had been narrowed to include few objects,
and through quickening of the intellect by her love for
those few, she had grown wise as to their needs.
The maternal instinct urged her to fly to her child
in trouble ; the maternal understanding forbade it,
saying, " You are kindest in letting her bear it
alone."

The story of the following weeks in Elizabeth's life
rings monotonous changes.   Not one iota of the home
details had suffered alteration, though something was
lost for which the mind searched vaguely.

In the process of becoming used to absence, you
go through the customary routine, but there are moments when the sense of loss remains in your heart as
a pain whose origin you half forget, and you wonder
at finding the old duties robbed of their sweetness.
You sit on the door-stone at sunset ; a belated hum-
ming bird takes one last sip from the vine at your side,
and you, too, inhale the fragrance from a thousand ·

hidden sources. Summer stirs her odors and sounds
in one delicious potion, but though you drink, the
pain at your heart never ceases. There is no delight
of the senses that is not robbed of its divine flavor by
this lethargy of the soul which should receive and re-
spond to it. At some such moment of happy con-
ditions, you wonder why the time should not hold its
former value. He was not always with you at this
hour ; it does not recall him by suggestions of a happiness shared. Ah, but he was near—in the garden,
or by the window, or you had a letter from him that
very day. You felt his presence, and now he is contained by no conceivable limits of time or space. So
Elizabeth was mocked by memory. It was well for
the health of her soul, at this time, that two sorrows attacked her at once. In her memory of Oswald, his
death did not hold the first place. If it could have
done so, the mystery and dignity of the change might
have forced out of consideration the mistakes and suf-
ferings of their life together. But, overshadowing
every thing, came the question whether they had ever
really loved each other, whether love had once existed
and she might have kept it, had she not somehow failed in her duty, or become less, by her very nature, where
another woman would have grown to be more. A
wrong lay somewhere, and her mind would not rest
until it had located it. Seeing him dead, so subject to
the smiting hand of circumstance, had overcome in her
all personal blame. She thought only of their having
somehow erred together. Had no purely dignified and
noble sorrow touched her at the same time, she must
have fallen into bitterness and self-pity, feeling herself

to have been shamefully misled by what she had trusted as her most womanly emotions.

Her religion of forms and traditions had no significance for her, in this hour of living questions. She wondered, rather listlessly, as at another strange experience, whether it was because there existed no fountain-head of inspiration or because her mind was too shallow a vessel to hold the living water. It did not come to her for years after the death of the pain which engendered the question, that religion had never been more to her than a decent observance. Never having felt the throb of its living heart, in her present spiritual chill she could not drag herself near enough for borrowing a little warmth. The thought of Victoria was often present with her, but it brought with it no sting of jealousy. That had died with love. She found herself wondering just what relation the actress had borne to her husband. Arguments balanced themselves. The woman might really have loved him and that not guiltily. Stay, that could not be, for Victoria was aware of his wife's existence. There could be nothing but guilt where one impulse of love was cherished for a man whose faith was pledged elsewhere. She started from her seat to pace the floor hurriedly, a great flood of remembrance scorching her face. What had been the meaning of the cry wrung from Felix Kewe's lips? Yet she had pitied and not condemned him. Were emotions then uncontrollable, and vows liable to become fetters when the fickle heart and spent fancy turned toward the new? Until now, it had seemed sacrilege to think of Felix. She would cherish the poor, pitiful fragments of her marriage vow without offense, even of thought, against what others would have pronounced right, for she was beginning to distrust her own judgment.

So the harassing debate went on in her mind, until she longed only for absolution from her marriage promises—a divorce of the spirit to accompany that separation which was a fact. According to her creed, marriage was an everlasting compact, second marriages or divorce something horrible. She saw herself trying, all her life long, to patch up a sort of loyalty of thought, keeping herself true to a dual life of feeling—a falsity against which her soul rebelled. Honesty rose indignantly, crying, " In spite of your vows, you make yourself a man of clay, when you conjure up something with which to keep your faith. This is an empty bond." But putting him out of her thoughts, ceasing to try to sorrow for him seemed faithlessness, a desecration of the ordinance which ought to be made invalid only by death.

Like a flash it darted into her brain that she would see Victoria. Elizabeth was scarcely more conventional than Victoria herself, though she had fewer impulses and was less daring. Without considering her thought long, she wrote the actress a note, sending it to the World. At first, she simply asked to see her, signing herself without explanation. Then it occurred to her that this might not be enough, and she chose a new phraseology which, stiff enough, seemed to be the only one for expressing the truth.

" I was married to Oswald Craig, and need to talk with you about him. If I go to Boston, will you see me ? "

By return mail came the answer, couched politely
and not necessarily to be considered cordial or otherwise, mentioning Victoria's room at the hotel as the
place of meeting, at a certain hour of any day Mrs.
Craig might name.   Elizabeth set the next but one. ·
Now that the deed was done, she felt, perhaps, a little
frightened, and certainly too much excited to post-
pone the interview.

CHAPTER XXXI.

IT is not strange that the two women should have felt so great a timidity before their meeting that either would have withdrawn if she had not given her word. A few minutes past the hour, came the knock Victoria had been expecting for thirty minutes before the hour. She opened the door, and Elizabeth came in without a word. Neither had arranged commonplaces for smoothing the way, and neither could think of any thing better to do than to look at the other.

"Will she let me take her hand," thought Victoria, rapidly. "No, I will not offer. Poor little soul! I couldn't hate you now." All this in a second; then she drew forward a chair, and Elizabeth took it, without yet opening her lips. She had, with no distinct purpose but one of ease in the old, gone back to the clothes she had worn before her marriage. She looked very old-fashioned and very sweet.

"I am not sure I can tell you just why I wanted to see you," she began, with a little smile which deprecated her inability to explain.

"I know, without telling," said Victoria, quickly, her deep tones a decisive contrast to Elizabeth's voice. "You think of me, and the thought troubles you. You don't know whether to blame me or not."

"No," said Elizabeth, with a sigh of relief. "I can't settle it alone. I didn't understand many things as—as he did, and the thought that I may have blamed him too much, or driven him on to care for other things, keeps troubling me. He told me, that night, that he loved you, and I have felt like a thief to take the place you ought to have had. But I didn't know—and another woman might ! "

She was not sobbing, but repeated the sentences with little breaks between, catching her breath piteously, before going on. Victoria felt the color come into her own cheeks. In spite of herself, she held her head higher, and for an instant looked joy in the face.

" He told you he cared for me ? "

" Yes, the night you were there, the last time I saw him."

" Why did he tell you that ? "

" Because I was angry, and asked what it all meant."

" I wanted to know what it all meant, too ?" said Victoria, proudly. "I never dreamed he had a wife, until that night."

" Then why did you come ? "

" Because he had just told me, and I was very defiant, very crazy," said the actress, humbly. "I thought you didn't care for each other—that you had made a mistake—and I wanted to see with my own eyes whether it was so."

" He told you so ? Yes, it was true ; we had made a mistake in marrying."

" Then I had a right to love him ! " cried Victoria. " Say it again. Tell me you have no claim on him. And what good will it do," she said, sharply, throwing her head back, " when he is gone ! "

"And suppose he could be here," said Elizabeth, all her hesitation swept away in righteous indignation at this threatening of holy things. "What could you or I do? We couldn't make an unlawful love any thing but a stained and wretched one. Suppose I told you I would go away and never trouble you two any more —would he have any right to call you his wife? What promise could you take from him after he had broken one to me?"

"Good God! is love to go for nothing?" cried Victoria, a sort of horror taking possession of her. "Here is my one life to live. Shall I shiver and starve because the man I love foolishly made a promise, before he knew I was in the world?"

"Yes," said Elizabeth, her tears beginning to come slowly. "Yes; it is better than the happiness we steal. Oh! we know so few things, we are so likely to make mistakes when we think ourselves greatest, and then we are taught that we must not dare choose!"

"So you would endure every thing?" asked Victoria, bitterly. "You are better than I am. Would you have staid with him for the sake of your promise, when you found out that you were the one thing that stood in the way of his happiness?"

Elizabeth waited a moment, while Victoria watched her, a little scornfully.

"You must not think me better than I am," she whispered. "I did leave him. I had gone home, and meant never to come back. I don't know whether I ever could have come back or not—I don't know whether it would have been right."

"Oh, you have suffered more than I!" cried Vic-

toria, a sudden flood of tenderness sweeping into her
heart. "Oh, if you could forgive me for it all! And
yet, I couldn't have helped it, unless I had known—but
forgive me for living, even! Forgive me for something!"

The actress sunk on her knees, and hid her face in
Elizabeth's lap. Elizabeth laid her hands on the
bright head and cried over it softly. It was very
sweet to find a woman who understood. It seemed a
long silence before Victoria rose suddenly, and brushing her eyes with a quick, backward motion of both
hands, said, "But I have known love. It is one
more emotion. I shall be the better actress."

The contrast between the triumphantly splendid
woman of the moment and the crushed one who had
been on her knees almost dazzled Elizabeth. What
had she to say to this marvelous creature of changes?

"It will lie in my heart and sting me forever!"
cried Victoria, the agony coming back into her face.
"I shall never hear Romeo's vows without bitter remembrance. I shall never drink my poison without a
prayer for death. And do you think I can ever groan
and lament on the stage without longing to cry out,
'These words are wretched babble. I have learned
them, I recite them. But if you could hear my heart
cry day and night, you would learn what passion is!'
Ah, I know the human heart, now! Art can teach
me no more. This great fire in me will burn as long
as I draw breath, and make what I have to say all
glowing." She had risen, and was speaking rapidly,
her face aglow, like her words. Elizabeth felt a deep
wonder and awe at her beauty.

"You are a strange woman," she said, in a whisper.

"A blessed woman!" said Victoria, in a glad voice, stretching out her arms to the distance, in welcome of something invisible, "because I have my art, my white statue of the ideal; I hold it to my breast as you women hold your babies. It is so fine and small that it nestles in my heart, and then so large and stately that I fall on my knees before it and veil my eyes. You have your homes and loves. I have a world to create."

"Then your work will comfort you?"

"Do you think my work will take me off the rack, bind up my wounds and keep me lapped in softness? It is only because of my work that I shall have strength to suffer. If I were not the vessel of the gods, I would not guard against being broken. I would not bear having been so cheated." Elizabeth watched her with a fascination greater than Victoria had ever inspired from the stage.

"Listen to me. I seem to understand his character better than I ever did before. He loved you once, didn't he? You were enough for him?"

"Yes."

"And then he grew tired. Perhaps he would have tired of me. It is only guess-work; I don't know. But I am sure of this, that he had that strange, inexplicable quality we call genius. He should have created, but he never did, and the wonderful current turned upon his character in revenge, and spoiled his life. He preyed on men and women. He made his heart act in the dramas his hand ought to have written."

"So you think he was unfortunate and not wrong?"

"Unfortunate to the brink of bearing a curse. And we are unfortunate, for we do not know whether a shadow met us and clung to us for a while, or whether it was a substance that could give human love. He will haunt me, sometimes my knight, sometimes the ghost who crossed my track only to wander away and cross other paths."

She was still standing. Turning her head slightly, she caught sight of her image in the glass and looked critically, arrested. Elizabeth had risen, too, meaning to take her leave. She followed the glance to the mirror and met it there.

"I shall play Mary Stuart, yet," said Victoria. "It will be a great part."

Elizabeth offered her hand, a little timidly.

"Perhaps my coming here hasn't done you any good, but it has helped me. You will remember I saw there was nothing to blame, and how much I admire you."

"For such a good woman, you are a very generous one," said Victoria, earnestly. "I hope you will be happy some time, if that isn't too much to expect."

"It is," said Elizabeth, smiling faintly at her. "It is enough to be able to live."

Neither spoke of meeting again, perhaps because they found little in common but their sorrow. After that day, Elizabeth no longer tormented herself with forced thoughts of Oswald. He went out of her life, as something that had had no place there.

CHAPTER XXXII.

TWO years after, Victoria Landor was sitting in a room of the St. John's Hotel, talking to her manager.

"You think it nonsense of mine," she was saying, somewhat sharply. "You think an actress cares for nothing but her personal reputation. As far as mine goes, it is miraculously established. But I care for the stage itself, yes, more than for Victoria Landor!"

"People have tried it before," said Rose. "Not one actor in ten thousand can be a successful manager."

"I don't want to try. I want you for my manager. The idea is mine. You are to carry it out with the help of my money and my work."

"I tried to get up a good stock company years ago," said Rose, with the moodiness induced by a further temptation to an old, impracticable project. "And I did have a fair one, too. But as for devoting seven performances a week to high dramatic art, it can't be done, you know. People don't want it. Why, even when there was the first *furore* about you here, I had to fill up your off nights with twaddle. The public will have it."

"The public must be taught not to want it," said Victoria, as firmly as if Rose could be expected to do any thing but groan at inconsequent theorizing. "You have not lost money by me, have you?"

"You're the best investment I ever made." Look-ing at her with the pride of a creator.

"You sent me starring because you thought it would be better for me.   I told you I was willing to stay with you as leading-lady, if you would go on building up the company we used to talk about.   When I left the World, you put on those popular, miserable French things, and oh! most wretched of all, American plays, made to live a day."

"Now, I beg of you, don't !   We've talked it all over before.   I know what's coming.   Lord ! did you expect me to put on Othello and Hamlet, with Kendrick or Sullivan in the leading parts?"

"Now, there's no reason," went on Victoria, "why a city should not support a theater that is as religiously devoted to high art as its pet orchestra is to the best music."

"I like to hear you talk, but you do occasionally re-peat yourself," said Rose, patiently.

"Do you know how I have invariably seen Shakes-peare played, sir ?   So outrageously in scenes when the star was not on, that the audience might have been ex-cused had it gone to sleep as one man."

"Good thing ! kept you fresh for the star when he did appear."

"It is not art ; it is wretched work, no matter who the star may be.   Oh, if I could see perfection on the stage just once before I die !   Perfect scene-setting, religious attention to details, subordination of personal vanity to the art ! "

"You never will.   Take my word for it."

"I shall not die without trying.   Now, you acknowl-

edge my starring has been a success. You've paid a
small fortune into my hands."

"Yes, I couldn't ask any thing better for you."

"What do you suppose has become of the money?
I've had no horses, no fine establishment, no yacht. My
dress off the stage, is as plain and inexpensive as a
lady's can be. I live like a Spartan, as far as an
actress may, and I do it to save money."

Rose was looking at her with interest, at last.

"So you see I have a small capital. You shall look
over my bank account, presently, and then decide
whether I'm to be considered as a partner. Now, I
offer myself to you as leading-lady of the best stock
company we can afford to pay, the stipulation being
that nothing but standard tragedy and comedy shall
be presented."

She had fire enough in eyes and cheeks to touch off
a less inflammable man than Rose. After all, it was
his pet project, too, though he never stated it to himself as ideally. He liked a good, honest article in trade;
he wanted, therefore, to offer the public, for its daily
consumption, the best material in the market. A trashy
play was too often a paying investment, but he knew
its intrinsic worth quite as well as another. He preferred to have such a play on his boards as would call
in Bigwig, the critic and Benham, the novelist; it
gave him a feeling of self-respect, for the lack of
which not all the dollars that go to the support of a
mushroom farce could compensate. Therefore, now,
when Victoria had come down to dollars and cents,
from what he had been wont to consider the airy regions
of declamation, he listened.

The conversation was carried on another and another day, to such purpose that, in a year, the World was to begin its season consecrated to Art and not alone to Mammon. Money might come ; money must come, or Art would die, but the Muses should no longer be insulted in their own temple.

Had Victoria continued faithful to her idea of love for Oswald ? That had been a battle of the emotions, blasting enough for the time being, but followed by temperate peace. She saw the moral lack in him, and, poetical novelist to the contrary though there be, no good man or woman continues faithful to the unworthy after it has been recognized as such. It was Victoria's hard lesson. She weighs social laws more justly, now; youth and splendid vitality are not as likely to lead her into considering the universe as made for Victoria Landor alone.

. . . . . .

In the two years, Stratford really had changed a little, and more than in the previous quarter century. No new houses were to be seen, but the woodbine smiled freshly from the old ones ; there were, perhaps, no strange faces to be met, but the familiar ones held more brightness and purpose. The reason for such change might be found in the fact that Stratford had been enthusiastically busy over its library, Elizabeth's gift to the town.

One summer twilight, as she was walking home from her duties as librarian, a figure came rapidly along the path from the sea. It was Felix. After the first glance, she waited, not daring to look. When he had reached her, it seemed a long time before he broke impetuously in upon the silence.

"I can't wait to tell you what I came here for—to beg you to take my love."

A shiver passed over Elizabeth. She had felt her only possibility of living well to lie in quiet days. Was the tide sweeping in again?

"I know it is sudden," Felix went on. "It shocks you. I can't bear to have you hurt, but I have waited so long! My love for you has grown too great for me. Only take it; let it lie in your hand."

"Please don't talk of such things," said Elizabeth, trying to shake off her own excitement. "It troubles me. I want to ask you about yourself; there are so many things to say."

"No, I should be a hypocrite if I tried to pave the way with talk of other things. That would be only to put you at ease before speaking of the only thing in the world there is for me to tell. Sit down here, please."

She took the stone under a great apple-tree by the roadside, and Felix threw himself on the ground at her feet, going on without looking up, but plucking a spear of grass now and then to busy his eyes and fingers.

"You have been in my thoughts these two years like a sealed memory; something I never dared to talk about with myself, even, for I had no right to love you. I have fought against thinking of you, oh, I have fought! And when I came back to find you free—tell me, did you really love him, at the last?"

"No," said Elizabeth. Her lips seemed quite numb and frozen.

"I was sure of that. Take my love. I don't ask

for yours. It would kill me. But let me take care of you."

"I, too, have things to do, and people to take care of. I never can leave my mother. I was selfish once ; help me not to be again."

When did Felix ever hear a cry for help without turning to listen ? "I was wrong," he said gently, reminding her of the Felix of two years ago. "Let us talk about it quietly. Do you think it would be possible to live well if we two were together ?"

Elizabeth paused a moment, then said slowly, "I think—I should feel as safe as I should with the archangel Michael."

A man ought to have have been satisfied with that, perhaps ; this hungry heart would have been better contented with one confession of tenderness for itself. When the admission tempted him to entreat her again, Felix pulled himself up sharply. "I have been hearing of you and all the things you have done for the town. I have seen Si."

"That is nothing, all nothing. I don't do it from fine motives. It is half to carry out what you began and half to keep myself busy ; I don't want time to think."

"You have been so unhappy ?"

"Yes—no, worse than that ; common doubting, not able to believe in heaven, sometimes not able to believe in God."

" "That is hard, but it will pass ; it does with us all, sooner or later."

"Do you think Philip is alive ?"   .

"Assuredly. I can't convince you with words. I

never can argue about that ; it is like an inspiration to me."

"But if it is all wrong, all black, not to be understood, and the world goes on forever and ever, and we die and other people live—oh, it makes me sick ! "

"It is not all wrong." The man's deep voice somehow comforted her by its very tone. "Think of the greatest feeling you ever have, and decide whether that can ever die into the squalid blackness of a universe gone wrong. The tremendous fact in my life is my love for you ; a man who can feel such love cannot sink into nothingness. See, here is something that has dignified life for me when circumstances have tried to belittle it. If this scheme of a God and immortality could be the figment of our own brains, think what Godlike creatures we must be to conceive such glory—the peers of the Creator we imagine. If we are not the sons of the Almighty, if we have no Father at all, we are too great to die."

Half an hour more, when their talk was all of Philip, they walked back to the house.

"I expected you," said Grandmother without preamble, as they went in, looking at Felix with surprising mildness.

"To-day ? "

"No, some time. I thought I should see you before I was called away. What have you been doing? "

"Shoveling coal in Albaville, giving a lecture once a week and holding a Sunday service."

"Do you call yourself a minister ? "

"Yes," with a twinkle in his gray eyes, "and a miner."

"How much salary do they pay you ?"

"We call it wages. It depends on the amount of work we do. Most of the men can earn more than I, because I take out half a day occasionally, for my own use."

"Don't they pay you for preaching?"

"No, I don't need any thing beyond my miner's pay. Besides, preaching was my own offer."

"I suppose you think you are doing a great deal of good."

"I think another man is," said Felix, waking to enthusiasm and turning to Elizabeth. "Do you remember Tim Ellin ? Almost every body knew him as Nellie, thanks to the college boys. Well, he has spent most of his income for the last two years on the miners at Albaville. He has built them a church, the one where he allows me to hold service. They have a reading-room and books and newspapers. And because I must earn my bread and choose to do it with the men, he is ashamed to have more leisure and shovels coal with the rest of us."

Elizabeth smiled at him, in a way which brought the suspicion of a blush to his face. Her glance said, "I know very well who has made the change in Tim Ellin."

Mrs. Nye came in, almost tearful at sight of him, and thinking at once of Philip. Still, her face was less worried than he remembered it. Elizabeth, who had made the home, the town itself, better worth living in, was the only one who seemed to catch no reflection of the new brightness.

That night, Felix staid at his old friend's, Mrs. Potter's, and was back again, early in the morning. He had considered his course and with such result that he was no longer impetuous nor faint-hearted. Elizabeth stood in his mind for the great jewel of the world, the one inestimable treasure. He would possess her. When they were alone, he began suddenly. " Do you trust me enough to belong to me ? "

" Yes."

" Then won't you let the trust be a bond between us till you feel something stronger ? I can wait."

" Oh, you don't understand ! " cried Elizabeth, stung by the impossibility of putting her feelings into words. " If I were a girl, if it was years ago and you found me first before I made a mistake! But I have belonged to some one else—I thought I cared—I am not good enough—"

" For God's sake don't go on, my princess," he cried, ready to fall on his knees before her there in the open day. " My darling, who has been wronged ! Oh, if you did not love me, you would not be jealous for me ! "

" No," said Elizabeth, looking at him, honestly, through streaming tears, joy shaking her voice. " I think I have loved you always. I think perhaps that is why my life has seemed so hopeless these years. After making so many mistakes how could I hope for any thing ? That ' too late ' has been death to me. Is it too late for me to live again ? "

" I have been telling people, all these years, that there is no minute of life when it is not possible to put the heel on dead mistakes. Is it true for other people and not for you and me ? "

Elizabeth turned to him, her eyes one brown glow.

"Is it true, sweetest of women?" whispered her
lover.

. . . . . .

When Felix came for his wife, months later, it was
because Mrs. Nye was free to go West with her children. She was released ; Madam Nye had indeed been
"called away," meeting the summons as grimly and
methodically as she had lived.

Though Elizabeth left a fund to pay the Reverend
Mr. Benson for combining her duties as librarian with
his own as preacher, it was another man to whom the
town was really confided.

"Si, I know you'll take care of Philip's grave. And
the library—you will see that the wood is hauled every
year? And O Si, do keep Stratford's head above
water! "

"I will, by Righteous!" swore the giant ; and it is
to be asserted that up to this present date he has loyally
kept alive every one of Elizabeth's plans which he
knew, working sometimes in the dark, but because she
had begun.

In Elizabeth's room stands always a little red chest.
It contains all Philip's papers, which she cannot help
hoping to see published some day, though as yet no
one has read them.

THE END.

www.ingramcontent.com/pod-product-compliance
Lightning Source LLC
Chambersburg PA
CBHW021218270326
41929CB00010B/1183